SOUND AND MEANING IN
ENGLISH POETRY

Sound and Meaning

in

English Poetry

by

Katharine M. Wilson

KENNIKAT PRESS
Port Washington, N. Y./London

SOUND AND MEANING IN ENGLISH POETRY

First published in 1930
Reissued in 1970 by Kennikat Press
Library of Congress Catalog Card No: 76-113352
ISBN 0-8046-1060-6

Manufactured by Taylor Publishing Company   Dallas, Texas

SYNOPSIS

BOOK I

SOUND

BOOK II

MEANING

v

Large portions of the first chapters of both books have appeared as articles in *Music and Letters*, whose Editor I sincerely
thank.

BOOK I

SOUND

EXPLANATION OF MUSICAL SYMBOLS

Accent is represented by a vertical line placed before the accented note. In the above example the last note (*a*) is accented.

Time is represented by the dots with stalks in the above example. The *direction* of the stalk up or down from the note is immaterial. The note marked (*b*) is the norm or average length of time, and is called a crotchet. The note marked (*c*) with a clear dot lasts twice as long as a crotchet, and is called a minim. That marked (*d*) with a pennon on its stalk lasts half the time of the crotchet, and is called a quaver. Another pennon on the stalk halves the time again and so on, so that (*c*) = 2 (*b*), which = 2 (*d*), which = 2 (*e*). To lengthen a note by half its own value we place a dot after it, as at (*f*), which lasts as long as (*b*) plus (*d*), or as three notes of the value of (*d*), while (*a*) is equal to three (*e*)s or to (*d*) plus (*e*). The three first symbols on the lower group of horizontal lines (*h*) represent silences of the respective duration of the notes above them.

Pitch is represented by the ten horizontal lines and the spaces enclosed. The dot of the time-symbol indicates the pitch of the note; the higher the dot on the stave, the higher the pitch. Thus on the highest row of notes in our example the pitch rises with each note from (*c*) to (*a*). When only five horizontal lines and the enclosed spaces are needed to indicate the pitch, we use only five; the curious-looking symbols at the beginning of each set of horizontal lines shows whether we are using the higher or the lower portion of the stave. To save unnecessary expense in printing, I sometimes use the *sol-fa* names to indicate the pitch—*do, re, mi, fa, so, la, ti, do', re', mi', so'*. The above example shows their relative pitches. Thus *ti* to *do'* indicates a very small rise in pitch, *do* to *la* a large one, while *so* to *do* represents a slightly smaller drop in pitch.

I think the reader ignorant of music will get a pretty fair idea of the musical illustrations from these explanations. But in case he should wish to play them on the piano, perhaps I should say that the first note in the example (*c*) is "middle C", the 27th white note from the right-hand end, the 24th from the left, and that space and line alternately indicate the successive white notes. The two "sharp" signs placed at the beginning of the lower stave (*m*) indicate that the black note immediately to the right of that indicated by the line or space is to be played, not the white one; or if there is no black note immediately to the right, then the next white one. This holds for the whole line unless contradicted by the sign at (*n*) placed before the note. The contradiction holds till the next accented note. The "flat" sign at (*o*) indicates that the black note immediately to the *left* must be played instead of the written one, or if there is no black, then the nearest white. Where the "sharp" or "flat" is placed immediately before the note as at (*o*), and not at the beginning of the line as at (*m*), it holds only until the next accented note. Notes placed in the same vertical line are played simultaneously. Thus the group marked (*x*) contains four "chords" (or groups of simultaneously played notes) of three notes each, one in the top or "treble" stave, and two in the lower or "bass". The notes marked (*z*) are quavers with their pennons joined, and therefore have half the time value of the crotchets in the group. This means that the second of the two notes takes the place of the first, half-way between the two chords.

CHAPTER I

MUSICAL SOUND IN GENERAL

Two things are necessary for music—noise and movement. Only less courage and intellect have gone to prove a monistic origin for music than to prove a monistic theology. In comparison with monism, dualism appears a failure of the intellect or of the heart. In both problems we find two obvious ways to unity; very probably God created the Devil and movement noise, as presumably the Devil did not create God, and, less incontrovertibly, noise did not create movement; or there may be no Devil, Devil and God being one, and noise and movement equally inseparable. Let us say that God is divinity understood, Devil divinity misunderstood, and, putting their relationship even closer, that noise is movement heard, movement noise made. At all events the reconciliation of either problem forms a very ticklish metaphysical speculation.

We need not attempt to solve these difficulties since they are purely metaphysical, but we can beat back the disputants on the outskirts of the problem to this blank precipice. According to the Bible, noise created; God spake and movement resulted; though modern science makes the more plausible creator movement. Examining primitive races for the answer is no use, man not being the first noisy or energetic creature; and happily the results are inconclusive. Two kinds of music obtain among primitive races, one tonal and usually vocal, the other instrumental, almost toneless, and purely rhythmical. Some primitive peoples beat tom-toms, and tom-toms are usually considered interesting rather for their rhythms than for their noise, but this needs proof. I can remember a nursery orchestra with trays and pokers, and the players interested rather in the noise than in the rhythms, though I have no doubt a disinterested observer might find the rhythms the more musical. Incontestably, primitive human beings like to make a noise, and find it easier to make rhythmic than arhythmic noises, but they may not be interested in their rhythms or conscious of them. It is, however, commonly assumed that we cannot act rhythmically without knowing it. Mr. Wallaschek* thinks man is the first rhythmic animal:

Even animals recognise and utter intervals but cannot make any intelligent use of them, because they do not understand rhythmic arrangement.

But animals do make intelligent use of intervals of pitch, just as they make rhythms of them; nor do they differ from human beings in not understanding rhythmic arrangement. Bird-song has often decided rhythms. Many of the blackbird's "catches" are in equal-bar rhythm. The low monotonous note of one bird, name unknown—for my natural history is very slight—a frequenter of riverbanks and sedgy, flat ground, sometimes persists in a regular beat long enough to get us on edge; any musical significance it has seems to lie rather in its rhythm than in its monotonous tone. And we must not call the free rhythms of animal music unrhythmical, any more than we may say the blackbird sings out of tune because it does not sing in equal temperament. But assuming that the rhythmic sense appears first in man, Wallaschek† goes on to say that the desire for rhythm arises from unapplied energy, consequently that rhythm precedes melody in history and

* *Primitive Music*, p. 233.   † *Ibid.*, p. 231.

psychology; the "time-sense" is the psychological origin of "music"* and melody arose to mark rhythm.† Wundt also says:‡

Because of the character of his locomotor organs, primitive man repeats the movement of the dance at regular intervals, and this rhythm gives him pleasure. Similarly, he derives pleasure even from the regularly repeated movements involved in the making the straight lines of his drawings, and this pleasure is enhanced when he sees the symmetrical figures that arise under . . . his movements. The earliest aesthetic stimuli are symmetry and rhythm.

Again the deduction is wrong. The dance may result from unapplied energy, and derive its rhythm from the character of man's "locomotor organs", but it does by no means follow that the first "aesthetic stimuli" are symmetry and rhythm; the first aesthetic stimulus is the desire to make a row, the desire to do something violent; and the chances are ten to one, perhaps one hundred to one, that the savage has no sense of symmetry or rhythm, that he remains unconscious of the symmetry and rhythm of his movements.

It is remarkable that when art grew thoroughly self-conscious in the eighteenth century, and men became emphatically aware of rhythm as a discrete entity, only the very simplest rhythms were felt as rhythmic. The eighteenth century found the complex rhythms of earlier ages too difficult. Even now our conscious sense of free rhythm has not fully awakened, and we still find some difficulty in grasping the movement of a five- or a seven-beat bar. The submersion of the imagination which accompanied the awakening to self-consciousness in the eighteenth century becomes all the more significant when we see the same thing repeated in the development of the child. Child

* *Primitive Music*, p. 275.   † *Ibid.*, p. 233.
‡ *Elements of Folk Psychology*, p. 103.

artists and poets lose their "inspiration" and their facility, when, at the age of about twelve or thirteen, they become self-conscious. The psychology of the artist or poet who retains, or regains, or discovers his creative ability after that age, differs from that of the small-child artist or poet. The eighteenth-century attitude to art in England shows a similar fundamental change of mentality, evident equally in its music and its poetry. We need not think of this change as retrogressive; it was not so much that the fire died down in their imagination and in their sense of music, as that their self-conscious intellect, having newly taken control, could not yet grasp and understand or even perceive more than the tamest facts of the imagination, or the very elementary rhythms. Milton and Shakespeare possibly did not know how complex were the designs of their rhythms; their command of rhythmic composition was intuitional, half-unconscious; they wrote more from a general sense of music than from a particularised feeling for the design of their rhythms. The eighteenth-century poets, with "reason" newly awake, knew all about the designs of their rhythms; the music of poetry to them meant two discrete things, the sound of the words plus the symmetry of the rhythm. Pope could have explained the rhythmic design of *The Rape of the Lock*, but not Milton that of *Paradise Lost*. Pope's "aesthetic stimuli" might well have been "symmetry and rhythm". What stimulated Milton was something more emotional, more imaginative, more intuitional, less capable of definition. At all events it has not been proved that the rhythmic sense precedes the melodic either in the history of music or in the psychology of man.

Progress in art psychology is from the general impression to a sense of the components, the unsophisticated, unself-conscious reader or listener perceiving but the general impression. One who has a particular perception of

all the elements of *Paradise Lost*, of its rhythmic peculiarities, of its erudition, of its architectonic structure, *etc.*
etc., before he gets a general impression of the whole, is
not a sincere, simple-minded, artistic reveller; he is a
student studying for an *exam.* or a connoisseur and critic.
Many learn to appreciate art in this way, reading with
their eyes on the particulars, so that any general impression
they receive is a fusion of all the particular impressions; but
to the unsophisticated reader the general is the first and
primitive impression, and particular perceptions need never
emerge. And indeed, if a perception of the particulars
within the general feeling of art were part of primitive
aesthetic emotion, we should not need to train and develop
our critical faculty, which is precisely the faculty of perceiving the particulars of a general impression. True, we
can develop this faculty until it usurps everything and we
get no impression of the whole, but this has nothing in the
world to do with the genesis of artistic feelings.

In one sense a plum-pudding has its most primitive
state as a collection of ingredients on a table, but our most
primitive perception of it is as a finished article in our
mouths; psychologically considered, this is the primitive
plum-pudding feeling. We find its origin by studying not
kitchen processes and methods of selection, but physical
and psychological processes. To take pleasure in the taste
because we notice the repetition and rhythm of each particular ingredient is a refined and intellectual, not to say
the cook's, enjoyment. In searching for the first essentials
of music we do two things—separate music into its components or ingredients, imagining them all set out on the
kitchen table, and go far back in the primitive mind to find
the birth of musical feeling, to discover the first stirrings,
the first glimmerings of artistic life. We follow two diverging roads, which get further and further apart the further
we go. These "origins" of music are different sorts of

origin, and "the elements of music" mean entirely different things according to which road we meet them on. Although we take our first step in chemistry by dividing the world into its elements, our first step in writing the history of the growth and formation of the world is to do no such thing; the world did not start plum-pudding-wise, and no more is music a plum-pudding formation. We should not assume that music results from two separate things put together, that either rhythm must have preceded melody or melody rhythm. Every melody includes its rhythm, the rhythm being but a particular aspect of the melody. When children learn songs by ear, they are conscious of the tune as a whole, the combination, not the rhythm plus the notes, just as the untrained listener hears a tune as one thing, not as a component of notes and rhythm. Perhaps to our emotions they are still not easily separated. Try to *feel* the melody of *God save the King* without its rhythm, or the rhythm without its melody. I can do neither. To think of the rhythm apart from the melody we make an abstract intellectual deduction, and realise it as a piece of analysis, not as a musical emotion. It is ludicrous going to the emotions of savages to find the discrete perception of these. Evolution in art, if art does evolve, is not towards synthesis, but from the primitive general impression to an analytic perception.

We live at least as much in a world of sound as in a world of movement; and just as our sense of rhythm functions in every movement, so our sense of sound responds to every noise. Our reaction to the universe of sound is prevoluntary; an express train racing with its terrible *crescendo* through an echoing station fills us with a sort of fear in spite of ourselves, and we feel relieved as from an involuntary pressure when it has passed. Sounds continually keep alive our sense of hearing. Absolute silence is a rare and, to some people, a terrifying thing. One holiday-

dweller in the remotest hills, living in a cottage on the
heather just beyond the sound of the brook, had to put a
loudly ticking clock in her room at night to break the fear-
ful spell of the stillness. We have only to look for an absolute silence to discover how rare it is. Think of the sounds
that come to you at this moment. Here birds twitter in the
garden; someone talks in the passage; a door slams far off;
when these noises cease I hear the bath tap dripping, the
drops fall on the metal waste trap with a clear *ping*; even
if the bathroom were further off I should still hear the fire
burning, the sound of my pen on the paper, and, if I shut
my eyes and concentrate on listening, the murmur of distant traffic, the ticking of my watch, the rustle of clothes as
I turn to take my pen again, and the whisper of a deeper
breath than usual.

Either sounds mould our sense of hearing, or our sense
of hearing determines what we shall hear, or perhaps both.
Certainly our ear determines what we shall hear. Notes
much below 20 vibrations a second or above 20,000 are
usually inaudible,* and as we grow old our sensitiveness to
high sounds becomes lower and lower. Animals have not
precisely the same range, cats and small dogs hearing
higher sounds than we can;† mice sing at a pitch just beyond what most of us hear,† so presumably have a higher
audibility. We miss sounds even within our range of hearing, and have to learn to discriminate closely. We can also
to a wonderful degree shut out sounds we do not wish to
hear, make our brains "positive" to them. It is almost as if
our minds had a secretary between them and the world to
select what is worth attention and what shall go in the
waste-paper basket. The discretion of our secretary varies,

* These figures leave a margin; 20 vibrations and 20,000 are well
within the range of audibility. Any reader who does not understand
will find an explanation on p. 205.

† Wallaschek, *Primitive Music*, pp. 239-40. He gets the informa-
tion about cats and dogs from Galton.

as do our instructions to him. We may remain "positive" to half the music in the world; or perhaps we each live in a world of our own hearing. Many noises which do not interest us escape unheard; and townsfolk who visit the country every vacation to play golf and fish and admire the scenery, can live through a resurgent fortnight in spring and never hear the lark. Yet it seems equally true that what we hear educates our ears. Sounds do bear in upon us, and those we are accustomed to, help to condition the impressions we get from music; they help to make our musical sense.

We are as vitally sensitive to noise as to rhythm, relying on our sense of sound as continuously and as discriminatingly as on rhythm, our sense of movement. And not only do we hear sounds everywhere; the sounds we hear are musical, or, when not musical, still capable of musical analysis. The most hideous noise can be divided up into absolutely pure tones, like those of a tuning-fork. We can shape blocks of wood to play a scale when dropped successively—a rather wooden one; and most of us have amused a vacant hour in childhood playing tunes on a selection of tumblers or cups. But not only can we draw music from inanimate nature, she plays tunes for us when we work with her. The forge delights our ears as much as our sight, and not for its rhythm alone. When we throw coal on the fire, the piece that strikes the grate sings out its note to us. Every motor-horn sounds its warning at its own particular pitch; an unusual note strikes us as unusual, even as funny. Water has an inexhaustible repertory. The scale of a filling bottle is familiar; a "singing" kettle sometimes plays with the music of fairy bagpipes. Water in brooks and rivers, on the roof, on leaves, in the sea, sounds pleasant to us. Being the most moving, it is also the most variously musical thing in inanimate nature. The songs of the wind cannot rival it in variety.

The noise of man's mechanical inventions is in harmony with nature's music. The tune of a cart moving along a highland track fits the general harmony* of the hills; it forms a suitable bass to the cry of the lapwing, the distant lowing of cows, the bleat of lambs, or the incessant hum of the millions of creatures in the spring heather. Even man's noisier machines make music, though at first we shut our ears to their too magnificent *fortissimos*—not that this could be held to make them any the less musical. In a remote northern district was a tramway service popularly believed to survive on the castaway cars of all the other cities in Scotland; in the worst of these the window-glass rattled in the sash, the iron mats slid on the floor, the seats jostled the sides of the car, the sides swayed with a different motion from either the roof or the floor, every screw in the machinery moved in a free rhythm and with an independent tune of its own, so that when a workman on the top deck let his tool fall out, it betrayed no undue nervousness in the lady who hastily got out, thinking that the car was coming to bits; yet the resulting noises were wonderfully polyphonic, like a metallic brook—slumbrously, monotonously, various.

In 1832 William Gardiner published his *Music in Nature; or an attempt to prove that what is passionate and pleasing in the art of singing, speaking, and performing upon musical instruments is derived from the sounds of the Animated World*, and has succeeded, at least, in showing a continuity between the sounds of the Animated World and our own music. He tells us† that musical sounds carry further than noises; the music of a fair is heard further than the noise of its traffic; and old fiddles, though their tone is softer, further than new ones; a chanted mass sounds through a church, where the spoken service would be inaudible. And we might add that music is the most arresting

* In its widest meaning.   † pp. 12-14.

kind of noise; it forces our attention, even in a tea-room. Gardiner gives examples, written out in our clef notation, of the sounds in Animated Nature, and gives so many that I cannot begin quoting. He notices* that the horse's whinny "passes through every semitone of the scale". Such a chromatic descent is common in nature. We hear it in the wail of a dog, who achieves the semitones ascending as well as descending, while the cat rivals him in expressiveness and flexibility; the gibbon ape, also, comes down in semitones, and† "effects . . . the descent with great precision", not to mention the howls of savages‡—all, presumably, sung *portamento*, more as an inflection§ than as a succession of notes. Consequently this is rather nature's speech than her song. But even birds, whom we regard rather as songsters than as orators, sometimes sing *portamento*. The crow has striking inflections, for it is a mistake to think that because he has only one word he has but one note. His inflections show the meaning of his call. "Caw" can be an imprecation of the most direful nature, an exclamation of satisfaction, an impatient ejaculation, a wailing lamentation; it can even express a sense of humour. The octave jump at the end of some bird-song is, or so it seems to me, a lightning *portamento*, as in the April blackbird's song in Aberdeenshire:

But the mysterious and fateful inflections of the sea-gull heard through mist, or the joyous Celtic cadence of the

* p. 203.   † Wallaschek, *Primitive Music*, p. 156.
‡ Parry, *The Art of Music*, pp. 53-4.
§ Throughout this book I use the word "inflection" as a technical term meaning the modulations of voice we use in speaking.
‖ In examples of bird-song I have written down the octaves to save ledger-lines.

mating lapwing are more expressive. Gardiner* gives a convincing array both of music like our own in nature, and the direct incorporation of nature's music in the works of our great composers.† So our music is not isolated and fortuitous, but essential in the nature of the universe.

By song or inflection practically every interval in our scales finds voice in nature. Some writers, however, think that animals, though they use the intervals of our scales, not our equally tempered ones,‡ yet have no scale sense. This seems to me a mistake. The song of the blackbird shows the scale sense very clearly, certainly a common chord sense. One in Aberdeenshire at the beginning of June revels in it:

The most developed song I have heard from a blackbird came from a Cambridge one in April:

It is interesting to find this bird escaping from the tonic common chord (*do, mi, so*) by way of the submediant (*la*), the submediant being a strongly felt note in much primitive folk-song. It has been said that the blackbird sings in a Celtic scale, but this is because Celtic folk-music was the

* Though Gardiner's work is out of print I have not quoted; if a public ever arise for this sort of study, his book will be reprinted; if it does not, I need not waste more time transcribing.

† See also Raymond, *Music as a Representative Art*, pp. 315-18.

‡ The piano is tuned in equal temperament, not in justly tempered intervals. Nature's singers, human and animal, do not sing a piano scale, which is machine-made, and as different from a real scale as margarine from butter. For explanation, see an encyclopaedia under *Temperament*.

only folk-music known to the educated people of these islands until comparatively recently.

Nature has a sense of "absolute pitch". Birds sing only in related keys, and some birds always in the same key till their voice breaks at the end of the season. The natural period (or pitch) of the dog's ear is supposed to be E; Helmholtz* quotes the opinion that "dogs are very sensitive to the high e'''' of the violin", and holds that our ears are tuned to notes between E and G. This does not mean that E is the only note or the chief note in dog music any more than it is in ours; but presumably it seems to the dog himself his most incisive one. E seems to me the very sharp, painful note we hear in the bark of some dogs. The irate impatience of one Irish terrier aroused sympathetic vibration in a bowl that sings out when E, a trifle sharper than the E of the nearest piano, is sounded.

Psychological investigations show that a sense of "absolute pitch" is more fundamental than a feeling for intervals of pitch.

Young children (and birds) when . . . taught a short musical phrase, tend to repeat it without any subsequent alteration of pitch. This . . . is favourable to a sensibility to absolute pitch, but it is soon discouraged, owing to the fact that they generally hear the same melody repeated in different keys. Sensibility for intervals replaces sensibility for absolute pitch.†

One notices, also, that people who do not consider themselves musical have no difficulty in hitting off the right pitch when impulse leads them to burst into a song or a whistle, whereas the more conscious musician doesn't know which note to begin on. The feeling that keys have each a characteristic atmosphere, and the fact that many of us have

---

* *The Sensation of Tone*, Ellis's translation, p. 169.
† C. F. Myers, *A Textbook of Experimental Psychology*, p. 50.

favourite keys, show a latent sense of absolute pitch.
Gardiner* characterised the different keys thus:

F major—rich, mild, sober and contemplative.
D minor—ditto, but heavier and grander, doleful and
          solemn.
C major—bold, vigorous and commanding, suitable to
          war and enterprise.
A minor—plaintive but not feeble.
G major—gay and sprightly, adapted to the greatest
          range of subjects.
E minor—persuasive, soft, tender.
D major—ample, noble, more fire than C.
B minor—bewailing, but too high to excite commisera-
          tion.
A major—golden, warm, sunny.
F♯ minor—mournfully grand.
E major—bright, pellucid, feminine.
B major—keen and piercing.
B♭ major—least interesting, not sufficient fire for majesty
          and too dull for song.
G minor—meek, pensive, melancholy.
E♭ major—full, mellow, soft and beautiful, the loveliest
          key, though less decided than some of the
          others.
C minor—complaining, something like whining cant of
          B minor.
A♭ major—loveliest of all, unassuming, gentle, soft, deli-
          cate, tender, with none of the pertness of
          A major.
F minor—religious, penitential, gloomy.
D♭ major—awfully dark; in this remotest key Beethoven
          has written his sublimest thoughts.

M. Lussy says:

it would seem a little hazardous, if not doubtful, to write
a piece of tender character in E major, that being one of
the most brilliant and vigorous keys.†

* *The Music of Nature*, pp. 439-41.
† *Musical Expression*, p. 7.

Everyone's experience will not agree with Gardiner's. We have different tastes, and our descriptions take colouring from these tastes. Green may seem a hideous colour to you and lovely to me, and yet we might both get the same sensation from green. D♭ is perhaps a favourite key of mine, and "awfully dark" wrong for my experience,* yet I may get the same sensation as Gardiner, describing it otherwise. I may likewise object to his calling the same key both religious and gloomy, gloom never having gone with religion in my experience. But if we allow for Gardiner's colouring of the keys with the colours of his taste, and if we allow that some people get no sensation from the colour either of physical tints or of musical tones, we may accept his descriptions. They agree well with Helmholtz, who believed the natural period of our ears was from E to G. E is Lussy's most brilliant key; E and A major Gardiner's bright, incisive keys; and E♭ and A♭ his mellow and lovely ones, where the edge of the tone is softened, blunted, muffled. When we talk of a remote key we probably mean a key far removed from E or A. And I need not remind the reader that the note a fifth above A (*i.e.* E) is more nearly related to it than the note a semitone below (*i.e.* A♭), that the "colours" of A and E are more alike than those of A and A♭. Yet this is admittedly very controversial ground, and the frequent changes in the naming of pitch through the centuries, the last within living memory, must be taken into account. It is conceivable, however, that we raise or lower the pitch of the note we decide to call A and tune from, to satisfy changed feelings about the quality of the pitch. The letter A in our pronunciation of, say, "father" changes its nature or the pitch of its resonant tone, phoneticians say, in every generation, the change being easily remarked in the third generation. The change depends on a change in the pitch of the resonating cavities of

* I have been told that D♭ is the note I use most in speaking.

the mouth, and may, if it does not result from a change in our feeling for pitch, bring about that change. This may have something to do with our raising and lowering of standard pitches. I have, however, absolutely no grounds for this conjecture other than that there must be some way of reconciling our feeling for different keys with the changes in standard pitch. At all events we shall see later* that only because we have a feeling for "absolute pitch" can we distinguish one vowel from another. Man did not create any new material when he developed articulate speech.

That animals can understand our speech and respond readily to our music proves human speech and song not so much distinct from the speech and song of nature as differentiated from them. We need not illustrate how animals appreciate our music; we have all heard of it being a lure for fish; Orpheus' power is no myth. And anyone fond of domestic animals knows how sensitive they are to musical inflections in our speech. We may calm a nervous horse most easily by talking to him with the sort of quality of voice and with the sort of inflections that calm and soothe. A terrier carried off in a tramcar, who went so wild with grief and impatience that a hysterical woman got into a panic and shrieked in sympathy, was reassured in an instant when one who loved dogs spoke to him in unexcited tones; but perhaps this is not a fair example, since dogs take meaning from our words as well. Cats rely more on the inflections. If you say, "You are a dear pussy", in the tones of voice with which you usually say, "You wretched thief!" your cat will take the inflectional meaning; if you try the experiment on your dog, the conflicting meanings will puzzle him. Then dogs and cats like our music, as well as understand our inflections. One rarely hears of a musical household where the animals are not musical too —and they have individual tastes in music, or at least dogs

* Chapter on "Our Alphabet".

have; they like some tunes better than others, and few of them can resist a lullaby. I am inclined to agree with those who say that it is excess of unwonted emotion that makes dogs, unaccustomed to music, howl when they hear it. Even human beings think beauty akin to tears; very lovely or very moving poetry or music makes them cry. And not only those animals we have half-humanised appreciate our music. Wild animals respond to it, and we are told* that the circus band certainly gives the animals as much pleasure as it gives us. Mice have more than once come out at a concert to listen to music, and in a humane and un-hysterical audience retired when the music ended. Experiments in the Zoological Gardens* proved that all the animals tested, except wolves and cobras, liked "soft, sad music", and preferred tunes in the minor to those in major modes, bears and ibexes alone excepted. An elephant on another occasion showed that he liked sentimental airs, and sometimes roared in unison. How like an elephant!

That animals prefer minor to major modes is interest-ing, since all primitive music is in either gapped† or modal or minor scales. Some writers do indeed tell us that certain primitive peoples have a major scale, and that tribal or racial taste determines whether major or minor scales are preferred. As an example of a primitive melody in a major scale, Wallaschek‡ gives this one, sung outside the hut of the dying:

We see that the scale is not major, but gapped. Under the heading *minor* we tend generically, and strictly speaking

* H. F. Gosling, *Music and its Aspects*, pp. 52-62.

† A gapped scale is one in which any of the notes that make our major or minor or modal scales is missing, e.g. *do, re, mi, so, la, do*. This one is common in Scotland.

‡ *Primitive Music*, p. 147.

wrongly, to class all scales not major; if we do this, then the natural scales are all minor. Wallaschek* possibly means no more when he says: "It is surprising how often savages sing in the minor key", but when he tells us that African tribes prefer the major, and the Fijians always sing in the major scale, he really means that their scale has the major third and not the minor. A gapped scale gives us a different sensation from a major, and to many a sensation more like a minor scale. Penny-whistlers tell us that a major key with a minor feeling about it suits the penny-whistle best. Tunes classed under this heading have no "leading note", which is a little awkward to play on the penny-whistle, the instrument being made to accommodate a six-note scale. Our modes and scales, then, are not arbitrary conventions, but the music of real and natural moods.

It is a commonplace that the more civilised, the less susceptible to musical emotion do we become, the harder the task of Orpheus. Mr. Antcliffe† draws a pretty picture for us of the ancient Britons:

> They had songs ... that were most affecting and peaceful. One Greek writer tells how on occasion, after two armies were ready for the charge, some of the British bards, with peaceful motives [and unintentional pun], stepped in between the fighting lines and "by their soft and fascinating songs calmed the fury of the warriors, and prevented bloodshed."

Plato's‡ emphasis on music in his educational scheme for the ideal state shows that it had more power over the ancient Greeks than it has over us. In our own age and cities we may see the contrast. If a string quartet were drawn through our streets playing Mozart, how many would leave their sober senses and follow in a mad glory,

* *Primitive Music*, pp. 145-6.
† *The Nature of Music*, pp. 209-10.
‡ *The Republic*, bk. iii.

with an excitement as wonderful as that of small unre-
fined children in the wake of a military band? But perhaps
we can explain our apathy creditably. A solitary melody
often moves us more than one accompanied with harmony.
The song of Wordsworth's highland reaper would have
lost half its emotional appeal if other reapers had sung
harmonies to it. The melody is stronger alone because
single and unperplexed. Harmony starts contrasting
strains of emotion which take away from the single effect,
making the music more complex, less all-absorbing in one
emotional line. In music such as that of string quartets,
where an energetic tune may go simultaneously with a slow
dreamy melody, the conflicting strains of emotion neutral-
ise each other. That sort of music moves us less, though it
may interest us more, than purely melodic music, or music
in parts where each has the same melody in turn with
cumulative emotional power, or even than harmonised
music where the melodies, though different, are related
emotionally, or where the melodic lines of the harmonies
are so feeble that they mean nothing at all. Wallaschek,*
however, holds that

the difference between people with or without harmonic
music is not a *historical but a racial one.*

He notices that "natives" often sing in "thirds", that the
Hottentots sing a descending common chord in canon.
But there is all the difference in the world between the
psychology of people taking their part in singing a canon
or in thirds and the psychology of an audience listening to
harmonies. Moreover savages singing in thirds may believe
they all sing the same notes, showing rather primitive
hearing than harmonic ability. And though it may follow
from Wallaschek's facts that some savages have a harmonic
sense, it does not follow that they hear the trend of two

* *Primitive Music,* pp. 139-44.

simultaneous melodies, not to mention that, as Dr. Myers*
puts it, the parts

are invariably permitted a freedom of movement which is
denied to our own music, and the different simultaneous
rhythms are allowed full scope for independent development.

And not only our music; we too are more complex. Though
as sensitive to the influence of music or to musical inflections of the voice as animals and primitive people, we
feel so many things at once, such a differentiated environment plays on us all the time, that the soothing or exciting
of one strand does not make such a difference to the whole
content of our consciousness. That music overwhelms
or transports us less may not really mean that we are less
sensitive to it, that it is less vital to us.

Perhaps this seems an alien discussion. What has all
this to do with poetry? It has everything to do with poetry,
because speech is an adaptation of music to serve utilitarian ends. As the mind grows, its activities become differentiated. To-day music and speech are far enough apart;
it may seem that we can talk of the *music of poetry* only as
a figure of speech indicating no more than the pleasant
noise of poetry, and not referring to a fact as we talk of the
mica in granite. Yet even to-day poetry is really a music,
and if we trace speech and music back into the past or
into the primitive, we travel along converging lines. Apart
from their intrinsic relationship, our vocabulary still shows
their common origin; we have *sonnet* and *sonata*, *ballad* and
ballet, and a *song* means either a tune or a poem. So late
as Elizabethan times, the arts had forms like the madrigal
in common, while Troubadour stanzas belong to both
equally. A *villanelle*, a *triolet* and a *rondo* were musical as
well as poetic forms, the musical *rondo* still surviving,

* *Anthropological Essays presented to E. B. Tylor*, "The Ethno-
logical Study of Music," p. 238.

though we have forgotten the poetic one. Before printing, the arts were necessarily closer than now, and another reason why music has dropped out from everyday life lies in our more adequate vocabulary. As speech becomes fitter to cope with the desires of expression, the importance of music dwindles. If we can say all we wish in words, we do not require music; if we can get all we wish from the written arts, we are not interested in heard ones; the novel banishes music from our idle hours. Once the novel was a ballad, and the ballad was sung. When all poetry had to be rendered aloud, song made a more natural way of rendering it than speech. The minstrel was essential to the early middle ages as the newspaper to us, and the minstrel was both a poet and a musician, not more one than the other. Earlier still—wasn't it in the days of Bede?—they despised an educated man, that is, a monk, who could not sing and compose a song; and a song meant a poem as well as a tune. The further back we go the more commonplace becomes music— a breakfast companion so to speak, and not a concert star. Once upon a time the Kings of England wrote music. The halo of romance round Richard I takes deeper colouring because he was both poet and musician; but Henry VIII, whom we accuse neither of romance nor of sentimentality, who was fat and practical, wrote music which is still sung. And so back we go till Plato could define* an educated man as one trained to sing in a chorus, or till we come where everyone composes their own songs, as musical children do, not to mention the natives of the Andaman Islands.† So in our backward course music becomes more essential and poetry creeps nearer it, till we arrive where we can no longer separate them, and the only poetry is song. If we go but a little further, not only poetry and music but speech and music become indistinguishable, or very difficult to distinguish. Then a curious problem

* *The Laws.*   † Wallaschek, *Primitive Music*, p. 279.

arises. Did speech develop out of music, or did music come from speech, or did they start together from a pre-music, pre-speech ancestor, and become differentiated only later? Just as we do not find rhythm existing before melody though we find it apart from melody, or melody before rhythm, and, though we may differentiate them, cannot say one grew out of the other, so, far back in distant psychology, perhaps speech had no pre-music existence nor music a pre-speech, but both were parts of the same thing.

This problem did not arise among theorists. It presented itself at the suggestion of observed facts. These observed facts are relevant to our study, and the most interesting introduction to them is through the theories. The discussion, it seems to me, attempts to solve two problems, which have been "tackled" simultaneously and as if they were the same. Before we set out to discover whether speech arose from music or music from speech, we must determine where the difference lies. We may do this in at least two ways—one according to their subjective aim or purpose, the other by their intrinsic objective difference. Although Wallaschek, like many others, clouds his reasoning by confusing the two, he tends rather to the first distinction. He says:*

We can see in almost all the examples furnished by ethnology that music is the expression of emotion. There is no doubt that emotion is one . . . of the sources of human language. . . . Music is an expression of emotion, speech the expression of thought. . . . Many cases of aphasia prove† that an expression cannot be emotional and intellectual at the same time, the one kind of expression arising in and spreading through different parts of the brain and nervous system from those occupied by the other. It may be, however, that in a very primitive stage of mental development thought and emotion have not yet become

* *Primitive Music*, pp. 250, 253-4.
† He does not say how.

clearly differentiated . . . music and speech did not arise the one from the other, but . . . both arose from (or together with) an identical primitive stage in one of their common elements.

This final conclusion is probably the right one. It is almost certainly right that in primitive mentality thought and emotion are not differentiated; but the deduction from the aphasia case is risky. Doesn't the point in aphasia consist in its abnormality, partly in the abnormality that thought and emotion do not work together, that the portion of the brain that expresses one is atrophied? That abnormally emotion and thought can be disunited does not prove that normally they can never be simultaneous. Nor does Wallaschek define the end of speech and music safely. Both music and speech can and do convey emotion, and perhaps music, too, can convey thought. We may differentiate between them more truthfully by saying that in speech we use sounds to convey meaning or emotion, in music (including poetry) to express that quality in life which we call its poetry. When weighted down with this significance or elated by this consciousness, the poet writes. Whereas inward necessity occasions the outpourings of emotion we call music, utilitarian or outward necessity occasions speech. The artistic or musical necessity comes from some deep part of our being; speech is a surface thing made necessary by the facts of our environment.

We must determine whether the artistic or the utilitarian first prompts nature's song. Is the blackbird's song speech or music? Is it a declaration of love, a revel in lovely sound for its own sake, or in his primitive *psyche* is the declaring of his love the same thing as the unburdening of his ideal or beauty-yearning impulses? Wallaschek* says that bird-song is not music but speech, and points out that gregarious birds are garrulous, solitary species silent. Mr.

* *Primitive Music*, pp. 247-8.

Garstang,* on the other hand, tells us that though gregarious birds chatter, "a certain isolation or aloofness" is necessary for song. Starlings, as he points out, sometimes sing if they are solitary, never otherwise. Wallaschek calls every sound a bird makes its song, and since some bird-sounds are not music, concludes that none is; he does not consider, what Garstang assumes, that a bird may both speak and sing. To prove one origin he refers to Mr. Witchell's statement that the call note or song, and the danger cry of birds originate from the same sounds. But Witchell was only proving his case; this is his idea rather than his observation. Wallaschek says further:

If the third frontal convolution of the bird's brain is stimulated by an electric current, the bird begins to "sing". Now this third frontal convolution is the *speech*-centre, on which our musical faculty does not at all depend.

This is interesting; it might prove almost anything. If we take bird-song as speech because of this experiment, and remember that the blackbird's speech sounds like our music, it will prove that music arose from speech. If we refuse to believe that the blackbird's song is speech, it will prove that speech arose from music, or that speech and music once inhabited the same house, were part of the same mental process. But it need not even prove a connection. The skin, speaking very loosely, of the most primitive animals acts as their eyes and ears, again speaking loosely; but this does not mean either that our hearing grew out of our sight, or our sight from our hearing. My recollections of Wundt† tell me that as the brain evolves, the mental processes proceed to new apartments. Man and dog do not necessarily use the same part of the brain to carry through the same mental act. The difference is much more physiological than psychological. Still it is interesting

* *The Songs of Birds*, p. 25.
† *Principles of Physiological Psychology*, p. 263.

that our speech-centre should grow out of what is the melody-producing centre in the bird, that perhaps in primitive brains melody and speech come out from the same depot—not that we did evolve from birds; we were only reptiles together. But we must remember that an electric current is not a psychological motive. If my right hand were stimulated with a red-hot poker I should probably scream, but this would not mean that the screaming agent of my mind were situated in my right hand. Suppose birds sing because they are happy, and suppose having an electric current passed through one's speech-centre makes one feel hilariously joyful, then the bird's song, being psychologically and not physically conditioned, would express excitement. Normally the song-centre comes into action by a volition which need not emanate from the song-centre and probably does not. A bird may work both its danger signal and its food call from the same centre, and the psychology of the impulses differ. If the blackbird makes its disagreeable *chirr-chirring* sound from the same centre as it sings with, the *chirring* sound may remain utilitarian and the song music. At all events, anyone who has followed the blackbird's song from its rise to its decline may see that it is not speech, but music. Nor is it an unpractised, spontaneous outburst of feeling. Listen to the first pained strivings of the blackbird learning his jump of a fifth. You can hear the diffidence of it, see him hesitate when he has not taken the interval up to pitch. No one could call these preliminary efforts either speech or song; they are deliberately practised exercises. A human whistler can beat them in precision of interval and in quality of tone, as the bird knows. If you mock a blackbird who has taken his fifth just wrong, with a patch from his last year's song, and are lucky, he will feel foolish, ruffling his feathers and drawing in his neck as a hen does when you stare it out of countenance, or he may fly away in a rage *chirring* at you as he does at the cat. When you live in a garden with black-birds and hear their daily progress, after the fifth, the third, then variations on the common chord, with improved tone, flexibility and ease, you cannot help seeing that only as a final consummation do their songs seem un-practised and spontaneous miracles. You can watch the songster keeping a critical eye on his production; if the first attempt does not please him, he tries again more carefully. He follows an ideal all the time, tries to sing beautifully, referring his song to an aesthetic or artistic sense, as if he made it after a pattern imagined beforehand, or at least in accordance with some subjective feeling. This is art, the catching of a heavenly music and the guiding of it through physical channels to earth; we cannot listen to his early strivings when he cuts out the channel, and doubt it. His song is not utilitarian; and if emotional, it is emotion devoid of earth, clear heavenly emotion.

We are not so sure as we used to be that bird-song is a mating phenomenon. The lark sings in January and February and does not mate till March; robins sing in autumn and winter, and thrushes in November. Herbert Spencer* concludes from this that "the singing of birds results merely from an overflow of energy". If a bird moults out of season he sings while the others moult. Caged birds sing longer than when wild. This looks as if bird-song, like human art, results from leisure. It is a spending of overflow vitality in the hunt for the beautiful. Witchell,† who believes that however bird-song may have originated, its final impulse is aesthetic, tells us that:

A Sedge-Warbler singing at ten o'clock at night reproduced exactly the fast-fading cries of a Chaffinch flying away. This Warbler then repeated in succession all the vehement alarm-cries which announce the arrival of a

* *Mind*, October 1890, "The Origin of Music."
† *The Zoologist*, 1890, "The Evolution of Bird Song."

Hawk, and continued his song with the single "tell" cries with which the male House-Sparrow, watching as a sentinel, warns his neighbourhood that the Hawk is very near. Then these sounds ceased. Suddenly the usual song of the Sedge-Warbler was resumed. The song of this bird was, in any event, evidence of his acute memory; but might it not have been an intentional picture, in sound, of an incident of bird-life? I submit that there are grounds for supposing the latter view to be correct; and if it should be so, may not all bird-song be to a variable extent intended to suggest pleasing impressions of surroundings to the objects of the song? Human songs are full of suggestions of surroundings, in which the sounds uttered by creatures are often imitated in the names of those creatures; and in the songs of birds we find an analogous reproduction of the notes of surrounding animals. May not the purpose of this mimicry be in both cases the same?

Even if we think Witchell has opened too many probabilities all at once, or generalised too much, still, that a scientific observer could arrive so far is striking.

We need hardly consider the speech of the animal world, its utilitarian noises. No one will deny that birds have food calls and danger cries; and the danger cries are nearly the same for many varieties of birds, or at least intelligible to them. There is something approaching a universal tongue, an Esperanto of birdland, for birds have international aims and agree in a sort of reciprocal protection policy, as in the *entente* that combines against the owl and the cat. We set ourselves to see whether primitive speech is music applied to utilitarian ends, or music the development of nature's utilitarian sounds to an artistic end; is speech an outgrowth of musical sounds to communicate meaning, or music a development of speech sounds to give pleasure? Wallaschek* gives music, or the emotion-relieving function, the original place:

* *Primitive Music*, pp. 240-52.

The monkey's tones of voice [he tells us] are so distinctly varied when these animals are on duty as posts or scouts on the flanks or rear, that a person much accustomed to watch their movements will at length fancy that he can understand their signals. Mr. Garner actually succeeded in understanding them, and by catching and reproducing these sounds by means of a phonograph got the apes to do the corresponding action. But this, and so many examples of the animal's call, proved that the vocal utterance, originally produced as emotional reflex, has been used later on with . . . a special meaning, *i.e.* in an intellectual way.

We still prefer music to a megaphone for army orders. As a further argument, he shifts over to the other problem and tells that in primitive peoples language lags behind music and gesture in powers of expression, drama dawned with music and action, words came only after, that in fact opera is older than drama. Thus speech has grown out of music to give precision and definiteness to meaning already there.

The other problem concerns the objective difference between speech and music. How does read poetry differ from sung poetry? We give up something when we sing; we abandon the inflections of speech in exchange for the melody of music. A melody can follow the inflections of a spoken poem, and a poem sung to such a melody differs from the read poem only in moving from note to note in jumps instead of by slurring. In a melody we sing the interval of a "third" ( ) as two clean, distinct, separated notes; in speech we make the movement from pitch to pitch by a very rapid *portamento*; the spoken "third" is not strictly an *interval*; the voice in going from one note to the other slides through all the intervening pitches ( ). Then, in song we stop on the delimiting pitch we have jumped to; in speaking we do not rest at the limits; the pitch of our speaking voice moves continuously. To many this seems so obvious as not to require saying; but in our survey of the music of poetry we are apt to overlook the fact.* It is important that we

* This is an accepted fact, as much as anything is accepted these days, though an experiment by Dr. Scripture seems to throw a few drops of cold water on it. He tells us (*Volta Bureau Reprints of Useful Knowledge*, No. 308, "Inscriptions of Speech") that music takes intervals less cleanly than we think:

"A subject spoke *sleepy* into the phonograph and was then asked to sing it. The notes on which he chose to sing the word resembled the inflections he had used in speaking. His voice was a quite untrained one and the result came out not so very unlike the curve for his inflected pronunciation. The vowels are observed to be much longer; otherwise the inscription appears little different. The voice starts at about 170 vibrations a second [*i.e.* 𝄢]. In writing out the notes I have used the table in the Appendix to Scripture's *The Elements of Experimental Phonetics*] and rises to 188 [*i.e.* 𝄢]. This tone is maintained with only one waver for a considerable time. As the note comes to an end, the voice drops downward to about 150 [or 𝄢]. The second note continues the slide downward to 120 [𝄢], and maintains this pitch for a while. The latter part of the note is at a pitch of 110 [𝄢]. This voice was a quite untrained one. It evidently aimed at two notes, falling by an interval of a major third. The voice misses the correct interval slightly. The sliding up to and down to a pitch are the common defects of an untrained voice. If the word could be sung on two notes with mechanical precision . . . Even the best trained human voice can never accomplish this; the melody constantly varies from the mechanical melody indicated by the written notes. This is required by the very essence of song, as a means of human expression; the slides, variations, wavers and inaccuracies are all elements of expression."

I learnt from the same experimenter that records from well-known singers showed such things as that their letters were not properly articulated, that the interval of a trill was less than a semitone. He remarked, recollectively, that it was funny how angry singers got when you told them what they sang. In this curious annoyance lies the argument against the results of the experiment, namely, that it *ought*

should realise how close speech is to song, and just where they differ. Every sound produced by the vocal cord in speech or song has a definite pitch; it is a note. In speech the pitch of the vocal cord's note never remains for one moment steady, the voice moving over musical intervals in lightning *portamentos*, flying up and down the ladder of melody so quickly that we do not see its feet on the rungs, hardly for one instant resting on any of them. In song the pitch of the vocal cord's note moves by definite jumps from rung to rung and rests its foot an appreciable time on each. That is the only essential objective difference between speech and song.*

---

to have been a semitone, that the letters *ought* to have been properly articulated, that the intervals *ought* to be precisely taken, and taken in a clean jump, and that the pitch *ought* not to waver. Indeed, learning to sing includes the learning not to do all those things which the records showed were done.

* Aristoxenus, as quoted by Mr. C. W. L. Johnson, describes the difference thus:

"In the continuous movement the voice appears to the senses to traverse a certain space in such a way that it rests nowhere, not even, so far as our conception of the sensation goes, at the bounds, but is borne along continuously until the sound ceases. . . . In the other movement, which we call intervallar, the contrary process takes place. For the voice seems to rest at various pitches, and all say of a man who seems to do this, that he no longer speaks, but sings. Therefore in conversing we avoid having the voice rest unless we are forced at times by reason of emotion to resort to this style of movement; but in singing we do the reverse, for we avoid the continuous and strive to make the voice rest as much as possible. For the more we make each of the sounds one and stationary and the same, so much the more accurate does the singing seem to the senses." *Studies in Honor of L. Gildersleeve*, "Accent and Accentual Arsis and Thesis."

Johnson remarks:

"In fact the line between speech and song could not be drawn with any degree of sharpness in ancient theory. The very fact of a formal separation of these two kinds of utterance according to the character of the vocal motion points to the existence of a manner of speaking resembling singing, and a manner of singing resembling speaking."

And if we were more observant, we could not draw the line any more sharply in modern theory.

We do not need to go very far to discover speech turning into song. When we wish to make our voice carry we

tend to give up the *portamento* and sing it.

sings my friend when the noise in the passage is so great I do not hear her speaking, or inflected invitation. In moments of more impatience, or effort to be heard, the drop is a minor sixth (*do'* to *mi*). The same thing happens in street cries. Dr. Carter Blake, as quoted by Wallaschek,* says these are always in minor keys, for which Mr. Joseph Kaines gives a pretty explanation; the street crier "utters his burden in pain"; more likely it is because the inflections of speech are in minor (in the wider, unacademic use of the word) modes. Plain-song, whose scales also are modal, had the same origin;† there we see the inflections of the voice being converted into musical notes. Both the intonations which we use to mark punctuation and those of pronunciation were copied, or if plain-song melodies arose unselfconsciously, evolved themselves.

‡Attentive observation on ordinary conversation shows us that regular musical intervals involuntarily recur. . . . A bass voice would say:

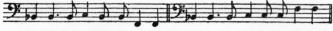

I have been walking this morning.   Have you been walking this morning?

. . . In the old Romish Church, the Gregorian school had the following rules:

* *Primitive Music*, pp. 149-50. Wallaschek objects that they are as often in major keys, that only one of Gardiner's seventeen examples is in the minor. He is thinking only of the "third". They are really in gapped scales.

† H. B. Brigg, *Elements of Plain-song*, pp. 8, 46.

‡ Helmholtz, *The Sensation of Tone*, Ellis's translation, pp. 364-5.

Sic can - ta com - ma, sic du - o punc - ta:
Thus sing the com - ma, thus sing the col - on:

sic ve - ro punc - tum, sic sig - num in - ter - ro - ga - tio - nis.
Thus sing the full stop. Thus sing the mark of interrogation.

It is easy to see that they strove to imitate the natural cadences of ordinary speech.

We can watch them following the pronunciation inflection in such phrases as:

* Lau - da - te.................... Do - mi - num,

or :

† Per om - ni - a sae - cu - la sae - cu - lo - rum. ℟ A - men.

℣ Do - mi - nus vo - bis - cum. ℟ Et cum spi - ri - tu tu - o.

If we consider how naturally the music goes with the Latin words, and hear how artificial it sounds with English, we realise how intimately these melodies are bound up with the Latin inflections. Folk-song, too, is but melodised speech, or rather poem, inflection. Mr. Cecil Sharp, speaking on folk-music in Cambridge on 25th October 1921, said that folk-singers often do not realise they are making music, are not conscious of the melody they sing, only of the words, and cannot sing the melody apart from the words; if they forget a song it is because they have

* Benedictines of Stanbrook, *Grammar of Plain-song*, p. 24.

† *Ibid.*, p. 67. Readers will remember that in plain-song notation time values are not represented.

forgotten the words; folk - song airs are unconscious emanations from, or crystallisations of, the inflections of the words. He said also that characteristic national differences in folk-tunes result from characteristic national "accent"; the peculiar Hungarian folk-song cadences come from a peculiar cadence in Hungarian speech; French has patter-song because its speech has no stress and does not inflect on emphatic syllables. So closely related are speech and song that we find speech taking every opportunity to turn itself into the more beautiful music.

On this resemblance between song and speech, Herbert Spencer bases his theory of the origin of music; music developed from speech inflection. He bases his argument rather on physiological than historical grounds, though history seems in his favour. Anthropological investigations are against him in so far as they have proved that song is probably older than speech. To consider the problem will throw the musical basis of speech into further relief, and emphasise facts in our study which require emphasis. Here again our province is not to umpire the contest, even if we felt sufficiently impartial to attempt it. In his article on the "Origin and Function of Music" in *Fraser's Magazine* for October 1857, Spencer rests his theory on physiology, and tells us:

that recitative . . . grew naturally out of the modulations and cadences of strong feeling, we have indeed still current evidence. There are even now to be met with occasions on which strong feeling vents itself in this form. Whoever has been present when a meeting of Quakers was addressed by one of their preachers (whose practice it is to speak only under the influence of religious emotion) must have been struck by the quite unusual tones, like those of a subdued chant, in which the address was made. . . . *If music, taking for its raw material the various modifications of voice which are the physiological result of excited feelings,** intensifies,

* My *italics*.

combines, and complicates them . . . it produces an idealised language of emotion; then its power over us becomes
comprehensible. But in the absence of this theory the expressiveness of music appears to be inexplicable.

This is the core of the theory, that music has evolved from
the modifications of voice which are the physiological
result of excited feelings.

Spencer's theory aroused opposition. It was new. We
do not want to believe that the most heavenly of the arts
had a common origin with speech in our physiology. Poor
mortals, we feel afraid when heaven comes up out of the
earth instead of descending from the sky, and cling to the
belief that what is divine can come only through an exclusively divine channel. But if Spencer's theory makes
prose of music, it makes music of prose; *we* have no
quarrel with it. Perhaps not unnaturally, the credit of
being its most deadly enemy belongs to a musical critic,
Mr. Ernest Newman. His objections* are answerable. Let
us look at them in order:

Stricker in his *Du Langage et de la musique* has . . .
made out a good case for believing that the organs of
speech and the organs of song are controlled by different
cerebral spheres.

I believe there is as good a case for believing that different
cerebral spheres control the organs of writing and speaking, yet no one would deny that writing is an offshoot from
speech. Newman objects that the musician thinks in sound
as the literary man thinks in words. It seems unlikely that
the literary man does think in words. Many psychologists
oppose the idea, and, as Mr. Keary† says, "a poet can think
his line before he knows of what words it will be made
up". If words are emotional they must be "supplemented

* *Musical Studies*, pp. 193-8.
   † *Fortnightly Review*, 1906, "Some Thoughts on the Technique
of Poetry."

by a *something*, by gesture or intonation". This is true of prose-writing also. The feeling, or subjective experience of writing, is not that of putting one word on to another word, but a rush of sound that comes all of a piece. The writer with command of his pen does not normally translate his meaning word by word, he thinks in a stream of sound. If we contrast this native writing with our first attempts in a foreign tongue we realise the momentous difference between merely writing in words and thinking in the sequence of foreign sounds. The musician thinks in sounds which may not include the sounds of words, but this is no argument against Spencer, who holds that music is precisely the stream of sound we feel in when there are no words. Newman says further: "No demonstration could deduce a Bach fugue from excited speech." A Bach fugue is founded on a single melody; if melody grows out of speech inflections, it is demonstrated that a Bach fugue can be derived from the intonations of excited speech. This is but another way of contradicting Spencer, not another argument against him. Fugue form or any other complex musical form may, or may not, be deducible from inflectional melodies, but this is wholly irrelevant. Spencer does not say it can. The finest cathedral has its origin in the earth, and could never be built if its material were not in the earth, but this does not mean that the imagination of man had no share in determining its form. Next we find a reference to Wallaschek, where he tells us that the words of the most primitive songs are nonsense words:

It is impossible [says Newman] that in these cases music arose as a direct imitation of the natural accents ready made in speech.

We anticipated this argument. It proves that melody preceded meaningful words, that a meaningful or emotional use of melody preceded the pointing of its specific application in words and in so far as the question is chronological is possibly unanswerable; but though Spencer, through not anticipating Newman, does not make the distinction, his theory is not so much chronological as physiological, though even chronologically we can defend it. He states his real position very clearly:

Using the word cadence in an unusually extended sense as comprehending all the modifications of voice, we may say that *cadence is the commentary of the emotions upon the propositions of the intellect.**

The function of music is, he thinks, to develop this language of inflection. We may agree that melody, whether as inflection or as song, preceded words. Then on Spencer's view, the inflected or *portamento* melodies preceded the sung melody, and music has developed from howls and wails, which, being *portamento* cries, are inflections and therefore speech rather than song. At all events Spencer does not hold that "music arose as a direct imitation of the natural accent ready made in speech", though he avails himself of the justification or analogy which musical history provides. He says that speech is compounded of two elements, the words and the tones in which they are uttered, the signs of ideas and the signs of feeling; and it is from these tones, which he regards not as the "natural accent of words", but as the result of excited feelings—a point he labours—that music derives. He contrasts not so much words and music as inflection and song. Newman hardly considered the real theory Spencer puts forward. Its battle-ground should more properly be scientific, neither musical nor prosodical. But the theory has value for us in proving that music is a natural thing, part of our fundamental constitution, not in any sense arbitrary; it shows that our sense of tonality, of melody, of scale, is

* His *italics*.

innate and intrinsic, that our scales cannot be mere conventions arbitrarily determined by such things as the construction of primitive pipes*—a curious idea when we come to think of it. It suggests also that the same principles which govern musical melodies govern the inflections of poetry; since both rely on the same sense of tonality.

This leads us on to ground of common interest to musicians and prosodians, the setting of music to words and of words to music. Poetry and Music, being sister arts, fight very often, but this does not necessarily mean that they hate each other. Poetry's zealous following resent Music's share in the squabbles, even disclaiming the relationship: Poetry is an art by itself, distinct; why must Music come butting in and upset everything? That the inflections of poetry form part of its quintessential loveliness has hardly been recognised by theorists, although the musician recognises it, or at least some do. We talk rather as if poetry had no inflection, or as if such inflection as it has were incidental and an accident; yet this, though unrecognised, is the real quarrel the partisans of Poetry have with Music, that Music substitutes its tune for Poetry's. They owe their grudge to the misfortune of coming upon the sisters always at the wrong time; they have often seen them quarrelling, and Poetry, being the gentler, has usually got the worst of it, but have never seen the reconciliation, when Music, being the more generous, has given over everything to the words. The most unfriendly admit that in Gilbert and Sullivan the one art has not prejudiced the other; the music has given a soul to the words, the words a body to the music; both poet-humorist and musician were sensitive to the inflections of speech. In the best songs either the musician deifies the poem by forming his melody on inflections native to it, or the poet writes

* Wallaschek, *Primitive Music*, p. 157.

words whose inflections fit the melody, so that the music
and the poetry sound in more than harmony, they sing in
unison. But the musician may not only follow the characteristic tunes of speech and so make a song of a poem, he
may discover the more essentially expressive inflection and
crystallise it in his song, perpetuating a finer interpretation,
making, as it were, the tones of the inspired reader im-
mortal. Poetry sung well to a good tune is much beauti-
fied; it is then emotionalised, song being the expression of
more elated feeling than speech.

Lanier claims* a falling fourth as the commonest inflection for the end of a sentence; and it is interesting after
reading him to recollect this falling fourth, as the cadence
in the recitative of Bach's *Matthew Passion*, that most lingers
in our memory. Within sixteen consecutive bars we find so
many as three:

* *The Science of English Verse*, p. 267.
† *Matthew Passion*, No. 8, "When Jesus understood it," edited by
C. V. Stanford (Stainer & Bell). I have written the introductory
phrase in the bass clef to make the relative position of the pitch clearer
to the reader unaccustomed to musical notation.

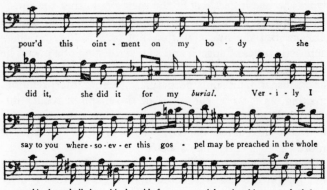

pour'd this oint - ment on my bo - dy she

did it, she did it for my *burial.* Ver - i - ly I

say to you where - so - ev - er this gos - pel may be preached in the whole

world, there shall al-so this be told for a memorial that this woman *hath done.*

Even one who cannot read musical notation will see that the music follows the inflections of the words if he remember that the higher the dot of the note on the stave the higher is the pitch. No intonation could be more expressive than that of "the whole world". But the expressiveness is all the more remarkable when we recollect that Bach wrote the music to German words. The English translation has been very carefully made to fit the music; but even so, it is remarkable that music which follows the most expressive inflection of one tongue can remain expressive in translation—a point in favour of Spencer's theory, for the Germans are our first cousins. The music of Debussy's *Blessed Damozel*, which fits the French translation, sounds inexpressive with the English words, not inexpressive as music, but inexpressive as inflection; it is English sung with a French "accent". Our folk-songs sometimes catch a local "accent". I do not think it fanciful to detect a Highland, or is it West of Scotland, "accent" in *Lizzie Lindsay*. This is not the only place I have heard

Ron - ald Mac - don - ald

That music can follow the inflections of poetry is not wonderful; but it is significant that music following the inflections of poetry should make such lovely melodies as our folk-tunes, or, more notably, this music—there is no adjective to describe its loveliness—from Purcell's *Dido and Aeneas*:

We need hardly comment on these expressive intonations, on the breaking of the voice, the shuddering of it on "darkness", or the inflectional quality we feel where two notes come to a word, on "bosom", "would" and "death". "Welcome" has the most emotional, as it has also the most lovely inflection. The sound of tears is in it; we talk like this only at the extremity of speech.

Here we shall not discuss the setting of poetry to music accompanied by instruments, or poetry sung in more than one part. That is another problem. Something may be said, and indeed much has been said, against giving words a full musical setting; nothing can be urged against singing poetry, rendering it in the native style. But perhaps the setting of words to music is the more interesting study. To our sophisticated minds this way of making a new song seems a wonderful, difficult, almost an unnatural thing, yet it is no less natural than the other way, being less ambitious, more primitive and naïve. Writing poetry to a tune is obviously a good way for the poet with an insecure "metrical" technique, to give definite form to his poetic impulse. The tune keeps the form of the poem, the metre, the phrasing, the stanzas, right. Many poets of Scottish newspapers write with this aid; after the title, they tell us their tune—(To the tune of *The Blue Bells of Scotland*), (To the tune of *Charlie is my Darling*). These are not freak or acrobatic poets, but humble shoemakers and house-maids. But the poet must have a feeling for the inflectional meaning of his tune to make a good song thus; and many of the poets who have given us the words for our Scottish national airs did so with a very sure instinct in using melody as significant inflection. An essential part of Burns' genius as a song-writer lay in his appreciation of this. Many of his songs inevitably suggest their melody; we cannot read them without their tune, and this not because we have never heard them save as sung, or that we hear them as songs before we read them as poems. It is not due to mere association; they were indeed written to the melody. The tune forms part of the material of the poem; the poem in-cludes the tune. In place of an inflectional sense when he wrote, the poet had a consciousness of the tune. So skilful is Burns in fitting words to music that we often feel rather as if the music were written to fit the words, but of course it is not so. Among the many dances of Scotland he knew where to find a tune for his mood, for in Scotland a dance played slowly may become a song, just as a song played quickly may become a dance. The annotator of the 1877 edition* of Burns, tells how *The Diel's awa wi' the Excise-man* was written. One day of incessant rain, Burns, with an insufficient force, was watching a smuggler's boat till his colleague exciseman returned with more men; one of the

* Blackie & Son.

party wished the "Deil" had the absent exciseman for
being so slow, and suggested that Burns should indite a
song on him. Burns, after taking a few strides by himself
among the reeds and shingle, rejoined the party and sang
this:

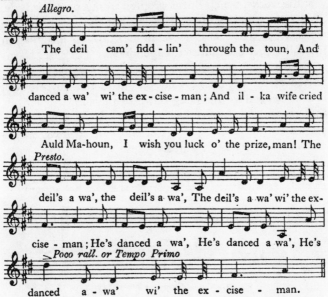

The deil cam' fidd - lin' through the toun, And danced a wa' wi' the ex - cise - man; And il - ka wife cried Auld Ma-houn, I wish you luck o' the prize, man! The deil's a wa', the deil's a wa', The deil's a wa' wi' the ex-cise - man; He's danced a wa', He's danced a wa', He's danced a - wa' wi' the ex - cise - man.

He could not have found a better tune than *The Hemp-
dresser* to express the impish, unrestrained jubilation, nor
could he have fitted the words better to catch the excited
intonations of the music on the right place. Besides a
genius for finding the right tune for his sentiment, he
seems to have had the genius for finding the right sentiment for his tune. If it is true that the writer of the air of
Ye Banks and Braes o' Bonnie Doon, James Miller of Edin-
burgh, was a man with no music—which is hard to believe
—who got the melody by acting on the suggestion that the
way to write a Scottish tune was to amuse oneself with the

black notes of the piano, and that Burns offered to write words to the result, and this origin is too picturesque to be lightly put aside, it proves him versatile in this other way. In any case, the song shows the most marvellous ingenuity. Though the music suggested the reference, it did not suggest the words, which Burns adapted from a previous lyric, in its turn a mosaic of older lyrics; but the music and the words fit so well that it needs an effort of our imagination to realise that each arose independently. They feel so inseparable that we tend to overlook the miracle which united them. Yet this was not an out-of-the-way miracle; it is as natural as the going down of the sun. The singer, too, respects the inflectional quality of the tune. When played on the violin as a sort of *presto* or, at least, *allegro* dance, we may hear it phrased thus:

It is sung *andante* thus:

Ye banks and braes o' bon-nie Doon, How can ye bloom sae

The inflection comes on "braes", "Doon", "can", instead of on "of", "how", "ye", as it would if the instrumental phrasing had been kept.

CHAPTER II

THE INFLECTIONS OF SPEECH

[The word "inflection" as used throughout this book means
the modulations of voice with which we speak, *never*, even in
the chapter where I have had to consider them, conjugational
or declensional endings.]

WE think this an elusive study at first, irreducible to rule
as a will-o'-the-wisp, not solid enough for practical investigation, though nice to talk about in the air. But when
we come to think a little more, we see that the inflections
of poetry are already of practical account, that literary
critics have been talking about them for centuries, and that
they influence our judgments of poetry. We often refer to
the "cadence" of the *Faerie Queene* stanza, and can recognise it when by chance any of Spenser's imitators catches
his tune; we talk about the "lilt" of Jacobean lyrics, and
so on, actually mentioning the "tunes" of poetry, and yet
we do not always realise how literally true such references
are. We tend to think them only metaphorical, using words
and musical terms to paint impressions. They are true in
fact, using words with prose significance. We have not ex-
hausted the musical facts of *Lycidas* when we enumerate
its rhythms, its rhymes, its consonant echoes, its vowel
modulations. Who ever felt he had found the *loca* of its
wonderful music? And yet prosody has not ranged the
whole floor of its ocean till it can point at this with its
prosaic finger. The unaccountably beautiful music of

Lycidas, which fills us with a sense of melody uncloying and insatiating, lies more than in anything else—the *onomato-poesis*, the choice of words beautiful in themselves, "Neæra", "enamel", "Lesbian", "Amaryllis", "mellow-ing", "violet", "laborious", or the subtle music of the tapestry they weave—in the melody of the inflections. It is the unwritten magic we hear and yet cannot find when we force ourselves out of its ecstasy—a difficult task—to look critically in the words and tangible construction of the poem; it eludes us then, because represented by no hiero-glyphic.

An analogy will illustrate the difference between the old way of looking at things and this new way. In the *Journal of the Folk-Song Society** occurs an illuminating passage about folk-singers:

They enjoy the singing; but how far are they conscious of any of the notes or tunes? I do not believe an answer to that question is possible. . . . The words are the beginning, middle and end of a song. . . . However minutely a song may be discussed, only the vaguest references to the tune will be heard. The tune is an elusive essence, the mysteri-ous soul of the words. It has no independent existence. It is part of the singer's secret, indistinguishable from his voice. . . .

Only experience in the country and long conversations about songs will bring you to this conclusion: that the people hardly know anything at all about their tunes. Certainly to-night, as we listen to our second singer, we do not feel inclined to believe it; for he is a great exponent of the local art, tuneful, precise, masterly. You would think that he had studied every effect with professional care; it will be a great shock to you, when you know him better, to find that he is largely unconscious of music. Yet so he is. If you tell him that two of his songs have the same tune, he will answer that that is impossible, since they are different

* Vol. vi, No. 23, p. xxiv, in an article on "An Irish Concert" by Mr. A. M. Freeman, whose permission I have to quote.

songs.* If you then say that the tunes are very much alike, he will agree, and look upon you as a musical genius for having noticed it. "What a marvellous thing," he will exclaim, "for a man who was not brought up in Irish to know so much about our songs!"

"The tune is an elusive essence, the mysterious soul of the words." We are all folk-readers of poetry and think of the tune merely as an elusive essence, the mysterious soul of the words.

Perhaps this music appears more real in bad poetry, where no longer a mysterious essence but a commonplace tune, as in much Christmas-card poetry:

> To wish you the season's gladness
> In greeting I send this line,
> For time and space cannot sunder
> The friendship of Auld Lang Syne.

The sentiment of these lines is laudable and sincere, the wording simple and inoffensive, but the melody of it does not bring us any pleasure. We find another trite tune in:

> †Not now can the nightingale sing
>   Expecting a stellar reply;
> No fugues intergarlanded ring
>   Of the earth and the clusters on high—
> Sidereal echoes that bring
>   The crystalline tears and the sigh
> For the end of a beautiful thing
>   That soldered the earth and the sky.

This, also, has something to recommend it, "fugues intergarlanded" being a pleasing description; but the tune is impossible.

How came the tune there? How far do we all hear the

* This, curiously enough, is an answer I got when I suggested that Milton's *Nativity Ode* and the song of Shelley's referred to on p. 118, have the same tune at the cadence.

† John Davidson, *Holiday and Other Poems*, p. 106.

same tune? Anyone who is musical and accustomed to analysing the impressions he gets from poetry must recognise the melody of these verses. The poet is almost bound to have written to it, at least subconsciously, though he, like many of us, may not locate the whereabouts of his tune. The Christmas-card poet is like Burns in writing to a ready-made tune, unlike him only in having it in the background, not the foreground of his consciousness. Milton differs from both in making his own tune. Some writers of free verse object to metre and rhyme as sophisticated, and write what they say is the only essential of poetry, "cadence". Among them Mr. Flint* cannot quite explain what he means by "cadence", but from his poetry one would say he meant an inflection tune:

> *He is sitting beneath a cherry tree in bloom,
> And the thought of the ripe cherries is in his mouth,
> And his eyes love the tall daisies in the grass
> And the children playing in the meadow.

Indeed, since the tune, more than anything, determines the form of a poem, the poet can hardly write without some consciousness of it,† unless he count his syllables on his fingers and decide where to end his sonnet by noticing the number of his line. Sometimes in the rise of poetry to consciousness, the tune emerges in the poet's mind simultaneously with the words and as distinctly. Some of Campion's songs were almost certainly written in this way,

* *Otherworld Cadences*.

† When discussing whether singing preceded coherent speech, Keary said (*Fortnightly Review*, 1906): "The unit of singing cannot have been a single sound; it must have been the phrase. Emotion must have evoked the (musical) phrase—containing, that is to say, some sort of cadence and contrast of sound—before language was formed into the words that made the phrase. And there is nothing unreasonable or fantastic, but most probable, in the notion that the same sequence is followed still when emotion provokes us to any metrical form of speech."

music and words simultaneously. Mr. Wallace says* that
in this way the words and music of a lyric may arise in the
mind while we are reading the music and words of another
lyric, and we gather that he speaks from personal experience. Probably all poets are musicians subconsciously, as
perhaps Mr. John Erskine recognises when† he says that
"music and poetry separate where poetry becomes
musical"; he thinks that completely musical poetry holds
its own music, has its own melody. On his view, *Music
when sweet voices die* would make the ideal poem for a song:

> Music, when soft voices die,
> Vibrates in the memory;
> Odours, when sweet violets sicken,
> Live within the sense they quicken.
>
> Rose leaves, when the rose is dead,
> Are heaped for the beloved's bed;
> And so thy thoughts, when thou art gone,
> Love itself shall slumber on.

With its transparent musical framework, its feeling as if
the inflection tune were an albino, colourless gossamer,
this cries out for the support of music. On the other hand
we should expect poetry with the fuller music to attract
the musician, since he would have but to catch the melody
already there. Presumably *Lycidas* set to Milton's own
melody would make a more magnificent music than is possible to *Music when soft voices die*.

We do know enough to talk about the inflections of
poetry in a solemn, *quasi*-scientific way. But we may have
been too positive about optional readings, and should discuss them first. The tunes we hear must almost inevitably
have small differences, just as a folk-song tune has different
versions; and just as the same folk-singer varies his tune,
the same reader will not always get precisely the same

* *The Threshold of Music*, pp. 188-9.
† *The Elizabethan Lyric*, p. 301 and elsewhere.

tune from a poem. This we must, I think, admit, and may then neglect. We need not clog our argument by being too generous with *perhapses*. Having admitted this, we must not exaggerate it. Different versions of folk-tunes do not destroy the identity of a tune. Besides, our renderings may be more uniform than we at first imagine. Dr. Scripture says* that:

> A study of inscriptions† of "Ein Fichtenbaum steht einsam im Norden auf kahler Höh'" spoken by thirteen persons from different parts of Germany showed that all of them used the same melody although they came from regions where the melody of ordinary speech differed greatly. Of course, this was the result of their education in speaking the language of their culture, namely modern high German. No matter how differently they spoke at home, they all spoke nearly alike in a matter of literature. The laws of variation in melody as an element of verse were the same for all.

This is a most striking and gratifying result for the psychologist and the student of poetry, yet we should be rash to assume such uniformity out of Germany. But granting that people with a local accent tend to render English poetry with the characteristics of that accent, and that even in standard-English inflection individual idiosyncrasies remain, poems may yet tend to suggest the same melody to every reader. Dauney, writing a hundred years ago, and talking of the close similarity of Scottish folk-poems and their airs, writes:

> ‡The very rhythm and measure of a verse, together with the sentiment, often seems to carry a certain intonation or air along with it, and Mr. Allan Cunningham has gone so far as to say that when he was a boy, and committed to memory many ancient and modern songs, he never learned

* *British Journal of Psychology*, January 1921, "The Nature of Verse."
† An "inscription" is a phonograph record or something of the sort.
‡ *Ancient Scottish Milestones*, pp. 40-41, his *italics*.

any of them without making himself master of some kind of melody which re-echoed the words, and that *most of the airs which the words suggested corresponded in a great measure with the proper tune.*

So, differences in the spoken rendering of a poem need not stagger us. Our silent reading may differ from our spoken. Self-consciousness, and, more ineradicable as an an obstacle, individual habits of intonation, and racial or physical peculiarities of speech, obstruct the poet's melody in our spoken rendering. This must be common experience. Not only is the voice no longer the poet's voice, the tune is different; and indeed we had almost said that whereas we now but speak, in our silent reading we sang. Consequently in the hunt for the melody of a poem experimental methods help us little. Nor need the reading of the poet himself satisfy us; he may suffer from the same infirmities in translating the imagination of his own music into physical sound, especially if he has a phonograph for audience.

We cannot know whether the unspoken music is the same for all, or more uniform than the spoken music. Milton does not read himself to the Scot with a Scottish accent, but we cannot prove this. Perhaps it makes the Englishman laugh to think that a Scot can imagine he hears an English accent in his silent reading of English poetry; but it is not really a contradiction. A child, not necessarily unmusical, may sing lustily on one note, thinking all the while that he sings a melody, and may get the same impression from his performance as if he really sang what he believes himself to sing; it is not that he cannot hear the difference between one note and another, or that he cannot imagine it,* but that he cannot translate it into his voice. We easily imagine ourselves imitating the accents of another, without perhaps being able to imitate them

* Some children learn to write down the notes of songs from ear much sooner than to sing them.

actually. But this is not mere speculation. I have amused myself, who am Scotch, putting the melodies of English poetry into musical notation, trying to find the melody I do hear; those from my spoken recitation come out in Scottish intonations, those from my unobjectified imagination usually in English. In the spoken music there is less variety, the pitch does not tend to rise for the accents, and where it does move, tends to move in tones and semitones, not in those big jumps we hear in the so-called standard-English inflections.*

We may find another reason for supposing that we hear the poet's melody in his poetry. Most people will grant that the music in the following is somewhat "flat"; it gives the sensation we get from hearing someone singing consistently out of tune, the impression of the musical interval being always just wrong:

The old brown thorn trees break in two high over Commen
    Strand,
Under a bitter black wind that blows from the left hand;
Our courage breaks like an old tree in a black wind and
    dies,
But we have hidden in our hearts the flame out of the eyes
Of Cathleen the daughter of Houlihan.

The wind has bundled up the clouds high over Knock-
    narea,
And thrown the thunder on the stones for all that Maeve
    can say,

   * Spencer notes a similar contrast: "The Italians, who have varied and expressive speech-intonations, have . . . free and flowing melody; and . . . the Scotch, with a more monotonous (not necessarily, however, an inexpressive) mode of speech, have . . . limited and monotonous tunes."

   It depends on the dialect, of course; dialects differ as much in Scotland as in England; lumping them all as one, besides leading to a libel on the tunes of the Scot, is as wrong as classing the London and the Yorkshire dialects as one. I take the quotation from Spencer from Gurney's *The Power of Sound*, p. 493.

Angers that are like noisy clouds have set our hearts abeat;
But we have all bent low and low and kissed the quiet feet
Of Cathleen the daughter of Houlihan.

The contrast between the out-of-tuneness of the body of
the poem and the perfect tunefulness of the refrain, "Cathleen the daughter of Houlihan", is marked. In Yeats'
poetry we often feel this flatness, as if the tones were in
between the intended notes instead of on them, and it is
interesting to discover that he is:

*quite tone-deaf—or perhaps I should say tune-deaf—
though of fine ear for all sound values other than pitch.

That in our own silent reading we should perceive this
tune-deafness is significant. The only difficulty lies in
locating the mistuned feeling, which I should attribute to
the inflection, since we feel it not so much in spots—the
letter music, so to speak—as in a general lack of precise
intonation. That the poet's tune should read itself alike
to every reader is not such a wild idea as we might at first
think.

If this music of poetry is something definite, then perhaps we ought to be able to write out the tune of any poem
in musical notation. But besides the practical difficulty of
discovering what the notes we hear are, a greater obstacle
stands in our way. There are, roughly, two ways of reading
poetry. First, with a critical eye, the way of the man who
has to form a judgment and is engaged in the process of
judging while he reads. His individuality, being at work on
the poem all the time, almost inevitably tinctures the impression he gets, and consequently is of no use to us. The
more natural, passive reader opens his mind to receive, not
so much holding out tentacles to grasp the whole matter,

* MacDonagh, *Thomas Campion and the Art of English Poetry*,
p. 52.

as allowing the poem to imprint itself on his limp, "negative" consciousness. This purely receptive reader, making no effort to absorb the poem, obtrudes nothing to prevent the music of the poet conveying itself, forms no other music to usurp its place. If he is unmusical he may not hear the music, or if his ear is not sensitive, may remain unhurt by mistuned poetry, but so long as he reads passively he will not substitute for the poet's music another created partly by himself. We are not all equally sensitive to the music poetry reads to us; some hear more than others, and some are more conscious of what they do hear; but it is not such a huge assumption that when reading passively we shall not hear what is not there. Once more this cannot, by its very nature, be proved. When we ask, "What do I hear?" we awaken our positive, critical personality, which is not trustworthy. Most of us have been both types of reader and know the difference between the two readings. If we read a poem to discover its metrical structure or to determine which interpretation of it is right we usually have a sneaking conviction of not reading the poem at all. By obtruding our discriminating and inquisitive personality we cut out certain effects, pictorial and emotional, and alter others, so that we see everything through our personal film; it is the same with the music of poetry. And this personal film is as obstinate as the film of individual tastes, which, whether we read actively or passively, determines our judgment on a poem. Two passive readers may hear the same tune, and while one thinks it beautiful, the other may think it banal; but there is more than this at stake. The critical reader is in danger of altering the tune when his critical eye turns on it, of composing the tune instead of merely transcribing it. Thus we cannot represent the inflection of any poem in musical notation save at a tremendous risk. After granting so much, we might almost conclude this not a proper study for prosody.

Still, the risk may be worth while, and at all events there remains to prosody, a servile study at the best, the unbaked dough of the music of poetry.

We may write out "rules" for variations of pitch in prose and speech. In English, words tend to have a tune. "Very", "solitary", "expedition", even monosyllables like "no" and "yes" are said on more than one note. "No" covers an appreciable interval; a minor third is not too large on the average (*fa* to *re*). If we wish a "rule", then standard English inflects up on the accent, and as English accentuates rather early in the word than late, mono-syllables usually have a falling inflection. Perhaps the marked inflections of southern English have something to do with the trend towards diphthongisation. The first step of "no" in the direction of the Cockney diphthong is a wide interval in its inflection, as we may hear in the speech of many Englishmen, where "no" has the same vowel as the Scot's "no", only it is said on two notes instead of on one. Conversely, where a letter like *r* is being lost, its inflection tends to linger, at least for a little. "Are" without its consonant has commonly a different tune from "ah", and the tune of "where" is probably influenced by the recollection that it used to have more than one consonant; indeed, throughout its whole vocabulary southern English prefers inflecting the vowel to articulating the consonant.

In many languages such inflections are as important as vowels and consonants in characterising words. Even to-day one or two Swedish words are distinguished only by their inflections, while in Chinese this is the common practice.* In one of the poorest and least developed tongues, the Dahomian, meaning depends almost wholly on intonation; thus "so" means to-day, to-morrow, a horse, bring,

* Scripture, *Elements of Experimental Phonetics*, pp. 486-7.

a stick, thunder, according to the modulation of the voice.* Tylor† tells us that:

to sing a Siamese song to a European tune makes the meaning of the syllables alter according to their rise and fall in pitch.

Wundt‡ says that in the Ewe language—that of the peoples of the Togo—the same word means both "large" and "small", only for "large" the tone is deep and for "small" high, that a deep tone in "indicative signs" signifies remoteness, a high nearness; that in some Sudan languages the inflections determine the degrees of proximity and size; "yonder" has a very deep note for the far distance, a note neither low nor high for the middle distance, while a high note turns "yonder" into "here"; so "sweet" is differentiated from "bitter" by coming on a higher note, passive verbs from active by coming on a low one.

Although in English the tune is not essential to the word, and English is understood spoken with un-English inflections, still, in comparison with languages such as French, its words have characteristic tunes. Scientific measurement of records from French vowels shows that as a rule both vowels in a two-syllabled word have the same pitch.§ As far as I know, the vowels of English have been studied scientifically only in Americans.‖ One American experimenter¶ discovered that most people consider a high

* Wallaschek, *Primitive Music*, p. 185.
† *Primitive Culture*, vol. i, p. 169.
‡ *Elements of Folk Psychology*, Schaub's translation, p. 66.
§ Scripture, *Elements of Experimental Phonetics*, p. 276.
‖ Scripture says of these (*ibid.*, p. 485): "Vowels of sustained or constant pitch are not very common in the cases I have studied. . . . Yet some of them are approximately constant; the vowel *i* in *see*, *needle* . . . etc., is approximately a sustained vowel although it generally falls slightly." Nearly all the other vowels had a rising pitch with a slight fall at the end, a circumflex inflection.
¶ *Amer. Jour. of Psychol.*, vol. xii (Squire, "A Genetic Study of Rhythm").

pitch more emphatic than a low, yet a considerable min-
ority felt lowered pitch more emphatic, while to others
change of pitch makes no difference; but none of those
tested varied in their judgment, feeling sometimes the high,
sometimes the low pitch the more outstanding. Writing a
century ago, William Mitford says:*

> With ordinary English pronunciation, the *strengthened
> syllable* has always the *acuter tone*, or, in musical phrase,
> the higher note. . . . It is the striking peculiarity of the
> Scottish dialect of the English language, unknown, as far
> as I have had opportunity to observe, in any dialect of any
> other language, that the distinguishing accent of its vowels
> is a proper grave; a lower note than is given to any other
> syllable of the word. In that dialect, if the penultimate be
> the strengthened syllable, the concluding syllable rises in
> tone considerably, so that the word ends with something
> approaching to a squeak. To those who, themselves speak-
> ing proper English, have had opportunity to observe the
> Lowland Scottish pronunciation, this strong peculiarity
> cannot fail to have been striking.

Perhaps the exceptions in the American experiment were
originally of northern extraction. Incidentally, Mitford
makes two mistakes. Scots is no more a dialect of English
than English is a dialect of German, both languages en-
shrining in them the marks of an independent national
history.† And he cannot have broken his journey to Scotland in Yorkshire, which is the real home of "the proper
grave"

---

* *Inquiry into the Principles of Harmony in Language*, p. 58.
† It is extraordinary how many make this mistake. Scots differs
from English less because of its distance from the influence of London
as English dialects do, than because its education came from Paris, not
London. Many Scots words are French, *e.g.* "grossart" = gooseberry.
"Dinna fash yoursel(f)" = *ne vous fachez pas*. Its borrowings from Latin
also are original. Its old state documents and philosophical writings
when not in Latin, are in Scots, not to mention the poetry of its
peasants and kings.

Scottish methods of inflecting do, however, form an interesting study. I do not know what happened in 1804, but to-day about half the people of Lowland Scotland are bilingual, they talk both Scots and English; most of those who "have" only one, "have" English, if such a way of stating it be not too great an anachronism. In mixed communities such as the universities, or at least in the most northern of them, it was common a few years ago, and probably still is, to hear Scots and English spoken in alternate sentences according to the listener; one even heard a sentence begun in English and finished in Scots, forming such horrid mongrelisms as, "I don't ken". Not only the words, the inflections may alter with the language,* the "proper grave" being dropped in compliment to the sister tongue, though heightened pitch is not much used except in an "Anglified" accent, which sounds as contemptible as it is ugly in the ears of the Scot. Indeed, the anomaly arises of the Scot who is not bilingual, speaking English with a Scottish accent, and attempting his native tongue with an "English" accent. We may even travel north in the Scotch Express with a chatterbox who entertains chance comers south of the border in English and an "Anglified" accent, those across the border in English and a Scottish accent, and greets her friends at the station in Scots and the real Doric music. Though some of this is mere artificiality, part of it is a logical recognition of the difference in the characteristic tunes of the two tongues. When we speak French or German we attempt the same thing.

Such differences in the tunes of speech make themselves felt in poetry. Not only so, their tunes help to determine the poet's choice of words, especially when poets are musical in more than mere sympathy. This sensitiveness to the inflections of words helped the Elizabethan lyrists

* This happens also when English people who normally speak in dialect use standard English.

to their lovely melodies. Lanier* points out how Shakespeare uses the different inflections possible to "Oh Lord,
Sir!" for humorous effect in *All's Well that Ends Well* (II.
sc. 2). In modern times some writers make the distinction
between metrical and logical accent on this ground: that
the logical is a pitch one. When poets write on prosody
they often recognise the importance of inflections. Campion, in his *Observations on the Art of English Poesie*, and
Daniel, in his *Apologie for Ryme*, always mean by "accent"
an alteration of pitch. Daniel says:

And though it [*i.e.* English verse] doth not strictly observe long and short sillables, yet it most religiously respects the accent; and as the short and the long make
number, so the accute and the grave accent yeeld harmonie.
And harmonie is likewise number, so that the English
verse then hath number, measure and harmonie in the
best proportion of musike.

Campion's observations on accent are valuable not only in
showing that the intervening centuries have left the
melody of English undisturbed, since his observations are
correct for English of to-day, but in being the observations of the ideal observer, the man who is equally a poet
and a musician:

In words of two sillables, if the last have a full and rising accent that sticks long upon the voyce, the first sillable
is always short, unlesse position, or the dipthong, doth
make it long, as *dĕsīre, prĕsērve, dĕfīne, prŏphane, rĕgard,
mănure*. . . . Words of two sillables that in their last sillable
mayntayne a flat or falling accent, ought to hold their first
sillable long, as *rīgŏr, glorie, spirĭ, furў, labŏŭr*; and the
like; *ăny, măny, prĕty, hŏly*, and their like, are excepted.
. . . All words of two or more sillables ending with a falling
accent on *y* or *ye*, as *fairelĭe, dĕmurelĭe, beawtĭe, pittĭe*; or in
ue, as *vertŭe, rescŭe*, or in *ow*, as *follŏw, hollŏw*, or in *e*, as

* *The Science of English Verse*, pp. 258-9.

parlĕ, *Daphnĕ*, or in *a*, as *Mannă*, are naturally short in their last sillables. . . . Words to two sillables ending with a rising accent in *y* or *ye*, as *denye*, *descrye*, or in *ue*, as *ensue*, or in *ee*, as *foresee*, or in *oe*, as *forgoe*, are long in their last sillables, unlesse a vowell begins the next word.

All monasillables that end in a grave accent are ever long, as *wrath*, *hath*, *these*, *those*, *tooth*, *sooth*, *through*, *day*, *play*, *feate*, *speede*, *strife*, *flow*, *grow*, *shew*.

The like rule is to be observed in the last of dissillables, bearing a grave rising sound,* as *devine*, *delaie*, *retire*, *refuse*, *manure*, or a grave falling sound,† as *fortune*, *pleasure*, *rampire*.

To all this we must add a contradictory *coda*. Such a small proportion of Englishmen speak standard English that one would almost say there is no such thing as a standard "accent". We start willing to agree with those phoneticians who take the educated brogue of the capital for the standard; that at least is a practical way. But we soon discover a sort of implication that the "standard" is more correct, or more educated, or more refined, or more something that all Englishmen would desire to be, than the music of other dialects. Then, as a deduction from this, comes a hint that they speak standard English in the great centres of education. We may spend the mind-roving spaces traversed in lecture-rooms studying the inflections, not to say the pronunciation of the speaker. Alas, I know not how it may be in Oxford, but this learned man will in a generation or two have lost the *h* of his "hat"; this other comes from Glasgow without any doubt; a "proper grave" in yet another leads to subsequent inquiries, which are answered by "Yorkshire", and another has the south-west of England music. In spite of this we may grant a standard pronunciation. We may say that "hat" ought to have a

* *i.e.* circumflex, or falling accent that rises first.
  † I think he means—has two falling notes in it. Cf. *Pleasure* with *fairly*.

good *h*, but we cannot say the Yorkshire "proper grave" or the west of England intonations are wrong. It seems rather as if inflections, especially if we include differences in the intervals as well as in the direction of the pitch, are essentially local rather than standard, if not indeed individual as well as local. We can very often trace characteristic inflections not only to their county but to their town; and perhaps the astuteness of the phonetician in *Pygmalion* is not solely farcical; not only each street may have its own music; family likenesses count. Though we cannot lightly assume standard inflections in English speech, there may be no great harm in postulating an idealised imagination of the inflections of English poetry since other than prose considerations condition them,* but we must not forget the inevitable discrepancy between the real and the ideal, not to say the legitimate or even beautifying individualisations of the ideal.

The second rule for English intonations is even more disturbing than the *coda* to the first: the English sentence does not observe its word inflections consistently. Southern English inflects down on occasion, and Northern English up, sometimes the only ostensible reason being a desire for variety. If there is any law behind these inflections it must be musical; we speak with a sense of music which imposes its inflections on the words. Why do the feminine rhymes of *Gae bring to me a pint o' wine* sound equally natural inflected to a rising or a falling pitch?

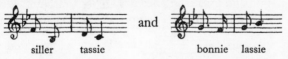

siller   tassie   and   bonnie   lassie

If Mitford is right for Burns' dialect, we should expect the pitch of all the accents to go down, and that of all feminine rhymes to inflect up. The light syllables of Burns' feminine

* See Chapter III.

endings do usually inflect up, but not always. On the other hand, in Purcell's *I attempt from Love's sickness to fly* only one light final syllable has a rising inflection, "ruin"

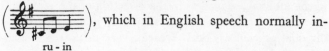

), which in English speech normally in-

ru - in

flects up; all the others, and there are many of them, have

falling inflections

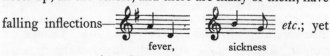

etc.; yet

fever,   sickness

we cannot say that this is the rule for Purcell, since *Fairest Isle* has very obvious exceptions. Though both are characteristic enough of their mother tongue to make an interesting contrast, neither Burns nor Purcell inflect uniformly for accent. The reason may be partly musical, yet we do not notice any discrepancy between the music and the tunes appropriate to the words; we are used to hearing the same sort of contrast in everyday speech.

We can, however, ascertain some reasons for this contradiction. Their study is not so much a part of phonetics as of grammar, and one grammarian—Henry Sweet—has worked out the rudiments of it. Indeed, it would probably be more logical to say that words derive their tune from sentence melodies than that sentence melodies are formed from the tunes of words. Mr. F. N. Scott* outlines the general principles of sentence melodies. The characteristic intonation of a prose sentence is roughly a circumflex with a pause [we should say *caesura*] at the highest pitch or

apex, like this: , *e.g.* "When he narrated the

scene was before you." The *caesura* and apex come after "narrated". Or, "The consequences of this battle were

---

* *The Scansion of Prose Rhythms*, pp. 720-25 (Publications of the Modern Language Association of America, vol. xx).

just of the same importance as the revolution itself." The *caesura* and apex come after "battle". I should rather say that the highest pitch or apex comes just before the *caesura*, on the second syllable of "narrated" and the first of "battle". Scott notices another type of sentence melody where this happens on a bigger scale: "His passions on the contrary, were violent even to slaying, against all who leaned to Whiggish principles." "To" comes at the highest pitch; the pause is after "slaying". He goes on to say that these descriptions are abstracts, stereotyped exaggerations of what really happens. The pitch neither rises steadily to the apex nor falls steadily, the curve representing only the general trend of the inflection. If in the diagram following we indicate the circumflex curve by the equal sides of an isosceles triangle, then the real inflection for the last sentence quoted will follow the course of the dotted line thus:

A = "His passions on the contrary";
B = "were violent even to slaying";
C = "against all who leaned to Whiggish principles". The fall in pitch from "to" through "slaying" is, he says, a fourth (*la* to *re*). These two types can be compounded:

Gliding up to the apex, the voice drops through an interval of a fourth without pausing; but instead of descending further it rises again, pauses at the maximum, and then descends to the tonic, *e.g.* "An infinite ∧ joy / is lost to the world / by the want of culture of this spiritual endowment."

(/ = *caesura*, and ∧ = apex.)

The diagram would be something like this:

"An infinite joy is lost to the world by the want of this spiritual endowment."

A second type of compound [inflection] arc is formed

by joining the pathetic [⌒] to the suspensive [⌐] type, *e.g.*
"The office of Paymaster-General during an expensive war
was, in that age ∧ / perhaps, the most lucrative ∧ situation
/ in the gift of the government" (Macaulay, *Earl of
Chatham*). Here the voice rises to the apex at "age",
pauses, descends through "perhaps the most", rises
through "lucrative", descends a fourth through "situation", then pauses, and finally descends through the concluding phrase.

Scott states and illustrates the general tendencies, in a
bird's-eye sort of way, showing how the land lies. We can
reconstruct his tune from his analysis—a good test. He is
talking about facts, neither exploiting a theory nor letting
his imagination run loose, but analysing types of sentence
inflections actually heard, and rendering them so faithfully
that we can re-read the inflections from his script. His
analysis is at least correct for his own reading, whether that
reading agrees with ours or not.

Another influence on sentence melody is *onomatopoesis*,
if we may stretch the meaning of the word a little, our
inherent dramatic instinct. We alter the usual sentence
tones for dramatic effect. As an example of the suspensive
followed by the pathetic type of inflection, Scott quotes
this from *Prince Otto*:

The sound of the wind in the forest swelled and
sank ∧ / and drew near them with a running rush and
died away ∧ and away / in the distance into fainting
whispers.

He says that the highest notes come on "sank" in one clause,
on "away" in the other. A better way of reading this is to
follow the meaning with an inflectional gesture: "the wind
in the forest" should have an undulating music, up and
down, the pitch rising in "swelled" and falling in "sank";
in the second phrase it should rise suddenly and *crescendo*
to fall away again in "died away and away" right down to

"whispers". This sort of *onomatopoesis* influences the melodies of speech; we see its effect in word inflections too. The most expressive inflections of "down" and "up" follow the meaning. Such inflectional gestures are most important in distinguishing homophones, and indeed help to account for their survival. Bridges laments the multiplication of homophones caused by loss of trilled *r*; "gnaw" becomes "nor", "roar" "raw", "shore" "shaw". But in expressive talk, which is the only thing that matters, "gnaw" has a different inflection from "nor". In "roar" we tend to echo the deep sound of the meaning, while "raw" is more expressive with a sharpened, heightened pitch; in "roar" we dwell on the first half of the diphthong and slide into the second, in "raw" we dwell on neither and make the change in pitch more suddenly, with a less gradual *portamento*. Nor can we read "shore" in a line of Milton's or Tennyson's without making it sound like the sea, and it sounds all the more illimitable, vague, and vast for the loss of the stubborn trilled *r*.

If Scott draws the bird's-eye outline, Sweet* is the more detailed grammarian of this study. He formulates such rules as the following:

> The *level* tone is plaintive—especially the high level tone . . . not much used in English. . . . The *rising* tone is . . . cheerful, animated, surprised, expecting, and is used in questions.

We have musical examples of this questioning inflection in *Lizzie Lindsay*, or in *Gin a body meet a body*—

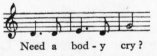

Need a   bod - y   cry?

—and might add that it is also the angry or excited

* *English Grammar*, Part II, chapter on "Intonation".

intonation, and when it goes up in sequences, the hysterical—

Presto.

—though we do not commonly hear this, except when a small child is going to end its plaint in tears. Sweet continues:

The falling tone is the natural expression of dogmatism, resolution, command, and suggests the ideas of completion, finality, certainty and of answer as opposed to question.

Appeals or remonstrances often rise, *e.g.* "I wish you would let me alone". Compare "all right" \ (with falling tones) meaning it is all right, and "all right" / (with rising tones) meaning why don't you start?

A rising tone often softens a contradiction ("Now you'll remember what I have said" /) or gives a general cheerfulness or geniality to what is said. "Well (/), goodbye (/). Hope to see you again soon" /.

If a general interrogative sentence is uttered with a falling instead of a rising tone, it expresses command or impatience. "Will you do as you are told \."

Dr. Scripture* took measurements of this sentence spoken into one of his recording instruments with the stress on "will" and expressing remonstrance, pleading and command. It began high, rose about a major third and fell at the end. Bach uses the impatient question in the *Matthew Passion:*†

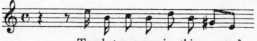

To what purpose is this waste ?

When a question falls to the close, the pitch rises at the beginning to give the interrogative gesture; the climax in pitch comes where the query focuses. "To what purpose is this waste?" is more reproachful with "is" on the higher

* *Philosophische Studien*, vol. xix, "Studies of Melody in English Speech", p. 607.   † Chorus No. 7 of Stanford's Edition.

note than if it had come on the same pitch as "purpose"

and "this". 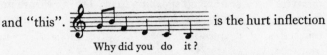 is the hurt inflection

of a disappointed child, children's inflections being often
both more expressive and more musical than grown-up
people's. It is nearer to angry tears thus, with, as it were,

a double interrogation: ..... . In the

same context as the last quotation from the *Matthew
Passion** we find the double interrogation, but with a
different feeling: "Why trouble ye the woman?"

When we talk in a general sort of way of rising and
falling inflections we are only on the outskirts of the subject. The emotional or expressive effect of inflection depends not alone on whether the pitch goes up or down, but
on what interval is taken in the rise or fall. These give
particular expressive colouring to speech. The inflections
of the *Matthew Passion* Jesus appear to come from a calm
and stable temperament, and have a sense of repose; they
influence our attitude to the personality in the same way
as the inflections of people we meet influence us, indicating
not only their temporary feeling, but what sort of people
they are generally. A proper study, a real grammar of the
inflections, should be able to tell us why. An exhaustive
research ought to answer such questions as:

Is there any special virtue in the rising major third (*so*
to *ti*) which we often hear in questions?

What does the difference between the falling fourth (*fa*
to *do*), the falling fifth (*so* to *do*), and the falling third (*mi*
to *do*) signify at the cadence,† if it signifies anything?

---

* See above, p. 45.
† In these pages I use the word "cadence" to mean the approaching

Do we fit the music of our inflections into the music of one who has just finished speaking to us? I think we are influenced in this way, but how far? We sometimes imitate the tones of a question when we give the answer in mockery.

Do we speak in different modes or keys? Many writers, of the few who write on such topics, have suggested that the inflection of a sentence is a sort of melody in one key, ending on the tonic. Even Joshua Steele,* writing some centuries ago, implies this. Hence the Spencerians would deduce our sense of tonality. A coherent melody is not a fortuitous juxtaposition of promiscuous notes, but seems to establish some sense of scale and gives us a feeling of significance. It has possibly some connection with our practice in speech. When speaking we are conscious, if half-unconsciously, that one note has a feeling of finality; we end on the tonic. In reading a list of names we come down on the last from the dominant pitch to the final. Every note in our inflection is felt in relation to this final; we start with a feeling of it, and order the cycle of notes we traverse in our effort to grip the attention and convey our meaning, with a relation to it. Our audience knows we have not finished till we come home to our last note. In music most tunes start on the mediant (*mi*) or dominant (*so*), a few on the tonic and not very many on any other note; practically all end on the tonic, or *do*. We can easily see why it should happen so in speech. When we have said our say we relax and sit down, the note sits down too and we end on the final; but when we are about to speak we exert ourselves, our mind starts working before our mouth opens, we wish to call attention to ourselves, and instead of saying "Lo" or using the vocative, we stand up or the pitch of our voice

---

of a melody or an inflection to the final note; as we usually approach the tonic from above, it generally indicates a *falling* progression.

* *Prosodia rationalis*, p. 36.

stands up, and we start on the mediant or dominant. Very few would question the final cadence to the tonic in speech, but it is also generally assumed, though I think wrongly, that we start from the tonic. Many of Campion's melodies and some folk-songs do, and they probably follow the inflections of the poems. But when we think of it, or rather when we listen to what happens, we discover that the starting pitch is usually higher than the finishing. We start on the mediant as a rule, just as plain-song does, or perhaps the dominant, as many folk-melodies do, though when a folk-melody starts thus it often jumps immediately to the tonic (*so* to *do'*), which may mean that it starts below rather than above the tonic.

Do we ever modulate [change our key] from sentence to sentence, coming back to our original key and ending on its final at the end, or are different modes and keys the result of different moods or temperaments?

Do dialects have their own characteristic modes? What difference do racial or language peculiarities make to the types of interval used or in the keys or modes used? In music sprung directly from the inflections of speech, as in Greek music, in plain-song, and in folk-song, the same modes appear. These modes were originally named after the Greek states. Is this because they arose from the dialectal inflections of these states, from the virile Doric inflections a virile mode, from the soft Ionian speech an Ionian mode? In the *Republic** we find this passage:

And you will grant that the mode and the rhythm ought to follow the words?
Undoubtedly.

* III, *c*. 398–400. The *italics* are mine. I quote from Davies and Vaughan's translation, save that for "harmony" I substitute "mode". The translators add a footnote saying that "*harmony* does not strictly correspond in sense with the technical acceptation of the English use". "Mode" is the word they wanted.

But we said you know that in the case of words we did not require dirges and complaints.

No, we do not.

Which then are the plaintive modes? Tell me, for you are musical.

Mixed Lydian and Hyperlydian and such as are like these.

Then these must be discarded; for they are useless even to women that are to be virtuously given, not to say to men.

Quite so.

And will you grant that drunkenness, effeminacy and idleness are most unbecoming things in guardians?

Undoubtedly they are.

Which of the modes, then, are effeminate and convivial?

The Ionian and the Lydian [our major scale!] which are called "lax".

Will you employ these then, my friend, in the training of men of war?

By no means; and, if I mistake not, you have only the Dorian and the Phrygian left you.

I do not know the modes myself, I said; only you see you leave me *that particular mode which will suitably represent the tones and accents* of a brave man engaged in a feat of arms or in any violent operation . . . leave me also another mode, expressive of the feelings of one who is engaged in an occupation not violent, but peaceful and unconstrained. . . . Leave me these two modes, the one violent, the other peaceful, *such as shall best imitate the tones of men in adversity and in prosperity, in a temperate and in a courageous mood.*

Well, said he, you are recommending me to leave precisely those which I have just mentioned.

But we need not go to Plato for evidence of a connection between modes and moods. Practically everyone feels the change from a major to a minor mode as a change of mood, witness the number who think minor modes sad. Incidentally, it does not follow that minor modes are sad; it may follow only that many people do not like to be in the mood of minor keys, and find them depressing, in its full original meaning. Others, and perhaps especially those with a strain of the Celt in them, prefer the minor to the major mode. Celtic poetry, also, has been called gloomy, although it is not gloomy to the Celt, giving him a pleasurable sensation of subdued excitement not unlike that of a minor scale. In singing, some find the change not only from one mode to another, but from one key to another, if the change is sudden, much easier if they alter the complexion of their mood, simulate a changed attitude of mind, by which I do not mean their sense of tonality but quite literally their mood, whence the altered sense of tonality results. A fiddler whose emotional musical sense is superior to his musical intelligence sometimes finds it difficult to play in tune in a major key when he is in a minor frame of mind. Nor need we go to the Greeks to discover that certain types of tune have emotional colourings. We feel it in the music we know, and hear it in the inflections of speech. Certain types of tune characterise the speech of each one of us and of each dialect. More than that, we all rely on such tunes for meaning. One insensitive to inflections constantly misunderstands those who use a variety of tune to colour the feeling of what they say. It was not fanciful of Sweet to include this study in his English Grammar; he is only not precise enough.

English could give its meaning if it were mere conventional labels strung together, or at least it might; but English is not a language of labels; we need inflectional melody to help us out with the meaning or add an emotional significance to what we say. Sensitiveness to inflectional effects is not alone an ancient and primitive thing dead and dying. And, indeed, it is sometimes a practical difficulty in writing to make our word suggest the right inflection. Have you ever said something in fun on paper and heard it delivered by another with angry inflections, your light scoff turned into abuse? But transmission by paper is not necessary. We may repeat a conversation practically *verbatim*, and by giving the wrong inflections misrepresent the meaning worse than if we had used different words. We have all seen the fragrance of a joke or a witty remark evaporate when repeated without the spontaneous inflections of the original speaker's voice, or how a stupid joke which comes off when acted well by inflectional gestures reads in print like absolute drivel. This is partly why some comedy upsets our gravity in the theatre but cannot move us in an arm-chair, and why the best way of capturing an audience for any humorist is to read him aloud. A serious reader misses the ludicrous or ironical tones.

Though some use only a small part of this inflectional language, and as listeners are not sensitive to fine distinctions of tones, yet the meanings of inflections to those who do understand them are as definite as the meaning of words.* The rudiments of this study have been attempted. Experimental phoneticians and elocutionists† realise its importance. Though very valuable work can be done by experiment, examples of inflection collected by ear have the advantage over phonograph records in being spoken unaware by people moved with real feeling, or making a real effort to convey their meaning; theirs is the unconscious music of speech, the wild primrose. It is difficult to collect such evidence, since we do not normally analyse this music, but let it play on us almost unconsciously; thus we can hardly both partake interestedly in a conversation or listen sympathetically, and analyse the music that influences us. We are left with the inflections of public

* For further examples, see quotations from Sweet's Grammar in Appendix I.

† I believe to an elocutionist this chapter seems the most utter commonplace, spun out at needless length—the best argument in its favour.

speakers where it is not so natural, or that of bores where it is not enlivening, or those chance tunes of living talk which happen to catch our attention. It is also difficult, especially in rapid speech, to distinguish the intervals of pitch and to discover whether these are precise, though I am inclined to think they are precise, if only because the lack of precision in those few who do not talk in tune is so very evident. Some hold that musical people take their intervals more precisely, speak more in tune and perhaps with more musical modulations than unmusical people. I think this is unjust to the unmusical, but the whole discussion is very vague. What constitutes "being musical"? And it has got mixed up with an entirely different speculation. One writer says that musical conductors nearly always have raucous voices. But how is this to the point? The quality of the voice has got nothing to do with the sort of intervals taken or the variety of the inflections used.

Joshua Steele* was the first to transcribe the inflections of speakers. He noted Garrick's rendering of "To be or not to be", representing the pitch traversed by lines (\ or /) and the time values by ⊤ = crotchet, | = quaver and ⌒ = minim:

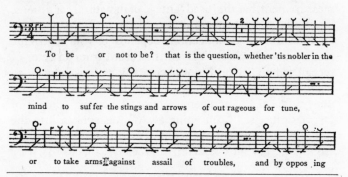

* *Prosodia rationalis*, pp. 40, 45.

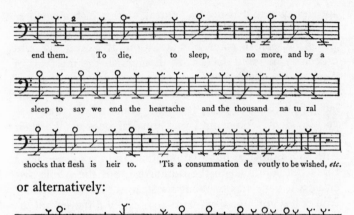

or alternatively:

Gardiner* gives us examples of Kean's declamation:

Oh . . . . not for Venice.

The scientific study, with the advantage of accurate measurement, has the disadvantage of unnatural conditions. The value of a phonograph record taken to discover how emotion influences inflection, depends on the histrionic ability of the "subject". Even the record from an actor of recognised ability need not necessarily be satisfactory—so many act with their bodies rather than their voice. In illustration of this danger we may take an experiment of Dr. Scripture's. "I am going away" was spoken into the recording instrument with different expressions, and for sadness he got no characteristic melody; the words were

* *The Music of Nature*, p. 50. Do you recollect Parry's savage, and the ape and horse?

articulated more slowly, that was all. It looks as if the "subject", in his effort to act grief repressed his gaiety, cut out the sprightliness from his speech, and was no doubt in so far right; but the melody of grief is not mere repression of the melody of happiness. Everyone with ears knows that grief has characteristic inflections, though happily we do not often hear them. Or if our memory does not, our imagination will tell us this. The *recitative* quoted from *Dido and Aeneas* at the end of Chapter I gives us a more trustworthy example of the tunes of grief; for we must not suppose that by putting an inflection through a machine and analysing the record, we give it authority over a record from Purcell's imagination. The dulled, stunned inflections which the instrument showed represent at best a controlled, that is, an unexpressed emotion. We rarely hear the melody of uncontrolled sorrow save in children, but where we do, cannot forget it. I have not heard the tunes of wholly unrestrained adult emotion half a dozen times. A mill-girl lamenting, and reviling another a hundred yards away, for going off with her "lad", absorbed my wonder by her spontaneous use of all the devices and subtleties of invective, and left no room for admiration of her music. Most of the others being tinkers and incomprehensible, the impression of their music lingers. It was as if someone had suddenly burst into song. One bewailing her unhappy lot under the pines in a highland summer, and the influence of too much whisky, is among the most musical of childhood's memories.

We have the following scientifically taken records* of incisive French inflections, that is, of French inflection where it is most interesting, in questions and exclamations:

* Quoted from Marichelle, *La Parole d'après le trace du phonographe*, by Scripture, *Elements of Experimental Phonetics*, p. 479.

Qui est là? C'est Paul. C'est Paul? Tiens! Voilà Jean. Ah!   Jean   Re - né!

Fer - di - nand!   Assez!   Très bien!

German "du" with various emotional significance gave:*

assertion   question   irritation   warning

In America† these results were got:

Oh!   Oh!   Oh!   Ah!
(sorrowfully) (admiringly) (questioningly) (sorrowfully)

Oh dear!   Oh my!
(sorrowfully)   (sorrowfully)

---

* Quoted from Victor, *Elemente d. Phonetik, ibid.,* p. 478.

† I use Scripture's tables to put the graphs in *Researches in Experimental Phonetics*, pp. 63-5, on to a musical stave. They are only approximate, it being difficult to convert them to a stave where every odd note is a space and the even only a line. "The sorrowful effect of the phrases 'oh dear' and 'oh my' is", says the experimenter, "due largely to the sameness and the general lowness in each phrase, and also essentially to the lack of convexity. This is in strong contrast to the plot for 'oh not really', where the surprise and possible doubt appear in the lively circumflexion of the three vowel groups. . . . It is interesting to note that the course of the melody in the sorrowful interjection is not smooth, but shows minor fluctuations. These tremblings of the voice are vital elements of emotional expression that are used by effective speakers particularly to excite sorrow, pity and religious feelings." If we put it into musical notation we get:

Oh not really.

"Sleepy" pronounced without emotion in another series of experiments* was inflected thus: ; spoken sadly,

thus: . A record† of continuous speech was analysed and gave this:

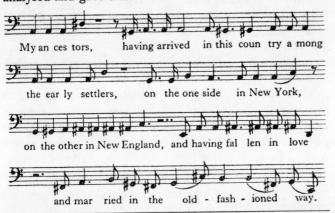

My an ces tors,   having arrived   in this coun try a mong

the ear ly settlers,   on the one side   in New York,

on the other in New England,   and having fal len in   love

and mar ried in the   old - fash - ioned   way.

<hr />

* Volta Bureau reprints, No. 208, Scripture, "Inscriptions of Speech."

† *Researches in Experimental Phonetics*, pp. 70-72. Of this he says: "The average tone is rather low. This form of melody gives a special emotional character to the phrase [my "ancestors"] for which no appropriate term exists ... we can define the expressive character of the melody here only by saying that it is the one appropriate for a solemn statement in an oration. The evenness of the melody gives it solemnity, the steady rise through the phrase gives it pomposity [still talking of the first phrase—the rise is not sufficiently wide to be marked in the musical notation], the sudden rise at the end makes it somewhat brusque and challenging. As only a few researches on speech melody have been made, little can be said concerning the change in emotional effect which such a phrase would undergo with changes in the melody. We know, however, that if the even melody had not the steady rise and had fallen at the end, the phrase would have had a religious intonation (see researches on the Lord's Prayer). If the evenness had been replaced by fluctuations, the melody would have lost its solemnity, even if it had retained the other characteristic of solemnity, namely,

In another experiment* Dr. Scripture noted such things as these: In a record of "Did you see him" the pitch rose from the beginning to the end and "the amount of rise is considerably less than an octave". In "Is he here?" "Is he" was of moderately high pitch, "here" showed a steady rise of one whole tone (7 : 8) during the vowel to a tone "maintained throughout". In "Where is he?" the pitch fell steadily throughout to exactly an octave from the first note; "where" had a slight circumflex inflection. "Where did you see him?" asked with emphasis on "where" had a circumflex rise on "where" and constant pitch thereafter save for a fall at the end. "Did you see him, John?" showed "a rise in pitch from the beginning to the end of the interrogative at "him". "John" began somewhat lower than the end of "him" and rose as a single interrogative word would. In "What! What did you say?" spoken as one startled by news might speak it, "What" had the circum-flex inflection usual in isolated words. He goes on to say:

The pitch is, however, in general very high for the author's voice and the change considerable. The

---

the general low pitch. . . . The entire effect of such a melody is dis-tinctly humorous—an effect that is increased by the very low tones employed, especially at the end. . . . It is a common device of humor to imitate solemnity in its chief traits and to change one of them into an inconsistency. Here the effect is that of a staid humor of a mild degree. Both these phrases might have been spoken with rising closure without destroying the general tenor of the impression, but the humor-ous turn and the contrast would have been lacking. Throughout the record the melody is one that is appropriate to ceremonial oration with a constant humorous twist to it. The unusually long pauses between the phrases, with the low and monotonous pitch, aid in the ceremonious expression. Some of the vowels are abnormally long, for purposes of emphasis." The same experimenter tells us that a mono-tonous intonation is supposed to distinguish American English as contrasted with Southern British English. This does away with much of the value of his records for *us*.

* *Philosophische Studien*, vol. xix, "Studies of Melody in English Speech", p. 608.

highest point is almost exactly as octave above the beginning.

After "What!" came a pause of about one-third of a second.

"What did you say?" shows a general fall with a circumflexion of pitch for the initial emphatic word as in the previous cases. . . . The interval between the highest and the lowest points is an octave.

In "Good heavens", "Good" was almost exactly the same as "What". "Heavens" had a very slight rise and a tiny fall in pitch. "How well he looks!" had a circumflex inflection with a sudden rise on "How"; the pitch was constant on "well" and fell gradually at the end. This, says Scripture, is the typical declarative sentence when the emphasis is at the beginning. "I've done all I can" was spoken with a resigned expression and the emphasis on "all". "I've done" showed a constant pitch . . . contributing to the expression by the monotony; in an ordinary narrative sentence it would presumably show a rise in pitch. The remainder of the sentence shows a circumflexion of pitch . . . [different] from most declarative and emphatic sentences in having a slow rise [to "I"] with a rather quick fall [in "can"]. The lowest and the highest parts have approximately the relation of 4 : 7 [i.e. a minor seventh, do' to re].

"I wish you'd let me alone" was spoken with irritation and remonstrance, the emphasis being on "wish" and "alone",

and gave this tune:*

I wish you would let me alone.

---

* Of this we are told: "The expressiveness seems to depend on the peculiar musical intonation in connection with the greater stress (intensity) at the time of the first elevation of pitch. The same modulation of pitch without the stress at the first elevation occurs in expressions of resigned agreement or reluctant consent, as in 'I suppose you can' with some such meaning as 'I wish you couldn't do it, but I suppose you can'; this phrase when uttered with stress on *suppose* expresses irritation as in the case just discussed."

This branch of the science of language and poetry does not appeal to Englishmen, so we have, I think, no record of English intonations.

None of the experiments on American English are directly to the point, but England's English cannot escape foreign investigation much longer. Such a study would be valuable even if it merely acted as a sort of check on our imagination, but there is much more in it than this. It does seem a pity that we cannot do this for ourselves, especially as the study needs just that touch of—shall we call it humour, or common sense, or imagination?—that Englishmen alone seem able to supply.

CHAPTER III

THE INFLECTIONS OF POETRY

How, then, does all this affect poetry? We must now ask that tactless question, the difference between poetry and prose, and may start inartistically by defining our terms. We limit ourselves to the difference between their music. Prose music is found in books of prose, poetry's music in books of poetry. De Quincey writes prose music, Browning poetic. De Quincey may be more musical or more poetic in another sense than Browning, but his writing comes under the heading prose, Browning's under the heading poetry. Why? Is there any musical reason for the distinction? It is easier to deny any essential difference between the two, and this answer has the virtue of being supported only by those who have thought about the matter. It has the disadvantage of being the one we do not wish to believe.

Prose and poetry have in common a word music, a rhythmic music, and an inflection music. No one has ever held that the distinction lies in their word music as such. The quarrel over "poetic diction" refers to words rather as meaningful symbols than as musical sounds. We might say that "castor oil", "epidermis", "inter-Germanic", "protozoon", "dolichocephalic", "Euclidean geometry" were not poetic words, but cannot deny them on account of their sound. Wordsworth's contention had its musical aspect, but has not been fought on that ground, and curiously enough if fought on that ground might become a plea for a poetic diction, a simple musical diction excluding the monstrous sounds of prose. There is such a thing as characteristic word music, but a catholic view cannot make this the distinction between the music of prose and poetry. Such words as "Tadpole-frog-theory",* "politic Old Macchiavelli",† "euphemistic",‡ "rhetorician",§ *Blackwood's Magazine*,‖ "psychologic"¶ occur at random in Browning's poetry; while "fair", "star", "sea", "sky", "rose", "lily", or "diadem", "diaphanous", "sulphurous", "ephemeral", "ethereal", "ocean", "Atlantic", or "rustic", "bosky", "browse", "sacred relics", "glebe", "marble monument", "sylvan", or even "faun", "swain", "Diana", "Aurora", occur in prose.

The rhythms of poetry and prose are clearly differentiated at the extremes. *L'Allegro's* rhythm is not in the least like the rhythm of this sentence; and they differ because one is poetry and the other prose. But at the means we cannot distinguish the rhythms of prose and poetry so easily; they have no final dividing line. And more, prose rhythms are made on the same plan, out of the same material, and on the same psychology as verse rhythms. We cannot say that poetry is necessarily more rhythmic than prose, or that it is prose in a higher degree, or that its rhythms are more pleasing or more lovely, or even more important to it than to prose. In general we may find differentiating characteristics, but when we come down to particulars and think a little more closely to the facts, we have to qualify our statements and dilute them too far.

* *Fifine at the Fair*, cxii.
† *The Two Poets of Croisic*, cxli.
‡ *Guido* (*The Ring and the Book*).
§ *Count Guido Franceschini* (Smith, Elder & Co.'s Edition, vol. ii, p. 88.)
‖ *Bishop Blougram's Apology* (*ibid.*, vol. i, p. 541).
¶ *Aristophanes' Apology* (*ibid.*, vol. i, p. 688).

Prose sometimes grows the rhythmic bloom of poetry, and poetry often has the leaves of prose rhythm.

Particular types of rhythm characterise a prose style as definitely as they do the poet's style. In original prose we have often to get accustomed to the strange rhythm before we can appreciate the writing; for the first paragraph or so, and even for the first essay, the unusual motion upsets us; we have to learn to keep our balance in it. Until we get into his idiom, Emerson's rhythm annoys us; we are pulled up, halted at every stride. Although prose tends more than poetry to allow of individual rhythmic mannerisms, and though on revision the prose writer is less careful to preserve the rhythm of his expression than the poet, disturbing the flow of his first writing for the sake of brevity, of point or what not, yet some prose writers do weave a rhythmic web as they write, and in revising, preserve it, while all writers of readable prose have a sense of rhythm, a faculty for rhythmic creation not unlike the poet's.*

Most theories of poetic rhythm work equally well with prose.† Mr. Patterson even applies the "isochronous foot"

* Abram Lipsky, *Rhythm in Prose*, p. 40, thinks that the "style and rhythm of prose are to a very large extent identical." He analyses prose rhythms to show us how authors differ.

† My own method of analysing poetic rhythms works for prose rhythms thus:

There are   no   fields of amaranth on this side of the grave;

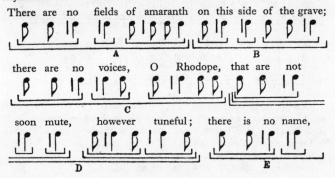

theory to prose.* Saintsbury,† who scans poetry by feet, scans prose by feet too, and picks out regular blank-verse rhythms in English prose, and rhyme from Ruskin:

> And the city lay
> Under its guarding hills
> One labyrinth of *delight*,
> Its grey and fretted towers
> Misty in their magnificence of *height*.

Ruskin's blank-verse rhythms nevertheless read like prose. Although their rhythms may be exactly like verse rhythms, we could not call such passages as the rhymed one just quoted, verse. However beautiful we may think this writing, it does not read like poetry, or give us an impression of poetic rhythm as De Quincey's prose sometimes does. So metre evidently cannot determine poetry from prose. The reader will perhaps agree with me that this treatment of the subject is superficial. I cannot establish an essential difference between the rhythms of prose and poetry. That there is no difference seems to me to require no proof, only a little study of the facts.

I wish we might prove that the inflections of poetry

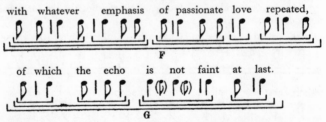

B balances A, D balances C; E, F, and G group. The same "laws" at work in *Paradise Lost* work here. The rhythm echoes, repeats itself with variations, and in every way responds to the same sort of analysis as I practise on poetic rhythms in *The Real Rhythm in English Poetry*.

* *The Rhythm of Prose*, c. p. 52.
† *History of English Prose Rhythms*, pp. 394-5.

differ from those of prose. This is the most obvious distinction to suggest and the easiest to prove, though I
rather hesitate to claim it as an infallible gauge. If we listen
to anyone speaking in a language we do not understand,
we can tell when he quotes verse by the changed inflections. I have noticed this for German. When we see words
printed in verses we tend to alter our inflections, almost
deliberately using intonations we should never use for the
same sentence written as prose. We feel bound to read
poetry in poetic inflections. "Follow, follow, though with
mischief armed, like whirlwind now she flies thee" has a
different inflection from:

> Follow, follow,
> Though with mischief
> Armed, like whirlwind
> Now she flies thee.

In the prose reading our intonation probably falls on
"armed" and reaches the highest pitch on "whirlwind".
Read as verse, the highest inflection comes on "Armed",
from which the pitch falls to "whirlwind". Certain factors
at work with the inflections of poetry do not affect prose.
The mere fact of its being written in lines and not in
paragraphs makes a difference to our reading of verse; the
lines influence the melody—an important consideration
in *vers libre*.

We expect poetry to speak to us with a different music
from prose. What is the music we expect from poetry? A
tune or song, to be sure. The inflections of prose must be
in some sort consistent, but need not make a melody. One
occasionally detects tunes in prose, wild untrained ram-
blers tangled together promiscuously, sown as the wind
sows them, scraps of song bursting in at random, but their
seeds come on the feet of uninterested travellers. The songs
which the inflections of poetry make are like roses growing in a garden with no entangling undergrowth, not the

wild uncared-for thing of prose, not music growing as it can, but music growing as it will. This makes a vital and important distinction. We must, however, remember some things not contradicting it, but still not to be forgotten. Using its own resources and relying on them alone, prose can have an inflection so melodious as to be a tune:

*And her eyes, if they were ever seen, would be neither sweet nor subtle; no man could read their story; they would be found filled with perishing dreams, and with wrecks of forgotten delirium.

Such prose considerations as the meaning, which is poetic, the emotion or imagination, which is poetic, the rhythm, which also is poetic, antithesis and onomatopoeic interpretation, *etc.* determine the inflection; and yet its tune makes as lyrical a melody as many of the tunes of poetry. It is poetic in every way to our subjective consciousness, yet not poetry, since the lineal control on the inflections is not required. We can write the passage out in lines and not alter the tune:

And her eyes, if they were ever seen,
Would be neither sweet nor subtle;
No man could read their story;
They would be found filled with perishing dreams,
And with wrecks of forgotten delirium.

We may heighten the pitch of "filled"—which we have no right to do—by splitting up the fourth line:

They would be found
Filled with perishing dreams.

So the distinction between prose and poetry resolves itself into the indisputable fact that poetry is written in lines, prose not.

When we enumerate the things which help to make De

* De Quincey.

Quincey's melody, we talk prose, we speak with the eyes (if we may) of the mere onlooker. What really happens is that De Quincey writes to a tune and lets it guide his pen; he writes not as the prose writer writes characteristically, but as the poet does, though without the poet's lineal instrument. De Quincey said he could have made his name writing poetry if he had liked. Here is corroboration, he could write, as the poets write, to a tune. The end of *Westward Ho!* has this song quality. Kingsley calls it "prose shaped into song". We cannot be sure if he meant this literally—prose, shaped into song—but if he wrote to a melody as the poets do, this is a literal description of the method, the shaping of prose to fit a tune. In Ruskin's passages with blank-verse rhythms the inflection does not form a song inflection. Ruskin did not write with a melody at the back of his mind, and his blank-verse rhythms do not make us feel that he is writing poetry, as Kingsley's and De Quincey's tunes do.

The poets, then, write to a tune, and use their lines to express it; but they also know how to absorb prose inflections into their melody. Browning often forms a characteristic poetic melody by stringing together the wildest prose inflection. I cannot help believing he did this consciously, that interjections, exclamations, questions and phrases of common speech which need meaningful inflections attracted him because of their music. Music interested him; he is one of the few nineteenth-century poets who knew something of its technique; his poetry owes its individual and vivid inflection more to absorbing prose music than to anything else; Browning possibly knew what he was about. I wonder why his readers once thought him unmelodious? Was it that they could not bring themselves to read his poetry with prose inflections, and could not fit it to poetic, or did they resent prose tunes? But perhaps it was only fright, mere rabbit timidity at something new.

*As for religion—why, I served it, sir!
I'll stick to that! With my *phenomena*
I laid the atheist sprawling on his back,
Propped up Saint Paul, or, at least, Swedenborg!
In fact, it's just the proper way to baulk
These troublesome fellows—liars, one and all,
Are not these sceptics? Well, to baffle them,
No use in being squeamish: lie yourself!

This is founded on prose inflections, but the lines influence the cadences; if we write the verse out as prose the melody changes. Here is a poetic tune, poetically conditioned; the form of the verses has modified the incisive prose inflections to make a melody.

In *A Toccata of Galuppi's*, where the inflections come first from prose, the form of the verse influences the tune even more:

Oh, Galuppi, Baldassaro, this is very sad to find!
I can hardly misconceive you; it would prove me deaf and
    blind;
But although I take your meaning, 'tis with such a heavy
    mind!

"This is very sad to find!" "I can hardly misconceive you;" " 'tis with such a heavy mind!" would have a vivid music even in prose; they call for an emotionally coloured inflection. But Browning's verse modifies their inflections to make a coherent tune of the whole. All the verses in the poem have much the same tune, and some of them exactly the same. This is partly because of the metre; the accents come on a plan, and accent tends to raise the pitch. But it is not all a matter of metre, as we see if we compare it with:

Leaping brooklet, swiftly running, far amid the mountains
    grand,

* *Mr. Sludge, "The Medium"* (Smith, Elder & Co.'s Edition, vol. i, p. 612).

How I long to wander by you, when the autumn evenings
    come,
Always singing dying music, like a song with slumbrous
    close.

Although this has the metre of the *Toccata*, their melodies
differ. The rhyme may help to determine Browning's
melody, but if we add rhyme, still these lines will not have
anything approximating to Browning's tune:

Leaping brooklet, swiftly running, far amid the mountain
    rows,
How I long to wander by you, when the autumn sunlight
    goes,
Always singing dying music, like a song with slumbrous
    close!

If we take the poet's point of view, the tunes differ because
the verses are written to different tunes. Browning's tune
helped to suggest the words he uses and in arranging the
emotional colouring of his sentences; it decided his metre,
his line, his stanza, and possibly his rhyme. If we take the
reader's point of view, things are the other way round; the
metre, the lines, the stanza, the rhyme, and the way the
emotional colouring of the sentence is arranged determine
the tune.

Christina Rossetti, and indeed many other poets, know
how to use the inflections of prose to make poetic music;
in *Winter: My Secret* these, as in Browning's poetry, suffer
a poetic change:

> I tell my secret? No indeed, not I:
> Perhaps some day, who knows?
> But not to-day; it froze, and blows, and snows,
> And you're too curious: fie!
> You want to hear it? well:
> Only, my secret's mine, and I won't tell.
>   Or, after all, perhaps there's none:
> Suppose there is no secret after all,
> But only just my fun.

> To-day's a nipping day, a biting day;
> In which one wants a shawl,
> A veil, a cloak, and other wraps:
> I cannot ope to every one who taps,
> And let the draughts come whistling through my hall.

The intervals covered by the inflections are less promiscuous in poetry than in prose; the music of poetry tends to set itself in recurring refrains, and the wider, wilder intervals of prose do not commonly occur. We might almost say that in the first instance poetry breaks itself off from prose and determines its tune without any reference to prose inflections; it certainly modifies prose inflections and sometimes excludes them. A regular metre has the most powerful effect on inflection—where there is no other influence, the poetic tune tending to an oscillating fourth. The other inevitable influence is the pull of the lineal cadence, or perhaps we should say the substituting of a lineal for the sentence cadence of prose, the lines, not the prose significance, determining the closes. Here is one of the simplest tunes we can have:

* Writing the melody as discrete notes is misleading. "Monarch" may not start punctually on *do'*, but on the slide up. The notes repre-

This melody is conditioned purely poetically, by the metre, and the oscillation to get a tonic and dominant contrast at the cadences. Begging the question whether we ought to read Cowper's poem like this—it is almost certainly our childhood's first tune for it—we may take the inflection as an example of a tune we often hear in badly commonplace poetry. I have made an attempt to render the commonplace tunes I hear in the poems quoted at the beginning of the last chapter. The same agents are at work, accent and cadence, though since these poems are less simple, the cadence has the stronger pull:

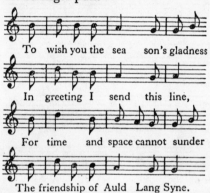

To wish you the season's gladness
In greeting I send this line,
For time and space cannot sunder
The friendship of Auld Lang Syne.

The attraction of the cadences keeps down the pitch of "season's", "cannot", "send" and "Auld". More than likely the feminine endings go up because of my Scotch "accent", or perhaps to get a contrasting cadence. The last line only finishes on the tonic. The cadence on the second line is less strong, coming to a note of the dominant chord, if this is not too sophisticated a way to talk of a melody. The first and third lines have the weakest cadences, which, therefore, bear repeating; if their raised pitch is purely northern, then the proper notes may be ;

gladness
sunder

sent what the tune would be if the inflection turned into a song, folk-song-wise.

even so the cadence is still weak,  being a

stronger ending than [musical notation]. Why, I shall not

pretend to know. The tune of John Davidson's poem,
also quoted at the beginning of Chapter II, is more difficult to catch. It has a wider sweep, eight lines instead of
four, and therefore more latitude for error. But I think,
though with less confidence, that I hear this melody in it:

Not   now   can   the   night - in - gale   sing

Ex   pect - ing   a   stel   lar   re   ply,

No   fugues in - ter - gar - land - ed   ring

Of the earth and the   clus ters on   high.

Si - de - re - al   ech   oes that   bring

The   crys - tal - line   tears and the   sigh

For the end   of   a   beau - ti - ful   thing

That   sol dered the   earth and the   sky.

The same influences mould very simple folk-song as very
commonplace poem inflection:

Simplicity is not enough to make a poem inflection feel
trite:

---

* *Journal of Folk-Song Society*, 1914–16, p. 227. Collected by Miss
Lucy Broadwood, who has given her permission to quote.

† *Journal of Folk-Song Society*, 1914–16, p. 83. Collected by Cecil
Sharp, whose permission I have to quote.

The melody of "Peas-porridge hot" is original, we have
not heard it anywhere else; it has in it, besides accent and
cadence influences, something characteristic of its words,
as has all good poetry.

Rhythmic balance as well as mere metre modifies the
inflection; the tunes of poetry reflect the *caesuras* as well as
the lines, a strong *caesura* bringing the melody to a strong
cadence and a weak *caesura* to a weak. We shall see this in
folk-song music later.* The *caesuras* in *Paradise Lost* have
much to do with its melody:

> Of Man's First Disobedience, and the Fruit
> Of that Forbidden Tree, whose mortal taste
> Brought Death into the World, and all our woe,
> With loss of *Eden*, till one greater Man
> Restore us, and regain the blissful Seat,
> Sing Heavenly Muse, that on the secret top
> Of *Oreb*, or of *Sinai*, didst inspire
> That Shepherd, who first taught the chosen Seed,
> In the Beginning how the Heavens and Earth
> Rose out of *Chaos*: or if *Sion* Hill
> Delight thee more, and *Siloa's* Brook that flowed
> Fast by the Oracle of God; I thence
> Invoke thy aid to my adventurous Song,
> That with no middle flight intends to soar
> Above the *Aonian* Mount, while it pursues
> Things unattempted yet in Prose or Rhime.
> And chiefly Thou, O Spirit, that dost prefer
> Before all Temples the upright heart and pure,
> Instruct me, for Thou knowest; Thou from the first
> Wast present, and with mighty wings outspread,
> Dove-like sat'st brooding on the vast Abyss,
> And mad'st it pregnant: What in me is dark
> Illumine, what is low raise and support;
> That to the height of this great Argument,
> I may assert Eternal Providence,
> And justify the ways of God to men.

* See pp. 145-7.

The full close (or cadence ending on the tonic with a feeling of full finality) comes only at the end of the paragraph. We might say that the melody is like an English psalm chant, all on one note with a tune for the cadences, only that every tiny *caesura* breaks away into a tune, so that the chanting note never sounds long, and the *caesuras*, coming so variously and calling for so many degrees of rest in the melody, make one of the most sustained yet beautifully varied inflections in English poetry. Whether the paragraph rhythms achieve this or whether these melodies give us the sense of paragraph rhythm, there can be no doubt about the coincidence of the rhythm and the melody; the closes and semi-closes and demi-semi-closes are equally melodic and rhythmic.

In *Paradise Lost* and in Milton generally accent tends to raise the pitch, though this tendency is sometimes overruled by the powerful cadence control, or in *Paradise Lost* obscured by the chant basis. In English poetry accent seldom sends the pitch down, but some of Wordsworth's poetry makes an exception. This northern inflection takes much the same place in many of his poems as the wilder prose inflections do in Browning's. I do not know that all poets enshrine the music of their local accent. I think probably not. Spenser, whose people came from Wordsworth's corner of England, does not write to the northern music, perhaps because he was born and brought up in London. But this may be merely a personal impression, and indeed I rather hesitate to risk it. Still we do feel that while the opening lines of *Lycidas** read with a falling instead of a rising inflection on the accents would be un-

* Yet once more, O ye Laurels, and once more
  Ye Myrtles brown, with Ivy never-sear,
  I come to pluck your Berries harsh and crude,
  And with forced fingers rude,
  Shatter your leaves before the mellowing year.

natural, un-*Miltonic*, not *Lycidas*, some of Wordsworth's poems sound trivial with a raised inflection for the accent. Milton gets many of his intense notes on the heights of pitch, Wordsworth's intensest notes are often deep. We can read *She dwelt among the untrodden ways* with a southern intonation, but both the music and the emotion are fuller in the northern:

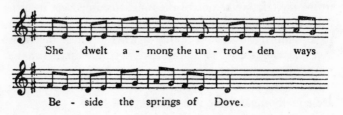

She dwelt a - mong the un - trod - den ways

Be - side the springs of Dove.

The accents go up and down alternately. If the downward accent is felt more strongly, then "dwelt", "untrodden", "Beside" and "Dove" have the important emphasis. If the heightened pitch is more emphatic, "among", "ways" and "spring" are the more outstanding. If we analyse Wordsworth's rhythms,* we see how the strength of his accented and unaccented syllables differ less than with most poets. Perhaps the northern tinge in his melody accounts for the level emphasis, or it may be the level emphasis that accounts for the tune. In the last verse of the poem—

> But she is in her grave, and, oh,
> The difference to me!

—"grave" and especially "difference" must come on deep notes, otherwise the ending is trite. A highly pitched accent on "difference" robs the verse of its solemnity. Similarly when the poet writes "Dear God" for an exclamation, a deep grave accent—say a drop of a fifth (*so* to *do*)—voices

---

* *The Real Rhythm in English Poetry*, by the present writer.

its solemnity better than a raised inflection. It makes all the difference between a sublimely calm and an hysterical excitement.

While we are talking about *She dwelt among the untrodden ways* we may notice another interesting feature in its tune. The poem has three verses. The second verse is in a contrasting key, its tonic or final note being, I should say, a third (*do* to *mi*) higher than in the other verses; its rhythm too is different, and its melody. The last verse returns to the rhythm, key and melody of the first, only with a more impressive cadence for the last two lines. This threefold division, a contrasting melody and key in the middle, is common in music. In the poem the changed rhythm may determine the fresh tune, and the change of mood the contrasting key. The first stanza tells us that she dwelt alone and few knew her, the last that she dwelt unknown and few lamented her; the middle stanza gives the poetry of her personality. So, besides rhythm and structural features, the arrangement of the moods, down to small details of feeling, determines the melodies of poetry. In what we may call "song form" the same mood recurs at the same spot in every succeeding stanza.

If a poet writes successive verses to the same latent tune, we should expect their form to resemble that of verses written to a given objective melody, and this is what we find. Starting with an objective melody, the poet has to fit new words and fresh sentiments to the same tune. We might imagine that if the first verse fits the tune perfectly, the other verses must fit imperfectly. It sometimes happens so, the first verse, or more often the refrain, making the best fit. But this need not happen. We can see the problem solved in some folk-tunes, where the words were probably the only conscious music, and yet the latent inflection must have guided the words. *Lizzie Lindsay* shows it well:

1. Will ye gang to the Hielands, Liz-zie Lind - say?
2. Will I gang to the Hielands wi' you, sir?
3. Liz - zie lass - ie, 'tis lit - tle that ye ken,
4. She has kilt - ed her coats o' green sat - in,

1. Will ye gang to the Hie - lands wi' me?
2. I dinna ken how that may be.
3. If sae be ye din - na ken me.
4. She has kilt - ed them up to the knee,

1. Will ye gang to the Hie-lands, Lizzie Lind-say?
2. For I ken na the land that ye live in,
3. For my name is Lord Ron - ald Mac - don - ald,
4. And she's aff wi' Lord Ron - ald Mac - don - ald,

1. My bride and my dar - ling to be.
2. Nor ken I the lad I'm gaun wi'.
3. A chief - tain of high de - gree.
4. His bride and his dar - ling to be.

Here the tune has probably crystallised out of question inflections, though there is a possibility that the melody was
there first and the poet set himself to follow it. The story is
told in questions, even the replies being stated in question
form: "I dinna ken how that may be"—a questioning doubt.
But we cannot tell the whole tale in questions, and the
questioning melody is used to express surprise: "If sae be
ye dinna ken me": "She has kilted them up to the knee".
"Ronald Macdonald" evidently pleased. The music of the

* Taken from *The Songs of the North*.

last two lines necessarily gives a sense of finality; it sums up the situation or culminates the sentiment. In each stanza the form is strictly parallel, and this parallel arrangement of the moods is what I call "song form". We might examine it where the poet has definitely written to a melody, in *Ye banks and braes o' bonnie Doon*.

The words we* sing make the third version or "set" as the Henley & Henderson writer calls it; but all three are in song form and were written to music. The poem had to be altered not so much to make it capable of the same melody in each verse, as to make it fit a given melody. It tells of the contrast between past happiness spent on the braes of Doon when the birds were singing, the woodbine twining and the roses blooming, and present pain made more sharp by the same pleasant surroundings. In all versions the lineal parallelism of the moods is fairly close, even in the last verse. The concluding verse of a lyric often, perhaps almost necessarily, differs a little from the others.

First Version:†

1st line ⎰(1) Sweet are the banks, the banks o' Doon,
of verse ⎱(2) Aft hae I rov'd by bonnie Doon,

2nd line ⎰(1) The spreading flowers are fair,
of verse ⎱(2) To see the woodbine twine,

3rd line ⎰(1) And everything is blythe and glad,
of verse ⎱(2) And ilka bird sang o' its luve,

4th line ⎰(1) But I am fu' o' care,
of verse ⎱(2) And sae did I o' mine.

---

* The annotator of the 1877 Blackie & Son edition says: "This sweet song is often desecrated by people taking a part in it, who have no more ear for music than a log, and whose voice resembles the creaking of a timber-yard on a windy day."

† Henley & Henderson's edition, vol. iv.

5th line ⎰(1) Thou'll break my heart, thou bonnie bird,
of verse ⎱(2) Wi' lightsome heart I pu'd a rose

6th line ⎰(1) That sings upon the bough!
of verse ⎱(2) Upon its thorny tree,

7th line ⎰(1) Thou minds me o' the happy days
of verse ⎱(2) But my false lover staw my rose,

8th line ⎰(1) When my fause luve was true.
of verse ⎱(2) And left the thorn wi' me.

9th line ⎰(1) Thou'll break my heart, thou bonnie bird,
of verse ⎱(2) Wi' lightsome heart I pu'd a rose

10th line ⎰(1) That sings beside thy mate,
of verse ⎱(2) Upon a morn in June,

11th line ⎰(1) For sae I sat, and sae I sang,
of verse ⎱(2) And sae I flourish'd on the morn,

12th line ⎰(1) And wist na o' my fate!
of verse ⎱(2) And sae was pu'd or noon.

This was written to a Strathspey tune, hence presumably the repetition of lines 5 to 8 in 9 to 12 to suit the repeated music. We see the same form in Skinner's *Tullochgorum* on page 202.

Second Version:

Opening lines
of verse

⎧(1) Ye flowery banks o' bonnie Doon,
⎪   How can ye bloom sae fair ?
⎪
⎪(2) Thou'll break my heart, thou bonnie
⎪   bird,
⎪   That sings upon the bough;
⎪
⎨(3) Thou'll break my heart, thou bonnie
⎪   bird,
⎪   That sings beside thy mate;
⎪
⎪(4) Aft hae I roved by bonnie Doon,
⎪   To see the woodbine twine,
⎪
⎩(5) Wi' lightsome heart I pu'd a rose,
         Frae aff its thorny tree,

Concluding
lines of
verse

(1) How can ye chant, ye little birds,
    And I sae fu' o' care?

(2) Thou minds me o' the happy days
    When my fause luve was true!

(3) For sae I sat, and sae I sang,
    And wist na o' my fate!

(4) And ilka bird sang o' its luve,
    And sae did I o' mine.

(5) And my fause luver staw the rose,
    But left the thorn wi' me.

Third Version:

1st couplet
of verse

(1) Ye banks and braes o' bonnie Doon,
    How can ye bloom sae fresh and fair?

(2) Aft hae I roved by bonnie Doon,
    To see the rose and woodbine twine;

2nd couplet
of verse

(1) How can ye chant, ye little birds,
    And I sae weary, fu' o' care?

(2) And ilka bird sang o' its mate,
    And fondly sae did I o' mine.

3rd couplet
of verse

(1) Thou'll break my heart, thou warbling
        bird,
    That wantons through the flow'ry
        thorn;

(2) Wi' lightsome heart I pu'd a rose,
    Fu' sweet upon the thorny tree;

Last couplet
of verse

(1) Thou minds me o' departed days,
    Departed—never to return!

(2) And my false lover stole my rose,
    But ah! he left the thorn wi' me.

There are one or two false quantities and accents, but
this did not trouble Burns. The same melody admits

small irregularities in the rhythm. The different phrasing of:

> But ah—he left the thorn wi' me,

and:

> Departed—never to return!

does not disturb us; both hang the cadence up, the pause after "ah" and "departed" being rather a suspending of the melody (not, of course, in the musical sense of *suspension*) than a *caesura* proper.

One need hardly say that not all the poems Burns wrote to fit music have this close parallelism. If the melody will bear a different interpretation in the second verse, the words give it, and Burns is not over scrupulous. The melody of:

> Gae bring to me a pint o' wine,

suits:

> The trumpets sound, the banners fly;

a certain common sentiment underlies both. The slight *caesura* after "me" and the strong break after "sounds" come at a tiny *caesura* in the music; we can hardly stretch a point and call it a cadence. The first verse is, therefore, the better fit, though we may suppose the speech of a warrior at the moment of departure—"The trumpets sound the banners fly"—moves without the halts an armchair reading suggests.

Many "Elizabethan"* lyrics have the song-form structure, and are more strictly true to it than Burns was. The tune of Wyatt's *And wilt thou leave me thus?* and *Forget not yet*, of Herrick's *Bid me to live* (save for the second verse), of the first three verses of Wither's *Manly Heart* and *Why so pale and wan, fond lover?* (save for the last) is identical in each verse.† And indeed, some of them read as if their

---

* Including lyrics before and after Elizabeth.

† If the reader wishes to check this, all these lyrics are in Palgrave's *Golden Treasury*, and *The Oxford Book of English Verse*.

inspiration were the melody of such chance tags of song as:

> Why so pale and wan, fond lover?
> Prithee, why so pale?

Mr. John Erskine* objects to this parallel structure and complains that the subject-matter of Elizabethan lyrics is often heterogeneous, Campion in one poem describing his mistress's face as a garden, a morning, a meadow, as heaven, death, youth and spring. Or again:

The music was repeated with each stanza, and as the end of the tune naturally called for a climax, the poet was tempted to make the effect by his wit. The result is a certain intellectual charm in every stanza, but the fundamental emotional unity of the lyric is lacking.

But this is to look at the thing from an unsympathetic angle. The emotional unity lies in the melody, whether of an actual air or of the inflection. If we had an emotional progress in each stanza we could not have the same tune in the inflection; and the very essence of the charm of these lyrists lies in their tune. Such poems as *Why so pale and wan, fond lover?* owe most of their poetry precisely to their tune. The music is the "taking" part of the Elizabethan lyric, and would in itself justify almost any words. The epigrammatic form fits the dainty grace of their melodies as no other form could, and the parallelism is essential to them. Besides, when we think of it, is the morning so very different a thing from a meadow or a garden, or heaven from youth or spring or even from death, when they all pay the same lady the same compliment? They have at least one thing in common, in all making the same bow. *Follow thy fair sun, unhappy shadow!* tells only of one contrast, that between light and darkness, sun and shadow. I shall write it out to show the parallelism:

* *The Elizabethan Lyric*, pp. 234-40.

1st line of verse
- (1) Follow thy fair sun, unhappy shadow!
- (2) Follow her whose light thy light depriveth!
- (3) Follow those pure beams, whose beauty burneth!
- (4) Follow her, while yet her glory shineth!
- (5) Follow still, since so thy fates ordained!

2nd line of verse
- (1) Though thou be black as night,
- (2) Thou here thou livest disgraced,
- (3) That so have scorched thee,
- (4) There comes a luckless night,
- (5) The sun must have his shade,

3rd line of verse
- (1) And she made all of light,
- (2) And she in heaven is placed,
- (3) As thou still black must be,
- (4) That will dim all her light;
- (5) Till both at once do fade,

4th line of verse
- (1) Yet follow thy fair sun, unhappy shadow!
- (2) Yet follow her whose light the world reviveth!
- (3) Till her kind beams thy black to brightness turneth.
- (4) And this the black unhappy shade divineth.
- (5) The sun still proud, the shadow still disdained.

Campion differs from some of the other lyrists; he is a problem. That he wrote in song form is not enigmatic. The difficulty lies in too many explanations; he is too easily accounted for. Perhaps he had the Burns quality and wrote poetry to fit his music, or the music of Rosseter and Coprario. Mr. Percival Vivian shows that he could do this;* but of all the possibilities it is least likely that this was his habit. The reason is rather musical than poetic. While we can see how the words suggested the music, many of his tunes and rhythms could hardly have suggested themselves apart from words. Moreover if Campion

---

* Introduction to Campion's poetry in "The Muses Library" edition.

wrote to a given tune, he made a singularly bad job of it—
too inconceivably bad—in one of the songs to Rosseter's
music. The second verse of *When Laura smiles* does not
fit, and we can explain the misfit only by saying that the
words were there first. Such misfits are rare in Campion.
If he usually wrote his words first their melody must have
been very near "the threshold" of his mind, if not above it.
He could hardly have carried out intricate metrical schemes
like those of *Hark, all you ladies that do sleep, Break now
my heart and die, Your fair looks inflame my desires*, so
naturally and spontaneously unless the melody of the
first verse were running in his head to guide him in the
others. He might, of course, have written the words of the
first verse, then its melody, and fitted the following verses
to that tune; but this is too utilitarian a method where
there is little inducement to utilitarianism. Vivian suggests that very often "the words and music were composed almost simultaneously"; and I do not think we need
be afraid of leaving "almost" out of it, even if in the
strictest logic we could.

Although I have not gone through his poetry sys-
tematically to verify this impression, I should say that
Campion's metre is more precisely the same for every
verse in those poems he himself set to music than in those
set to music by his friends. In his own songs he allows
himself certain freedoms; he gives false quantities but not
false accents to "and"s and "in"s; and he substitutes two
short syllables for one long ($\mathcal{C}\mathcal{C} = \mathcal{P}$); and he sometimes
phrases his verses differently. In the first verse of *Come, you
pretty false-eyed wanton*, the opening line ends with a
trochee, the second line beginning with a trochee:

> Come, you pretty false-eyed wanton,
> Leave your crafty smiling!

In the other verses the first line ends on the accented

syllable corresponding to the first of "wanton", the unaccented note coming on the opening iamb of the second
line:

> Sooner may you count the stars,
> And number hail, down pouring.

But these poems do not have discrepancies between the
verses such as we find in *When Laura smiles*, the tune of
whose first verse was certainly not running in the poet's
head when he wrote the second. It looks as if, in some of
the poems he gave to other musicians to set, the melody of
the inflections had not come into clear enough consciousness to keep each verse identical. Still we must not exaggerate the importance of this tiny contrast. If the poems
set to his own music had originally verses inconsistent
with each other, he might afterwards have altered them to
fit the melody. Yet, if he had made a habit of doing this,
knowing the necessity, he would probably have revised the
poems he gave Rosseter. Perhaps he never noticed the
contradictions in the form of *When Laura smiles*, especially as on the average the metres of Rosseter's poems are
not much less, if less consistent, than those he himself sets,
and since these poems, too, often suggest the same tune in
each verse, and must consequently have sprung from the
same latent melody. The inflection tune of *And would you
fain the reason know* is very vivid, while *Sweet, come again*
preserves an intricate rhythm throughout, with only one
false quantity and one substitution of two shorter syllables
for a longer.

But Campion has no monopoly of such intricate
metrical schemes preserved regularly in each verse.
Donne takes only one or two licences in *Sweetest love, I do
not go* and *Send home my long stray'd eyes to me*, and we are
very conscious of his inflection tune in such poems as *A
Valediction Forbidding Mourning* although the metres differ
from verse to verse. Nor is real song form confined to these

centuries; both Scott and Christina Rossetti know how to write in this form.

We have grouped two kinds of song form in one—the strict form where the mood retraces itself in each verse, and song form merely sufficiently strict to allow of the same melody. Out of the less strict form develops the stanza, which originated in the fitting of successive verses to the same tune. Stanzas necessarily result from this, and need no other explanation. Indeed, this fitting of words to a recurring tune seems to have been the reason for form in poetry.* In the earlier poetry of different civilisations we can trace the independent evolution of the stanza from this source. The simpler stanza forms in English probably arose directly from folk-song. The more artificial stanzas came from the troubadours, who in turn developed their art from the folk-songs of southern France, and indeed, most of them have perished with the perishing of the musical form, save as archaic, or at least scholar's experiments—*ballade*, *virelay*, *villanelle* and *rondeau*. The *rondo* form still survives in music, its "rules" still being identical with those of the poetic form. Details of the poetic form vary with the century; Schipper† gives this as an example of the old "roundel", as it was first called:

> Now welcom somer, with thy sunne softe,
> That hast this wintres weders overstake,
> And driven away the longe nyghtes blake;
> Seynt Valentyn, that art ful hy in lofte,
> Thus syngen smale foules for thy sake:
> Now welcom somer, with thy sunne softe,
> That hast this wintres weders overstake;
> Wel han they cause for to gladen ofte,
> Sith ech of hem recovered hath his make:
> Now welcom somer, with thy sunne softe,

* For illustration, see Katharine M. Wilson, *Mint Sauce*, section on "Poetry's Debt to Music."
† *History of English Versification*, p. 386.

> That hast this wintres weders overstake,
> And driven away the longe nyghtes blake.

A common French form, he says, was rhymed *ab* baab *ab* abba *ab*, the italicised *ab* lines being the repeated refrain.

The essential condition of this form, as used by the French poets, was that two, three, or four verses* forming a refrain must occur three times.

Of the musical form, Stewart Macpherson, in his *Form in Music*, says:

> The distinguishing mark of a Rondo has always been that of a principal theme occurring *at least three times*, the various appearances of this idea being separated one from another by passages more or less in contrast to it.

The separating passages differ from each other just as they do in the poetic *rondeau*. *Serenades*, *aubades* and *rondeaus* make artificial enough forms in English, but it is interesting that the peasants of the district that produced the *serenade* and the *aubade* still sing them beneath the window of their ladies as they did centuries ago†—so permanent are the foundations of art. The Latin hymns also may have influenced the early stanza-making in England.

We cannot appreciate the poetry of the Elizabethans to the full without some knowledge of their music. Not only did it still have a grip of their lyrics, their contact with music influenced the general outlook of their poetry. We missed some of the significance of their poetry till we rediscovered their music. Their p⋅etry about music meant no more to us than poetry about the moon means to a child who goes to bed at seven. Most of us remember the revelation when we first saw the moon in a poetic light, and realise the difference this makes to our reading of moon poetry.

---

* *i.e.* lines.

† J. Tiersot, *Histoire de la chanson populaire en France*, p. 107.

The same revelation of madrigal music illumines these
lines:

> Lap me in soft Lydian* Aires,
> Married to immortal verse
> Such as the meeting soul may pierce
> In notes, with many a winding bout
> Of lincked sweetnes long drawn out,
> With wanton heed, and giddy cunning,
> The melting voice through mazes running,
> Untwisting all the chains that ty
> The hidden soul of harmony.

"Lydian Aires" means something more concrete and definite when we have heard one. Here Milton has written not
vague poetic magic, but an almost scientifically accurate
description of the madrigal or motet music of his day. Each
"part" is a winding bout of linked sweetness—a beautiful
tune, running through the mazes made by the crossing
"parts"—with wanton heed and giddy cunning untwisting
all the chains that tie the hidden soul of harmony. It is
almost precise enough for an encyclopaedia, and fits this
sort of music and no other. We cannot really understand
the lines until we have heard that music, which is as much
more lovely than any other music as *Lycidas* is more
melodious than any other poem. Once we have seen the
moon and felt the emotion, a new lustre reflects from the
poetry of it. After hearing an Elizabethan madrigal or
motet we read *L'Allegro* as a new poem. It makes the same
difference to our appreciation as a botanist's knowledge
must make to an appreciation of Botticelli's *Spring*.

Spenser wrote his *August Eclogue* with a musical reference; he was thinking partly in music as he wrote. The
"roundelay" is a two-part song; Cuddie refers to Willye's
"part" as the "undersong". The two melodies run con-
currently, and we ought to read Willye's "undersong" and

---

* The mode starting on F, like our major scale, only with B natural
instead of B flat—different from the Greek Lydian.

Perigot's air as simultaneously as possible, otherwise we miss the feeling of it. Perigot's song goes without break:

> I saw the bouncing Bellibone,
> Tripping over the dale alone,
> Well decked in a frocke of gray,
> And in a Kirtle of greene saye,
>   *etc.*;

while Willye's follows continuously, perhaps a line late:

> hey ho Bonibell
> she can trippe it very well:
> hey ho gray is greete,
> and greene is for maydens meete.

If we know nothing of Elizabethan music we shall almost certainly misread the poem. The "roundelay" gives Saintsbury* an "antiphonal" impression. Reading it antiphonally he must lose something of its characteristic charm, the gaiety and daintiness. Cuddie's song, also, has a musical recollection. Its form, a simplified "sestine-stave", was invented by Arnaud Daniel, the famous troubadour. I know nothing about the music that went with this form, but if, as is possible, the order of the musical phrases went round in turn with the rhymes, the ingenuity would not be so merely ingenious, since it would be musical likewise. The form of the last verse reminds us of a musical convention still used; it is something like the idea of a *stretto*. At all events, the "sestine-stave" must have held musical associations for Spenser and his contemporaries we do not feel. Stanzas meant more when they usually represented musical forms. Herbert's quaint use of them as mystic symbols, which perhaps seems merely ingenious and has little poetic significance for us, represented more than we give him credit for. To symbolise mystical or abstract ideas by peculiar forms is a method more native to music than to

---

* *History of English Prosody*, vol. i, p. 356.

poetry. Writing a seven-lined stanza when the theme is Sunday, or a three-lined one when it is the Trinity, seems more artificial than representing the Ten Commandments by a tenfold repetition in music, or the Trinity by three themes. But if the Elizabethans connected the stanza with music, then Herbert's stanzas would have the significance of musical forms.

Though the stanza evolved from the fitting of changed words to the same recurring tune, whether conscious or merely latent, we can construct stanzas arbitrarily. We may sit down and write a so-called Spenserian stanza by copying Spenser's form, or invent new forms in an equally arbitrary way. But stanzas invented or copied arbitrarily do not sing themselves as the *Faerie Queene* sings itself. What strikes us about the stanzas of the Elizabethans, not exclusively but characteristically, is their song quality. Shakespeare's songs, whether heard with their melodies or not, carry the suggestion of their tune with them. He sometimes has two contrasting melodies in the same poem—an *andante* and an *allegro*, as in *Under the greenwood tree, Blow, blow, thou winter wind, O mistress mine! where are you roaming?*; the change in the tune makes its effect as vividly without the music as with:

(*Andante*) O mistress mine! where are you roaming?
    O! stay and hear; your true-love's coming,
     That can sing both high and low.
(*Allegro*) Trip no further, pretty sweeting;
    Journeys end in lovers' meeting,
     Every wise man's son doth know.

(*Andante*) What is love? 'tis not hereafter;
    Present mirth hath present laughter,
     What's to come is still unsure.
(*Allegro*) In delay there lies no plenty;
    Then come kiss me, sweet-and-twenty,
     Youth's a stuff will not endure.

Milton's *Nativity Ode* has a natural stanza, determined simply by the melody running in that form, though if we take the reader's viewpoint we must say that the arrangement of the lines conditions the melody. We can see that the stanza structure influences the tune for us, from the cadence of the Asia lyric in *Prometheus Unbound*, which recalls the *Nativity Ode* tune:

> My soul is an enchanted boat,
> Which, like a sleeping swan, doth float
> Upon the silver waves of thy sweet singing.

"Silver waves of thy sweet singing" has notes in common with the cadence of:

> It was the Winter wilde,
> While the Heav'n-born-childe
> All meanly wrapt in the rude manger lies.

Though I assume that most readers sensitive to the music of poetry hear the same cadence in these lines, even if they do not realise it, I do not assume that this cadence gives us each an identical experience. The same melody may affect us differently. Milton's stanza gives me the feeling of a Christmas carillon rung from some high tower; it is like the sound of bells hovering with an almost palpable consistency in the frosty air—a jubilant pealing, a swinging in the upper ether. But perhaps the effect results fully as much from the metrical as from the inflectional music, if we may separate them. The short lines ring the peal and the echoes die down in the final Alexandrine, which makes the bass, the "Heav'n's deep organ". The short lines clash like tumbling bells because their rhythms clash. A couplet like:

> The helmed Cherubim,
> The sworded Seraphim,

is rare. If one line begins with an unaccented syllable, the other usually begins with an accented:

> Only with speeches fair
> She woos the gentle air.
>
> But he her fears to cease,
> Sent down the meek-eyd Peace.
>
> Down through the turning sphear
> His ready Harbinger.
>
> The Windes with wonder whist,
> Smoothly the waters kist.
>
> The Stars with deep amaze
> Stand fixt in stedfast gaze.
>
> Nature that heard such sound
> Beneath the hollow round.
>
> Now was almost won
> To think her part was don.
>
> And let your silver chime
> Move in melodious time.
>
> And Mercy set between,
> Thron'd in Celestiall sheen.

The contrast comes too often not be deliberate, or to result from following inflectional tunes with this characteristic. In the last verse of all it is significant that neither of the short couplets have these contrasting rhythms; the close comes quietly; the tumbling bells cease. Milton's stanza is vital and expressive to the tiniest detail, its form being an essential part of the melody, essential to it not as its shape to a vase, but as its shape to a rose; it grew in that form, it was not made in that mould.

Stanzas of natural growth make an interesting study, perhaps especially the sonnet and the Spenserian stanza. Petrarch's sonnet may have grown out of the *terza rima*;* Saintsbury† quotes one of Christina Rosetti's as having "the real essence of the English Petrarchian sonnet as absolutely no others have it", and we see that it is rather in triplets than in quartets, not two quartets rhymed *abba acac*, but *abb aac ac* followed by two triplets *dce ecd*:

> Youth gone and beauty gone, if ever there
> Dwelt beauty in so poor a face as this;
> Youth gone and beauty, what remains of bliss?
>
> I will not bind fresh roses in my hair,
> To shame a cheek at best but little fair—
> Leave youth his roses, who can bear a thorn.
>
> I will not seek for blossom anywhere,
> Except such common flowers as blow with corn.
>
> Youth gone and beauty gone, what doth remain?
> The longing of a heart, pent up, forlorn,
> A silent heart whose silence loves and longs:
>
> The silence of a heart which sang its songs
> While youth and beauty make a summer morn,
> Silence of love that cannot sing again.

When her sonnets are in quartets, we sometimes hear a triplet cadence; the *abba* quartet being really a triplet, *abb*, with a *coda a*.

---

* I do not know that it did; I merely suggest the likelihood that the *terza rima* cadence may have helped to mould the form. The sestet was certainly in groups of three, and despite the division in the middle of the octave, there may have been a suggestion of a three-line cadence as in the first quartet of *After Death*, quoted below.

† *History of English Prosody*, vol. iii, pp. 358-9.

AFTER DEATH

The curtains were half drawn, the floor was swept
  And strewn with rushes, rosemary and may
  Lay thick upon the bed on which I lay,
Where through the lattice ivy-shadows crept.

He leaned above me, thinking that I slept
  And could not hear him; but I heard him say:
  "Poor child, poor child!" and as he turned away
Came a deep silence, and I knew he wept.

He did not touch the shroud, or raise the fold
  That hid my face, or take my hand in his,
    Or ruffle the smooth pillows for my head;

    He did not love me living; but once dead
  He pitied me; and very sweet it is
To know he is still warm though I am cold.

The first English sonnet was not a natural growth, but a
foreign imitation. *Terza rima* has never been assimilated to
English forms of thought.* Consequently English poets do
not construct their sonnets on *terza rima* cadences; they
find it difficult to bring the *terza rima* melody to its close.
But so various are the forms of sonnet in English that it is
almost a misnomer to class them all as one. Saintsbury†
says that Milton's are really little more than blank-verse
paragraphs. This is an exaggeration; they are blank verse
within a lyric shell. *When I consider how my light is spent*
starts off powerfully, almost heavily, in steady majestic
flight, and goes without flutter or hesitation to land at the
fourteenth line, just in the Miltonic paragraph way, but it
does give us a sonnet sensation. Its cadences evolve from
the Miltonic blank-verse cadence, but the sonnet form

---

* In his *History of English Prosody*, vol. iii, pp. 361-5, Saintsbury
points this out.   † *Ibid.*, vol. ii, p. 217.

modifies them. Similarly in *Methought I saw my late espoused Saint*:

> Methought I saw my late espoused Saint
>   Brought to me like *Alcestis* from the grave,
>   Whom *Joves* great Son to her glad Husband gave,
> Rescu'd from death by force though pale and faint.
> Mine as whom washt from spot of child-bed taint,
>   Purification in the old Law did save,
>   And such, as yet once more I trust to have
> Full sight of her in Heaven without restraint,
> Came vested all in white, pure as her mind:
>   Her face was vail'd, yet to my fancied sight,
>   Love, sweetness, goodness, in her person shin'd
> So clear, as in no face with more delight.
> But O as to embrace me she enclin'd
>   I wak'd, she fled, and day brought back my night.

The postponing of the cadence, which we expect at the eighth line, to the ninth, has an effect on the tune; the sonnet structure remoulds and transforms the blank-verse tune.

Some of Shakespeare's sonnets, too, are based on his blank-verse cadence,* but to his name is given the credit of the English sonnet proper. *Elizabethan* would have been a better name. The Elizabethan feeling for the sonnet developed from their feeling for song form, many of them being really lyrics of three stanzas with a final couplet.† Where the rhythms are not identical in each verse, the moods have often the song-form parallelism:

> ‡Were I as base as is the lowly plain,
>   And you, my Love, as high as heaven above,
>   Yet should the thoughts of me, your humble swain,
>   Ascend to heaven, in honour of my love.

---

* *e.g. The expense of spirit in a waste of shame* (No. 129).

† *e.g.* Shakespeare's, Spenser's, Daniel's, Drayton's on the whole, but not Sidney's on the whole.

‡ Sylvester.

Were I as high as heaven above the plain,
And you, my Love, as humble and as low
As are the deepest bottoms of the main,
Wheresoe'er you were, with you my love should go.

Were you the earth, dear Love, and I the skies,
My love should shine on you like to the Sun,
And look upon you with ten thousand eyes,
Till heaven wax'd blind, and till the world were done.

Wheresoe'er I am, below, or else above you,
Wheresoe'er you are, my heart shall truly love you.

The *Amoretti* have lovely examples:

One day I wrote her name upon the strand,
But came the waves and washed it away:
Again I wrote it with a second hand,
But came the tide, and made my pains his prey.

Vain man, said she, that dost in vain assay,
A mortal thing so to immortalise,
For I myself shall like to this decay,
And eek my name be wiped out likewise.

Not so, (quod I) let baser things devise
To die in dust, but you shall live by fame:
My verse your virtues rare shall eternise,
And in the heavens write your glorious name.

Where whenas death shall all the world subdue,
Our love shall live, and later life renew.

Men call you fair, and you do credit it (79) and *The famous
warriors of the anticke world* (69) make equally good illustrations. We need not quote from Shakespeare such sonnets
as *If music and sweet poetry agree,** Farewell! thou art too
dear for my possessing* (87), *Not from the stars do I my judgment pluck* (14), *When my love swears that she is made of
truth* (138), *Lo, as a careful housewife runs to catch* (143),

* *Passionate Pilgrim* (8).

How oft, when thou, my music, music play'st (128). Some of these have moods arranged in such strict parallels in all three verses that the final couplet comes unexpectedly, summing the thing up a little abruptly; it hardly feels like a sonnet. But the difficulty of the final couplet in the song-form sonnet can be solved. Drayton does it most beautifully in:

> Since there's no help, come let us kiss and part—
> Nay, I have done, you get no more of me;
> And I am glad, yea, glad with all my heart,
> That thus so cleanly I myself can free.
>
> Shake hands for ever, cancel all our vows,
> And, when we meet, at any time again,
> Be it not seen in either of our brows
> That we one jot of former love retain.
>
> Now at the last gasp of Love's latest breath,
> When, his pulse failing, Passion speechless lies,
> When Faith is kneeling by his bed of death,
> And Innocence is closing up his eyes,
>
> —Now if thou would'st, when all have given him over,
> From death to life thou might'st him yet recover.

The couplet follows more easily when it states a contrast to the preceding lines than when it condenses the previous themes:

> My mistress' eyes are nothing like the sun;
> Coral is far more red than her lips' red:
> If snow be white, why then her breasts are dun;
> If hairs be wires, black wires grow on her head.
>
> I have seen roses damask'd, red and white,
> But no such roses see I in her cheeks;
> And in some perfumes is there more delight
> Than in the breath that from my mistress reeks.

I love to hear her speak, yet well I know
That music hath a far more pleasing sound:
I grant I never saw a goddess go,—
My mistress, when she walks, treads on the ground:

And yet, by heaven, I think my love as rare
As any she belied with false compare.

The Spenserian stanza, though music goes to its making, possibly arose somewhat differently. It is not in song form, nor do the lineal or rhythmic arrangements control its melody as in the *Nativity Ode* tune. The Spenserian tune probably grew out of its cadence. The Alexandrine makes the origin of the Spenserian stanza. Guest says of it:

* The noble stanza which we owe to Spenser is formed by adding an Alexandrine to the ballet-stave of eight.

But we ought rather to say: "The noble stanza which we owe to Spenser is formed by prefixing the ballet-stave of eight to the Alexandrine." From the beginning Spenser had a new type of cadence, an individual tune at the close. We find a cadence very like the Spenserian in *Mother Hubberd's Tale*:

Some tolde of Ladies, and their Paramoures;
Some of brave Knights, and their renowned Squires;
Some of the Faeries and their strange attires;
And some of Giaunts hard to be beleeved,
That the delight thereof me much releeved.

The cadence is very long, comprising the whole of the last couplet; we feel the melody turn into the closing tune on "And some". This is of the very essence of the prolonged *Faerie Queene* cadence; the poet seems to be feeling his way back from it in his earlier works.

The Shepherd's Calendar, which was the first school of

* *History of English Rhythms*, p. 666.

the *Faerie Queene's* musical technique, had already a strong sense of stanza music. *The January Eclogue* is almost in song form, with a contrasting music like some of Shakespeare's songs; in the quartet the pace is quicker and on a higher pitch than in the following couplet:

Thou barrein ground, whome winters wrath hath wasted,
Art made a myrrhour, to behold my plight:
Whilome thy fresh spring flowrd, and after hasted
Thy sommer prowde with Daffadillies dight.
And now is come thy wynters stormy state,
Thy mantle mard, wherein thou maskedst late.

Moreover, the poem closes on an Alexandrine. Spenser shows as complete a mastery of simple stanza music here as he did later over the more subtle *Faerie Queene* music. *The June Eclogue* also keeps up a similar tune in each stanza despite the utmost variety in the placing of the *caesuras*. Then Spenser's rhyme-royal writing had a great influence in forming his *Faerie Queene* stanza. The rhyme-royal suits his mentality, for he loves the oddly balanced stanza—fives, and sevens and nines. His tunes run in lines like these. Where it takes five lines to meet the cadence, the close is hung up, the tonic-seeking melody prolonged. We have only to read a few stanzas of Chaucer's *Troilus and Cressida* to see how individually Spenser treats his rhyme-royal. Chaucer's cadence is not so vivid, and he groups his lines as frequently into three and four, or four and three, as into five and two:

> *She seyde, "O love, to whom I have and shal
> Ben humble subgit, trewe in myn entente,
> As I best can, to yow, lord, yeve ich al
> For ever-more, myn hertes lust to rente.
> For never yet thy grace no wight sente
> So blisful cause as me, my lyf to lede
> In alle joye and seurtee, out of drede.

* II, stanzas 119-120.

Ye, blisful god, han me so wel beset
In love, y-wis, that al that bereth lyf
Imaginen ne cowde how to ben bet;
For, lord, with-outen jalousye or stryf,
I love oon which that is most ententyf
To serven wel, unwery or unfeyned,
That ever was, and leest with harm distreyned.

Although Spenser, like Chaucer, varies the balancing of his
stanza considerably, he *tends* towards a five-line melody
with the remaining lines as a closing couplet—a tendency
perhaps inevitable to the Elizabethan in him :

*Why then dooth flesh, a bubble glas of breath,
Hunt after honour and advauncement vaine,
And reare a trophee for devouring death,
With so great labour and long lasting paine,
As if his daies for ever should remaine?
Sith all that in this world is great or gaie,
Doth as a vapour vanish, and decaie.

Spenser uses the stanza rather to fix a tune, than in
Chaucer's free way. His technique was essentially a stanza
technique, that is to say, he writes to a recurring tune which
varies only subtly, and conveys that melody by keeping
his stanza vivid; thus he has nearly the same tune in every
verse despite great diversity of rhythm. The later rhyme-
royal of the *Four Hymns* is even more remarkable than his
earlier rhyme-royal for this similar tune to a varying
rhythm, or, as hardly requires saying, the great poem itself,
for the *Faerie Queene* stanza has much of his rhyme-royal
feeling about it.

The music of the *Faerie Queene* is made by fusing many
cadences. Spenser arouses quartet or couplet or quintet
expectations only to slide out of fulfilling them, playing on
our sense of common forms to weave part of their music

* *Ruines of Time*, 50.

into his tune. This helps to give us a sense of unsatisfied longing and the lure of a promise never attained:

> A lovely Ladie rode him faire beside,
> Upon a lowly Asse more white than snow,
> Yet she much whiter, but the same did hide
> Under a veil, that wimpled was full low,
> And over all a blacke stole she did throw,
> As one that inly mourned: so was she sad,
> And heavie sat upon her palfrey slow:
> Seemed in heart some hidden care she had,
> And by her in a line a milke white lambe she lad.

Our expectation of a cadence at the end of the fifth line influences the tune that closes on "mourned". The Alexandrine also gives us a procrastinated cadence. The tune feels lazy and dreamy, always stretching idly to a shadow just a little further off. Saintsbury* comes near the secret of it when he tells us that Spenser's management of the *caesura* is one of the greatest devices of his art. Spenser controls his tune by an extraordinarily skilful placing of the *caesuras*, not like Milton in *Paradise Lost* determining the cadences on blank-verse principles, but using the *caesura* to modify the melody by playing it against our sense of stanza form:

> But full of fire and greedy hardiment,
> The youthfule knight could not for ought be staide,
> But forth unto the darksome hole he went,
> And looked in: his glistering armor made
> A little glooming light, much like a shade,
> By which he saw the ugly monster plaine,
> Halfe like a serpent horribly displaide,
> But th' other half did woman's shape retain,
> Most lothsom, filthie, foule, and full of vile disdaine.

Here the quartet melody which we anticipate comes early and unexpectedly to its cadence on an upward inflection at

---

* *History of English Prosody*, vol. i, pp. 411-12.

"looked in"; and a couplet tune is picked up and brought to its cadence at "shade". The beginning of the fourth line ends, or breaks off, the quartet tune, and the latter half carries on as if the beginning had started a couplet. The remaining lines lead to the final cadence whose lingering surprise is felt all the more strongly for ending another *quasi*-quartet. By playing the *caesura* and the stanza form against each other in the first five lines of the stanza, the poet has fused two melodies, which, following one another, would have taken six lines to complete, into one which runs for five. He can do this because his line-endings are real and vivid; despite the interlineal breaks, we never lose them as we do in *Adonais*,* where the interlineal cadences are of the blank-verse sort, and weaken rather than play upon our sense of the line. And not only his lines; Spenser's stanza form is vivid. The tune is conditioned by the stanza and modified by the *caesuras* just as the tune in Milton's sonnets is conditioned by the sense and modified by the stanza structure. We have another variation of his method in:

> * A pardlike Spirit beautiful and swift—
> A Love in desolation masked;—a Power
> Girt round with weakness;—it can scarce uplift
> The weight of the superincumbent hour;
> It is a dying lamp, a falling shower,
> A breaking billow;—even whilst we speak
> Is it not broken? On the withering flower
> The killing sun smiles brightly: on a cheek
> The life can burn in blood, even while the heart may break.

Saintsbury says that Spenser rarely has mid-line stops, while Shelley has (vol. iii, p. 106). It would be even more true to say that Spenser's mid-line stops do not bring the melody to a final cadence. Saintsbury tells us also (vol. iii, p. 98) that *Childe Harold* is really in couplets with rhymes in Spenserian order, and that the Alexandrine is Drydenian rather than Spenserian. He says this of the rhythm, but it is true of the inflection music as well, which is perhaps what he really hears: many writers talk of poems being very rhythmic, when they really mean melodious.

As gentle Shepheard in sweet eventide,
When ruddy *Phoebus* gins to welke in west,
High on a hill, his flock to vewen wide,
Markes which do byte their hasty supper best;
A cloud of combrous gnattes do him molest,
All striving to infixe their feeble stings;
That from their noyance he no where can rest,
But with his clownish hands their tender wings
He brusheth oft, and oft doth mar their murmurings.

The first quartet is completed. The second is curious; we just get into the quartet-like melody when we are cheated of its close, and led as if by an unforeseen magic to the Alexandrine cadence. This is how Spenser enchants us. Again and again he deceives, continually suggesting one form and ending in another. Despite its inevitableness, his close is unexpected, bewitching us with fresh wonder. When two quartets have gone to their cadence, the Alexandrine still follows consecutively as part of the melody, not as if extraneously tacked on, and still with a new delight:

At length they chaunst to meet upon the way
An aged Sire, in long black weedes yclad,
His feete all bare, his beard all hoarie gray,
And by his belt his booke he hanging had;
Sober he seemde, and very sagely sad,
And to the ground his eyes were lowly bent,
Simple in shew, and voyde of malice bad,
And all the way he prayed, as he went,
And often knockt his brest, as one that did repent.

Although we can go a certain length in explaining Spenser's tune, we cannot guess what makes his quartet or his couplet tunes sound different from anyone else's. Even his sonnets in regular song form have a Spenserian melody, the intervals and the progression of the intervals being characteristic. One gets the same sense of individual tunes in music. Some melodies could be written by Bach alone or his imitators, by Handel alone or his. It is not wonderful that poets should have individual types of melody, but it is surprising that we should catch them from their poems, from symbols with nothing to represent the inflection tune. This opens perhaps the most difficult problem we have to attempt. What causes Cadence?

CHAPTER IV

CADENCE

WHAT causes cadence? We have already seen the broad general causes. Meaning, sentence or phrase closes, line or stanza arrangements, and so forth determine where cadences occur, and to some extent the sort of cadence; but what determines the precise tune I do not know, unless it be the combination of these with the inflections suggested by the mood of the meaning.

We do know what a cadence is. There are two sorts, one ending on the tonic or final note, a "full close" as it is called in music, the other coming to a partial rest usually on a note other than the tonic. It takes at least two notes to form a cadence, and may take more than a line. In the crudest poem melody—the alternating fourth of our tune for Cowper's *Alexander Selkirk*,* which merely runs to and from the tonic and dominant—we see a sort of preparation for the cadence. The melody turns, lingers on the tonic before going to the dominant, and *vice versa*. It is possible by means of a preparatory note to give a sense of finality on the reciting pitch. In a quaint example of primitive (negro) declamation noted by Lanier,† a new and alien note (*fa*) makes the preparation for the full close on the declaiming note (*so*):

* Page 96 above.
† *The Science of English Verse*, p. 276.

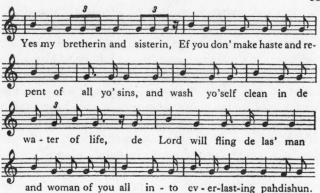

Yes my bretherin and sisterin, Ef you don' make haste and repent of all yo' sins, and wash yo'self clean in de
wa - ter of life, de Lord will fling de las' man
and woman of you all in - to ev - er-last-ing pahdishun.

At the half close on "water of life" the insistence on the
higher note gives a sort of turn to the melody. The repetition of this note again on "everlasting" prepares us for
the strong final cadence on the last two syllables. Most
people speaking in public emphasise the preparatory fore-
cast of their final. The adventurer on his first attempt often
finds it difficult to strike this warning note which lets his
audience know he is about to sit down. It is the difficulty
of getting out of a room, as it presents itself in the music
of life; the preparatory notes are the putting on of our
gloves, the diffusion of an atmosphere of about to be de-
parting before one absolutely goes. When we listen to a
list of names being read we can easily tell the second last
by its coming on the preparatory cadence note, especially
if we have heard the same reader deliver a previous list. A
digression accompanying the penultimate name need not
postpone the preparatory note. Only more conspicuous is
the absence of preparation when the reciter drops suddenly and awkwardly to his final. If we study the music of
tedious speaking—an entertaining occupation—we see the
young speaker going on too long because he cannot find
the notes to sit down on, the old speaker because he
achieves his final cadence so easily and unconsciously that

he does not realise how often he denies his assertion of having come to an end.

There are many ways of arriving on the tonic at a cadence, the usual one, according to Lanier,* being a drop of a fourth (*fa* to *do*), and this he tells us is "the sign for a full stop" in the Roman Church chant, and was as we have seen,† used by Bach; but most people would say a falling fifth was more usual (*so* to *do*). A drop of a fourth from the fifth note of the scale to the second and thence to the tonic (*so, re, do*) is one of the most emphatic cadences we hear in speech, the absolute final; we do not end every sentence with it, but a great many long speeches. In the *Monograph Supplement* of the *Psychological Review* for January 1910,‡ Mr. Van Dyke Bingham gives the result of an interesting experiment. He played the following intervals, and his audience, who were musical but not trained musicians, noted those which gave a sense of finality: *ti* to *do'*, *do'* to *ti*, *do* to *re*, *re* to *do*, *re* to *fa* or *la* to *do'*, *fa* to *re* or *do'* to *la*, *do* to *mi*, *mi* to *do*, *do* to *fa* or *so* to *do'*, *fa* to *do* or *do'* to *so*, *fa* to *ti*, *ti* to *fa*, *do* to *so*, *so* to *do*, *mi* to *do'*, *do'* to *mi*, *do* to *la*, *la* to *do*, *re* to *do'*, *do'* to *re*, *do* to *ti*, *ti* to *do*. *Mi* to *do* and *so* to *do* gave most sense of finality, then *so* to *do'*, *ti* to *do'*, and *re* to *do*.§ *So* to *do'* is not a usual melodic cadence in music, though it occurs often in the bass, nor is *mi* to *do* so common in present-day music as *re* to *do* or *ti* to *do'*; they possibly get their association of cadence from speech rather than from music. These intervals probably do not so much form the cadence as derive their association of finality from appearing often in the cadences of music or speech. *So* to *do'* makes a very common opening interval in folk-song melodies, and *so* to *do* or *mi* to *do*

* *The Science of English Verse*, p. 267.   † Page 45.
‡ Vol. xii, "Studies in Melody".
§ He gives the results in intervals, not in degrees of the scale as I have, to make the results intelligible to the reader who only knows a little about music.

possible and natural openings in music. A cadence depends less on the final interval than on the way of arriving at the tonic, and gets much of its strength from being the last note we hear. Coming at the end of the melody has more to do with the cadencing quality of intervals than anything intrinsic in the intervals themselves.

Rhythm may be very important to cadence, and this has led people to think that the "cadences"* of prose and poetry and even those of music are solely a matter of rhythm, that inflection has nothing to do with it, and that melody is guided entirely by rhythm. Mr. McEwen† says that "cadence" is an affair not of harmony nor even of melody, but of "rhythm"; thus

has a purely rhythmic "cadence", while

has no "cadence", though if we accent the second last note we achieve one. In short, McEwen proves that rhythm alone can make a "cadence". We hear it in drum rhythms. Similarly, we might prove that harmony alone or perhaps melody alone can make a "cadence". This is so obvious that it requires no illustration. But we can upset McEwen's rhythmic "cadence" by setting a melody against it, and yet leave his rhythm intact:

* I put inverted commas when "cadence" means a subjective sense of finality, such as we get from an inflected or melodic cadence, or at the end of a completely balanced rhythm.

† *The Thought in Music*, pp. 100-101.

By doing this we have made the "cadence" come a bar earlier; what was the close before is now the opening phrase of a new grouping. Harmonies giving a strong close on 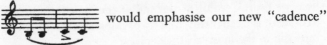 would emphasise our new "cadence" still more; but it is already stronger than McEwen's without the aid of harmony. Although rhythm alone can give us a "cadential" feeling, a melodic cadence is stronger than a rhythmic one.

In speech the end of a sentence, the full stop, brings a cadence into the inflection whether the rhythm is "cadential" or not; in good writing the rhythm and the inflection "cadence" together. Yet an exceptionally strong rhythmic close may sometimes force the inflection to a cadence in contradiction to the pull of the grammatical structure and the logical meaning:

> Oh, how comely it is and how reviving
> To the Spirits of just men long oppressed,
> When God into the hands of their deliverer
> Puts invincible might,
> To quell the mighty of the Earth, the oppressor,
> The brute and boisterous force of violent men,
> Hardy and industrious to support
> Tyrannic power, but raging to pursue
> The righteous, and all such as honour Truth!
> He all their ammunition
> And feats of War defeats,
> With plain Heroic magnitude of mind
> And celestial vigour armed;
> Their Armories and Magazines contemns,
> Renders them useless, while
> With winged expedition
> Swift as the lightning glance he executes
> His errand on the wicked, who surprised,
> Lose their defence, distracted and amazed.

Here the rhythms are too strong for the sense, and almost

compel the inflection to cadence at "Puts invincible might" or "With plain Heroic magnitude of mind". After these breaks we find it difficult to pick up the song. On our first reading we feel as if the musical inspiration had snapped, and Milton were "carrying on" with words merely as symbols of sense. After two or three re-readings we manage to avoid these cadences, to sing through the rhythm without letting the tune fall to the pull of its gravity, but at first we do so with an effort; the rhythmic inclination is very strong. Yet the rhythm is not so strong that, when we know the poem and can steer the inflection through it, the "cadential" feeling remains. Though the gravity of rhythm may pull the inflection to a cadence, we can destroy the "cadential" feeling of the strongest rhythm by deliberately setting the inflection against it.

A study of the effect of rhythmic "cadence" on the inflection would be interesting. Granting that when we come to the last word and see the full stop and *Finis*, we shall arrive at the resting note somehow, how far does the rhythmic incline sweeten the closing melody? We have only to look at some of De Quincey's cadences to see that rhythm has an effect. Though no one has attempted this difficult study, some work has been done on the rhythms we find in prose cadences, notably by Saintsbury and by Mr. A. C. Clark.* Perhaps the simplest and easiest verse "cadence" is the double iamb,† while the amphibrach makes a natural close, though not all rhythms will end gracefully on it. Yet we cannot say that these are cadence-inducing rhythms in poetry. No more are the rhythms of the Latin *cursi* cadential at the beginning of a sentence. The rhythmic and cadential effects depend on the context. The *cursus planus* (/ ˘ ˘ / ˘) does not necessarily make a cadence. If I say of

* *Prose Rhythms in English.*

† As illustrated in the analysis of "The Small Celandine" in *The Real Rhythm in English Poetry*, by the present writer.

my horse, "Dick is impatient," it does not follow that I have said all I shall say on that occasion; not necessarily, I might quite well add, "Do hurry up," giving the cadence on a sort of choriamb. Or the sentence might begin with the rhythm of my cadence, and cadence with the *cursus planus*: "Do hurry up, will you? Dick is impatient." Writers and languages tend to have characteristic rhythmic closes just as they have characteristic rhythms. These depend on characteristic mentality. Pater's rhythm oppresses me. It is limp and lackadaisical; I cannot bear the way his sentences trickle out, and feel tired and worn after reading a page of him. The rhythm of my mind lacks all the virtues his possesses.* To move with a graceful languor disagrees with my mentality; the unwonted motion makes me sick. Although we can get accustomed to rhythms foreign to our own, and though the thinking in such rhythms can exhilarate us like a cutting wind on the mountains, or delight us with the enchantment of a dream, we have all felt sufficiently repelled by an alien rhythm to realise that individual rhythmic idioms are matter of individual mentality. Consequently, though we ought not to say that the double iamb forms a "cadence", nor classify certain rhythms as cadence-inducing, we may assume that languages and persons have characteristic rhythms, and thus tend to have characteristic rhythms at the cadences. We ought not to say of the Latin *cursi*, "These rhythms make a Latin or a Ciceronian cadence," or classify the rhythms of English cadences and say, "These make an English cadence." We should state the facts more correctly if we said, "Cicero cadences on these rhythms, Pater on these. Latin often cadences on such and such rhythms, English on those others." Incidentally, if we wish to know

---

* To check this impression, I analysed and compared some of Pater's rhythms with those I wrote some time before I began this study. One could hardly find a contrast more decided.

the characteristic Latin "cadence" we shall find it somewhere else than in Cicero, the characteristic English
"cadence" elsewhere than in Pater. We should look for
the typical English "cadence" in the commonplace English
writers.*

In poetry also, the rhythm may characterise or help the
cadence.† Perhaps the types of rhythm suitable to the
beginning of the line were once more clearly differentiated
from those at the end than now, though even now we can
detect differences. Schipper‡ makes an interesting remark
on this stanza, which has affinities with the Burns stanza:

þe siker soþe who so seys	a
Wið diol dreye we our days	a
And walk mani wil says	a
As wandrand wiȝtes.	b
Al our games ous agas	c
So mani tenes on tas	c
þwich fonding of fele fas	c
þat fast wiþ us fiȝtes.	b

He says that the cadence lines of the stanza (the bs) have
the rhythm of the cadence portion of the Old English line,
while the rhythms which in Old English opened the line
form the non-cadential lines here. He finds this distinction
as late as *Gammer Gurton's Needle.*

The principal aids to cadence outside the sense are
repetition and contrast. The poet has this option: Where
the poem runs in a pattern, a sudden contrast will determine or ease the close; where it progresses by contrasts, a
return to the opening will help the feeling of finality. The

* Circumstances to do with the Latin *cursi* might make it necessary
to qualify this statement, but this does not affect the English cadence.
† In *The Real Rhythm in English Poetry*, last chapter, I show the
rhythm helping the cadences in blank verse or in poems like *Rose-
Cheek'd Laura*, and the play of the accents determining the cadences
of *Follow, follow.*
‡ *History of English Versification*, pp. 107 and 114.

couplet which closes the Elizabethan sonnet or the Shake-
spearean play makes some of its effect by contrast; and so
does a longer or a shorter line than for the body of the
stanza, such as the Alexandrine close or the short line in
poems like Pope's *Solitude*:

> Happy the man, whose wish and care
> A few paternal acres bound,
> Content to breathe his native air
> In his own ground.

Dr. Abdy Williams* notices the need for such a contrast
to bring what Guest calls the "fairy dialect" of England to
a close:

> On the ground
> Sleep sound:
> I'll apply
> To your eye,
> Gentle lover, remedy.

> When thou wak'st,
> Thou tak'st
> True delight
> In the sight
> Of thy former lady's eye.

This method, he points out, agrees with Greek theory:

The Greeks noticed that when the verses of poetry, or
the Rhythms of music (which with them were identical),
are divided into half-verses or half-rhythms, the rhythmical instinct seems to demand that the final verse or
Rhythm of the Period shall be complete and unbroken.
This instinct led Shakespeare to give the full number of
four feet to the last verse [*i.e.* line] of each period, and it is
remarkable how frequently instinct leads our musicians to
treat such periods as begin with half-rhythms in the same
way.

He gives a long list of musical examples, among them two
from Brahms's Clarinet Sonata, Op. 120 (in the second

* *The Rhythm of Modern Music*, pp. 141-3.

movement, and in the *andante con moto*). But this is not
the only way a short-lined rhythm may finish. Herrick
solves the difficulty by careful phrasing:

A ⎰ Thus I
  ⎨ Pass by,
  ⎱ And die:

B ⎰ As One
  ⎨ Unknown
  ⎱ And gone:

C ⎰⎰ I'm made
  ⎪⎱ A shade,
  ⎨⎰ And laid
   ⎱⎱ I' th' grave:

D ⎰⎰ There have
  ⎪⎱ My Cave,
  ⎨⎰ Where tell
   ⎱⎱ I dwell.

.... Farewell.

It is done by distributing the phrases into two groups of
three lines each (A and B) balanced by two groups of four
lines each (C and D)—a grouping made possible, or at least
helped, because the split rhyme of C and D (*grave, have,
cave*) assonates with the first C rhyme (*made, shade,
laid*), thus allowing "grave" to tone in with the other endings in C. This balance brings the poem to poise as it were,
leaving the final line to make the bow.

Recapitulation strengthens "cadence". The refrain
probably came first in primitive songs as it still does in
many old Scottish tunes, such as *Loch Lomond* or *The Skye
Boat Song*. The mind likes to end where it began, to feel
the circle complete; when we finish our adventure we cast
back to the beginning. Music also, to get a sense of finality,
ends in the opening key, just as the tune of *She dwelt
among the untrodden ways* does. Thus we often find echoes
of the beginning at the end of a poem, or even at the end
of a paragraph. Man has an echoing mind; the sounds

which the beginning of a poem rouses wait for an important place to shout back; towards the end they make themselves heard, summing up the opening music at the cadence, as we shall illustrate later. The psychology of it is connected with that of rhyme.

Rhyme had its birth in the echoing vault of our mind, and psychologists say the emptier the vault the more it echoes. Rhymes occur as often irregularly throughout the line as at the cadences, though we notice them more at the line ends, where the emphasis is strong. What emphasis they borrow from the cadences they return with interest, strengthening and sometimes even stereotyping them; but I do not think that rhyme induces the cadence. It has two functions, one origin. It arises from our delight in repetition, pleasing the ear as alliteration does, and is of use in gilding the form of the verse by marking the cadences and for the pleasure of its mere echo. At present we shall not consider the origin of rhyme, or its use as a thing pleasing in itself, but discuss it as an element in the forming of stanzas or cadence schemes.

Although they *can* occur on the same note of the inflection tune, linear rhymes do not as a rule strike the same note. They are important not in making an identical echo, but in that their identical echo emphasises the linear cadence. Assonance may do the work of rhyme, and the poet with a sufficient command of his material may induce his cadences and make them sufficiently felt without either. Campion shows what we may do in this way with lyric poetry. His contention was not that lyrics are prettier without rhyme; it was Samuel Daniel, his opponent, who said that the rhymed couplet "stuffs the delight rather than entertains it." Nor does he justify himself by the classics, though he could not fail to appeal there—an unfortunate appeal, over-emphasised and misconstrued by his opponents from Daniel onwards. On these grounds

Campion's position is easily attacked, but his central
citadel is better fortified, and has not been assailed. That
Campion had no quarrel with rhyme his practice shows,
and he needs no support from the classics. Here is his real
contention:

> *Some ears accustomed altogether to the fatnes of
> rime, may perhaps except against the cadences of these
> numbers [the poems he refers to include *Rose-Cheek'd
> Laura* and *Follow, follow*]; but let any man judiciously
> examine them, and he shall finde they close of themselves
> so perfectly, that the help of rime were not only in them
> superfluous, but also absurd.

In Campion's writing, "cadence" and "close" refer to the
tune of the inflection, and not to the rhythm. A century or
two ago they put the comparison exclusively: Should
poetry be rhymed or should it not? Is rhyme an ornament
or a blemish? The spice has gone from the controversy
stated thus. We do not ask now whether rhymed or unrhymed verse is the better, but granting equal citizenship,
giving to both equal rights, what difference does rhyme
make? The answer is not easy. Few things are more difficult in the whole range of this study than the relationship
of rhyme to cadence. Clearly it is not the first thing there
—prose has its cadences—nor does it strike the same note
in the cadence. Saintsbury† says of double rhymes that
they emphasise "whatever is the point". We may say the
same of single rhymes. They emphasise whatever is the
point, and the point of answering cadences is not their
identity so much as their contrast. We shall have to return
to music for its parallel. In the typical musical sentence of
16 bars (the equivalent of the octosyllabic quartet) the
cadence or half-close at the 8th bar (=the end of the 2nd
line of the octosyllabic quartet) commonly ends on the

* *Observations on the Art of English Poesie.*
† Reference lost.

dominant (*so*), which is answered by the final cadence at the 16th bar (=end of last line of the quartet) on the tonic (*do*). Less pronounced cadences may come at the 4th and the 12th bars (=end of the 1st and the 3rd lines of the quartet) while we may feel *caesuras* every second bar (=the interlinear *caesuras* of the quartet), but these are not so much cadences as very subordinate resting-places in the melody, marking the end of each "attention span". Some such contrast as these tonic and dominant cadences we find in all tunes. When we arrive at their half-close we feel we have come to a temporary resting-place, and expect the melody to proceed to a final close. Instead of the dominant at the half-close, we may have other notes of the "dominant chord" such as the second note of the scale (*re*), and not necessarily even these, so long as the cadences have contrasting degrees of repose.

Since these contrasting cadences play on our sense of tonality, we might call them tonality contrasts. In speech, when we wish a vivid antithesis we point our remark with a tonality contrast: "The more haste, the worse speed." We cadence up on "haste" and down on "speed". If we say, "You can't do it," with a high inflection on "can't" and a low on "do it", we add in emphatic confirmation, "There isn't time," with the lower inflection on "isn't" and the rise on "time". Cadence is prior to rhyme. Rhymes at the cadences only emphasise the contrast, they do not make the cadence. In couplet poetry like Pope's, the lines cadence alternately on the expectant half-close and the answering tonic, and so the rhymes do not come on the same note. In quartet melody the half-cadence usually comes at the end of the 2nd line, the 1st and 3rd lines having cadences less heavy. If the quartet is rhymed *abab*, none of the rhymes need come on the same note, and the *b* rhymes will answer as tonic to dominant. When we listen to any averagely musical reader, even if we do not recognise the cadencing notes, which are usually easily recognised, we feel the contrast. At the first *b* the tune arouses our expectation of the answering *b*; when we arrive at the second *b* our expectation has been answered rather than repeated.

We can study the relation of rhyme to cadence most easily and relevantly in folk-song. The melodies of folk-song emanate from the words often unconsciously, and are but the crystallisations of the inflection into song. The words necessarily determine the structure of the tune, as indeed, we can see very clearly when we compare the form of song tunes with that of dance tunes; action determines one,* words the other. In the first two illustrations I have turned the *caesuras* into line ends to show how they are represented by lesser cadences in the music. The lines are in couplets, rhyme being optional. From such long lines our shorter ones developed, the *caesura* being written as a line end like this:

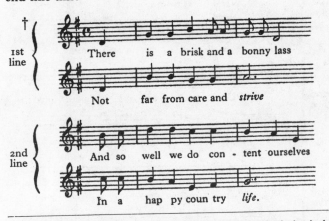

†

1st line

There is a brisk and a bonny lass

Not far from care and *strive*

2nd line

And so well we do con-tent ourselves

In a hap py coun try *life.*

---

* Except where a dance was originally a song and only derivatively a dance or *vice versa*.

† *Journal of the Folk-Song Society*, 1918–21, p. 4. Quoted with Mr. Frederick Keel's permission.

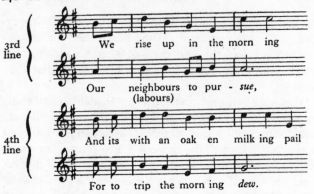

3rd line

We rise up in the morn ing

Our neighbours to pur - sue,
(labours)

4th line

And its with an oak en milk ing pail

For to trip the morn ing *dew*.

Each *caesura* has a cadence, though not as strong as those at the line ends. "Life" and "dew" come to the tonic; their rhymes, "strive" and "pursue", come on the super-tonic (*re*), which is in the dominant chord (*so, ti, re*).

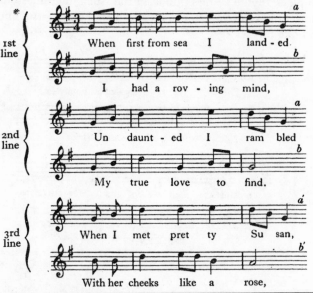

1st line

When first from sea I land - ed.

I had a rov - ing mind,

2nd line

Un daunt - ed I ram bled

My true love to find.

3rd line

When I met pret ty Su san,

With her cheeks like a rose,

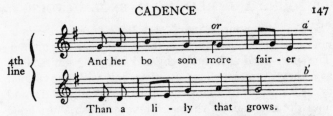

4th line

This song also is rhymed in couplets. The cadences at the cae- *suras* come down to the same note, the line cadences to con- trasting notes; yet the line cadences are much stronger than the interlinear, and give us a sense of answer. The cadence on "find" throws back to, or reminds us of, "mind", though "mind" is on a different note, and the nearest cadence—that on "rambled"—is on the same note. The weaker cadences to the tonic at "landed", "rambled", *etc.*, hardly attract our attention, certainly not sufficiently to interfere with the con- trasting cadences on answering notes at "mind" and "find", *etc.* We should get this sensation of the cadence at the rhymes answering without the words, if we whistled the tune, and might quote other folk-songs to show that the sense of answering is weaker when the cadences end on the same notes than where they have a tonality contrast. There are, however, many folk-songs with the rhymes, especially those of the first couplet in the stanza, coming on the same note.

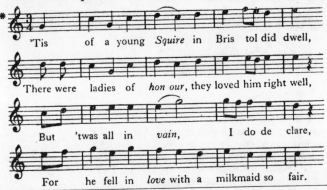

* *Journal of the Folk-Song Society*, 1918–21, p. 35. Quoted by per- mission of Lady Eva Ashton of Hyde.

"Squire", "honour", "vain" and "love" are on *caesuras*, not quite so strong as those in the longer lines just quoted. The short-lined alternately rhymed folk-song stanzas look as if they were really long couplets, only with one couplet to the stanza (or tune) instead of two, especially as the odd lines do not usually rhyme. There are also short-lined couplets, and even what may be the logical forerunner of *The Hall and the Wood* stanza,* the unrhymed line being a sort of refrain—but this study is really a research in itself, and we cannot go into it thoroughly.

We might strengthen the verdict of folk-song by hearing what Campion's airs—some of those easily accessible, at least—have to say.

†*Where she her sacred bowre adorns*	rhymes *xaza,*
the music rhymes‡	*abba.*
†*There is a garden in her face*	rhymes *ababcc,*
the music rhymes	*abcded.*
§*My sweetest Lesbia*	rhymes *aabbcc,*
the music rhymes	*aabccb.*
§*Though you are young*	rhymes *aabb,*
the music rhymes	*abac.*
§*I care not for these ladies*	rhymes *aabcc,*
the music rhymes	*aabac.*
§*Follow thy fair sun*	rhymes *abba,*
the music rhymes	*aabc.*
§*My love hath vowed*	rhymes *ababcdc,*
the music rhymes	*ababcdc.*
§*Follow your saint*	rhymes *aabbcc,*
the music rhymes	*aabcbc.*

* See below, p. 152.

† In Frederick Keel's collection of *Elizabethan Love Songs*, vol. i.

‡ That is, representing the same notes by the same letter. The cadences answer not *a* to *a* or *b* to *b*, but with a tonality contrast. In the first example the second *a* answers the first *b*, the form of the words and of the music being like the typical folk-songs quoted above.

§ *Campian*, in the "English School of Lutenist Song-Writers" Edition (published by Winthrop Rogers).

Turn back, you wanton flyer   rhymes *aabccb dde fge,*
     the music rhymes   *abaaba bca dbe.*

The music of the first three lines is repeated for the second three, and that to the last three lines of the poetry goes into one line of music.

It fell on a summer's day   rhymes *aabbcc,*
     the music rhymes   *ababcd.*
The cypress curtain of the night   rhymes *ababcc,*
     the music rhymes   *ababcb.*

No law forbids rhymes arriving on the same notes, and none commands it. Rhymes may come on the same note, but characteristically do not.

Certain scientific experiments illustrate the sort of obstacle which psychologists have to contend with in this study. Mr. Stetson† experimented to discover the essentially characteristic quality of rhyme. He presented his audience with practically the same sounds in each line save for different pitches, or intervals, in the rhymes. The only differentiating, characterising thing they heard was the difference in the pitch of the rhymes; the same interval gave the same sensation, a different interval a different, and the experimenter concludes, therefore, that we do not notice rhymes unless they come on the same note. To discover the effect of accent on rhyme he proceeded in the same way, with accent as the only varying factor, and got the same result, concluding that we do not hear rhymes if one comes on a strong accent and the other on a weak. On trying the same method‡ to discover the effect of rhyme on the pause at line ends he got the same result, that if rhyme marks the line end we do not need such a long pause as if there is no

* *Campian*, in the "English School of Lutenist Song-Writers" Edition (published by Winthrop Rogers).
† *Harvard Psychological Studies*, 1903, vol. i, "Rhythm and Rhyme."
‡ *Harvard Psychological Review*, vol. xix, pp. 423-64.

rhyme to mark it. In other words, his "subjects" noticed what he forced on their attention.

Such experiments tell us nothing about poetry. If we wish to discover the effect of accent on rhyme or of different intervals in the cadence, we must not eliminate everything else from our study. Added to the ordinary difficulties of scientific research, the psychologist has the almost insuperable one not only that the phenomena he investigates are artistic, but that the tools he works with are psychological too, and therefore variable. We can trust a spectroscope to split up the light that comes to it from distant stars, in the same way for each star, a difference in the spectrum necessarily indicating a difference in the star. But a human instrument suits its nature to its environment, analyses light differently for each star. Thus the psychologist has no constant to measure his results by; both the material he investigates and the instruments he uses are subjects, not objects. Rhyme may seem a concrete fact enough. If one line ends in "breeze" and another in "trees" you can put your finger on them and say, "Here is the rhyme," but take these words out of their context and you have altered not only their psychological effect but the musical facts about them. Artistic impressions can hardly be dissected. The musical effect of poetry is as illusive as air; you may divide it into its components, but then you have not air, but hydrogen and oxygen and some other things. To analyse the psychological effect of rhyme by scientific methods is not one whit less difficult than to "snap" spiritual essences on a *kodak*. We may achieve this some day, but as things are at present, the physical world is usually too stubborn, the spiritual too shy. To test the effect of accent on rhyme by repeating "ta ta, ta ta, ta ta, ta do" in different ways is like knocking on a table when you want the door of heaven to open. Not by abstracting the phenomena of poetry from their context, so much as by studying them in their context, can we hope to discover their psychology. When the experimenter analyses the record of a spoken poem his results are absolutely correct for the spoken sound, but where he not only has to put up with an artificial psychological environment, but eliminates the psychological factors he does not wish to consider at the moment, his results cannot be relevant to aesthetics, and are wrong even for science. If we wished to study how the oxygen in water affects iron, we should not begin by eliminating all the hydrogen from the water on the grounds that it is not hydrogen we wish to study; if we did, we should discover not the effect on iron of oxygen in water, but of oxygen by itself.

We have now come to the conclusion that rhyme rather emphasises than determines a cadence. For the poet this is true without exception, if anything can be so. But rhyme has an effect in re-creating the poet's music for the reader, just as in itself, apart from emphasising the cadence, it has an effect. It keeps the stanza structure vivid, and thus tends to fix the cadences. The typical English four-lined stanza, octosyllabic or decasyllabic, is rhymed *abab* or *xbyb* and inflected like this:

1st line: Word rhymes *a* or *x*, music rhymes *a*.
2nd line: Word rhymes *b*,   music rhymes Q (say *re*).
3rd line: Word rhymes *a* or *y*, music rhymes a or *o*.
4th line: Word rhymes *b*,   music rhymes *z* (say *do*).

The rhyme scheme *xbyb* admits the same cadence on *x* and *y* if anything more readily than the fuller scheme *abab*, and the rhyme scheme may affect the melody even further than this. The schemes of *Omar Khayyám* or of *In Memoriam* help to give their stanzas a different tune from the usual quartet, even if it does not alter the tonality contrast. Morris's *The Hall and the Wood* stanza, rhymed *aaax*, is curious, contradicting the usual habit of rhyme:

> Whence comest thou, and whither goest thou?
> Abide! abide! longer the shadows grow;
> What hopest thou the dark to thee will show?
> Abide! abide! for we are happy here.

A final cadence is always a felt one, and the denial of the rhyme surprises us, makes us feel a little uneasy. The *Omar Khayyám* rhymes more logically:

> Awake! for Morning in the Bowl of Night
> Has flung the Stone that puts the Stars to Flight:
>   And Lo! the Hunter of the East has caught
> The Sultan's turret in a Noose of Light.

The weak cadence at the third line gives a rather lovely effect.

Saintsbury* tries an interesting experiment with one of Waller's stanzas:

> Say, lovely dream! where could'st thou find   (1)
>   Shades to counterfeit that face;   (2)
> Colours of this glorious kind   (3)
>   Come not from any mortal place.   (4)

He is talking about the difference between couplet and quartet rhythms. Waller, he says, makes a good couplet-writer; but no good couplet-writer except Dryden is good in other metres; here the final line, which he calls iambic, upsets the rhythmic scheme, but rewrite the rhymes in couplets—(1) (3) (2) (4)—and the "iambic" rhythm fits beautifully. In couplet melody the cadences answer in lines, in quartet melody in couplets, the second and fourth lines answering. Saintsbury's couplets are all right because (2) answers (1), and (4) answers (3). Waller's stanza is not satisfactory because (3 + 4) does not make a graceful answer

---

* *History of English Prosody*, vol. ii, pp. 284-5. He rewrites the rhymes, not the lines.

to (1 + 2); the rhythm of the last line is unexpected and puts us out. If we rearrange the stanza again, writing "ah" for "come" so that there may be less doubt about its iambic tendencies, not the iambic but the final trochee-suggesting line disturbs us:

> Say, lovely dream! where could'st thou find—   (1)
> Ah not in any mortal place—   (4)
> Colours of this glorious kind,   (3)
> Shades to counterfeit that face.   (2)

The last line would be more graceful iambic to answer the second—"To counterfeit that lovely face." The first two lines set the type of melody; we expect the answering lines to answer in kind.

We may have a quartet melody with couplet rhymes, as in *Astraea Redux*:

> Now with a general Peace the world was blest,
> While Ours, a world divided from the rest,
> A dreadul Quiet felt, and worser far,
> Than Arms, a sullen Interval of War.

or Waller's *On a Girdle*:

> That which her slender waist confined
> Shall now my joyful temples bind:
> No monarch but would give his crown
> His arms might do what this has done.

In these, though the melody makes a quartet, the couplet rhymes have an effect. Cross rhymes suit a quartet tune better; they seem more native to it:

> It is not Beauty I demand,
> A crystal brow, the moon's despair,
> Nor the snow's daughter, a white hand,
> Nor mermaid's yellow pride of hair.

or perhaps more characteristically in Herrick's *Bid me to live*.

We can study the effect of rhyme very well in Spenser's poetry. Whether they influence his cadences or not, his rhymes are certainly an essential part of his music. But it sometimes happens that we can learn more from the failures of the poets than from their successes:

> There grewe an aged Tree on the greene,
> A goodly Oake sometime had it bene,
> With armes full strong and largely displayd,
> But of their leaves they were disarayde:
> The bodie bigge, and mightely pight,
> Throughly rooted, and of wonderous hight:
> Whilome had bene the King of the field,
> And mochell mast to the husband did yielde,
> And with his nuts larded many swine.
> But now the gray mosse marred his rine,
> His bared boughes were beaten with stormes,
> His toppe was bald, and wasted with wormes,
> His honour decayed, his braunches sere.

Here the couplet form governs the melody, which comes to repeat itself regardless of the sense, not even altering to form a cadence at "sere", the end of a paragraph. "Sere" *will* come on a high note. Matters would be helped a little if the vowel had been lower, "dead" or "down", but "sere's" vowel is high and encourages the voice to rise to the expectant note away from the tonic. In this *Eclogue* (the February) the rhyme has undoubtedly made itself felt; it has kept the rhythmic symmetry too vivid and stereotyped the tune. Yet that couplet structure does not always have this effect needs no illustration. In the *September Eclogue* the split rhyme at line 46 does not prevent or, happy term, interrupt the cadence, because there the sense rather than the abstract form of the verse controls the line. The *February Eclogue* shows Spenser immature; his couplet music ought not to have got beyond the control of the sense like this; by September he has learned something. In Chaucer's *Prologue*, the cadences of paragraphs ending on the expectant rhyme differ from those ending on the answering one; the rhythm and the sense are strong enough to force on the expectant rhyme a more conclusive cadence than is native to the first line of a couplet, but not strong enough to bring a full close. The rhythm and rhyme playing now against, now with each other, determine the melodies of Chaucer's paragraph. The *Prologue* was written by a surer and maturer couplet-writer than the young Spenser.

The Faerie Queene rhyme scheme was a work of genius, but once discovered, its virtue can be analysed. An *abab* quartet differs from an *abba* one; in the *In Memoriam abba*, the fall to the final cadence, coming immediately after the new impetus which results from the repeated *b*, gives a sense of repelled effort, not the great wave accumulated in the first quartet of a Miltonic sonnet and billowed out in the second, but a little tired wave spilt before it has gathered:

> I sometimes hold it half a sin
> To put in words the grief I feel;
> For words, like Nature, half reveal
> And half conceal the Soul within.

In a stanza of more than one rhyme, the first is often difficult to close on. Perhaps one reason why the *terza rima* remains unacclimatised in English results from this, since three-lined stanzas with identical rhymes feel at home:

> Whoe'er she be,
> That not impossible She
> That shall command my heart and me.
>
> (*Crashaw*)

or:

> Whenas in silks my Julia goes
> Then, then (methinks) how sweetly flows
> That liquefaction of her clothes.   (*Herrick*)

Just as an *abba* quartet differs from an *abab* one, so an *abab* quartet followed by a *bcbc* differs from an *abab* followed by an *abab* or a *cdcd* quartet. The recoil on *b* gives a feeling of renewed vigour or motion, not so very unlike the recoil of the Miltonic sonnet *abba, abba*. In the sonnet, after this octet with its abounding, accumulating force, the less vigorously rhymed sestet comes with a sense of withdrawing energy. But *abab, bcbc* is more difficult to bring to a cadence than *abba, abba*. The recoil on *b* gives a sense of turning to the stanza, but not the culmination of the Miltonic octet; it is as if we had reached the top of a hill and shut off the engine for the coming decline, whereas in the Miltonic octet the double throb keeps the engine going. How are we to bring *abab, bcbc* to a cadence? We cannot start the engine for the end of our journey, and yet we must cadence on a strong rhyme; we cannot make the end emphatic by withdrawing the energy, for we have already done that. Whereas *abba* added to *abba* strengthens a throb, *bcbc* added to *abab* changes the direction of a current—for what end? Eight lines rhymed *abab, bcbc* are apt to give us a sensation of having set out to do something and, when we have arrived, forgetting what we had set out to do.* We feel uneasy when the cadence rhyme is not the strongest in the stanza, and *b* appearing twice for any other rhyme is stronger than *c*. Even in an *abab* stanza the *b* rhyme is stronger than the *a*; in *abab, bcbc* it is still further strengthened. Rhyme-royal had to face this difficulty, and from rhyme-royal Spenser got his feeling for the Spenserian. We might think that having achieved *abab,b,* by adding another *b* we could close the stanza easily. But by turning back on *b* we take its cadence quality from it. The unexpected third *b* sets the stanza in the air; and once it has raised the stanza

---

* Perhaps all this is too vague and metaphorical; on the whole, I have avoided this way of describing facts, but where they are facts of feeling I do not know how else to describe them.

off its feet the *b* rhyme becomes ethereal and therefore unsuitable for a cadence rhyme. Since the couplet close makes the strongest cadence in English, rhyme-royal secured a sense of finality by adding a couple of *cs*—*abab*, *bcc*. Even an *ababab* rhyme scheme is difficult to cadence on *b*; the third *ab* weakens the cadencing power of the rhyme. *Ottava rima* and Spenser in *Muiopotmos* meet this difficulty in the same way as rhyme-royal by a couple of *cs*—*abababcc*. One of the Middle English stanzas quoted by Saintsbury* in his history helps the cadence by shortening the lines rhymed *c*—*abababcbc*:

Middel-erd for mon wes mad,	*a*
unmihti aren is meste mede;	*b*
This hedy hath on honde y-had	*a*
that hevene hem is hest to hede;	*b*
Icherde a blisse budel us bad,	*a*
the dreri domes-dai to drede,	*b*
Of sunful sauhting sone be sad,	*a*
that derne doth this derne dede;	*b*
thah he ben derne done,	*c*
This wrakeful werkes under wede	*b*
in soule so teleth sone.	*c*

Many of the rhyme schemes quoted by Saintsbury in his chapters on the early romances are interesting from this point of view; on page 116 is one rhymed *aaaaaaaabb*, another *abab*, *bbbc*, *dddc*; on page 117 are others ending on the *b* rhyme, *aab*, *aab*, *ba*, *ab*, or *ab*, *abab*, *ab*, and so on.

The Faerie Queene clinches its rhyme scheme with an Alexandrine *C*; the effect is subtle; this is not a final couplet of *cs*; *c* remains a weaker rhyme than *b*, as the second *c* rather answers the first *c* than forecasts the final *C*. The Alexandrine prolongs and forces the cadence, but its effect, as Saintsbury says,† is rather to launch the stanza "on

* *History of English Prosody*, vol. i, p. 115.
† *Ibid.*, p. 367.

towards its successor *ripae ulterioris amore*, or rather with the desire of a fresh striking out in the unbroken though wave-swept sea of poetry." The rhyme scheme fully more than the Alexandrine creates this sense of delayed or unsatisfied desire. Spenser's stanza cannot cloy, since he never gives us what we want, unless indeed, he gives it us in the next stanza:

*He making speedy way through spersed ayre,	*a*
And through the world of waters wide and deepe,	*b*
To *Morpheus* house doth hastily repaire.	*a*
Amid the bowels of the earth full steepe,	*b*
And low, where dawning day doth never peepe,	*b*
His dwelling is; there *Tethys* his wet bed	*c*
Doth ever wash, and *Cynthia* still doth steepe	*b*
In silver deaw his ever-drouping hed,	*c*
Whiles sad Night over him her mantle black doth spred.	*C*

Whose double gates he findeth locked fast,	*x*
The one faire fram'd of brunisht Yvory,	*y*
The other all with silver overcast;	*x*
And wakefull dogges before them do lye,	*y*
Watching to banish Care their enimy,	*y*
Who oft is wont to trouble gentle Sleepe.	*b*
By them the Sprite doth passe in quietly,	*y*
And unto *Morpheus* comes, whom drowned deepe	*b*
In drowsie fit he findes: of nothing he takes keepe.	*B*

We are not prepared to follow straight on to:

And more, to lulle him in his slumber soft.

The *ripae ulterioris amore* sensation has gone. We leave the first stanza with the *ee* vowel of "steepe", "deepe", "peepe", sounding in our memory; it comes out in the cadence of the second stanza; for once we have closed on the insistent vowel, finishing the stanza with a stronger sense of finality than usual. Shelley's Spenserians do not

* I, i, stanza 39.

create this feeling of postponed satisfaction. Not the rhyme
scheme but the management of it gives us this feeling. We
are not conscious of Shelley's rhymes as we are of Spenser's;
they do not shine out of their context like luminous win-
dows. This is partly because Shelley's line sense is weaker,
partly because his rhymes are often defective or their
vowels less pure and sounding, and also because interlinear
echoes of the rhymes distract us.

Perhaps I ought to say something about rhymed "blank
verse" such as we have in *Endymion*, or compare it with
real blank verse such as we have in *The Winter's Tale*.
Many readers lose the rhyme in the *Endymion* couplet:

> The very music of the name has gone
> Into my being, and each pleasant scene
> Is growing fresh before me as the green
> Of our own vallies: so I will begin
> Now while I cannot hear the city's din;
> Now while the early budders are just new,
> And run in mazes of the youngest hue
> About old forests; while the willow trails
> Its delicate amber; and the dairy pails
> Bring home increase of milk.

We may certainly read such poetry without being conscious
of the rhymes. If only the sense and the rhythm govern the
cadence for us, we shall no more notice them than we
should irregular interlinear echoes. But perhaps we deceive
ourselves, and the rhymes make their effect though we
remain unconscious of their agency. The poet presumably
wrote with a sense of the rhyme, or if his rhymes came unknown to him, then with a consciousness of the line-ending
as a place where the music culminated in some sort. If the
rhymes meant nothing they would not be there. Those who
do have a feeling of the rhymes read with an inflection tune
which gives tonality answers at the end of the lines. We
read *The Winter's Tale* on the "thought moment" or

"attention span" principle, the lines having only the tiniest
influence on the melody:

> *Apprehend
> Nothing but jollity. The gods themselves,
> Humbling their deities to love, have taken
> The shapes of beasts upon them: Jupiter
> Became a bull, and bellowed; the green Neptune
> A ram, and bleated; and the fire-robed god,
> Golden Apollo, a poor humble swain,
> As I seem now.

In *Endymion*, whose rhythmic groupings runs athwart the
lines as in *The Winter's Tale*, the rhyme takes the melody
out of the clutches of the logical "thought moments". The
sheer sense in *Endymion* is glamoured over if we allow the
rhyme to help decide the music, just as the sheer sense of
Christabel is glamoured over by the illogical emphasis of
its accents.†

When blank verse first came in, it was thought bombastic; Nash talks scornfully of "the swelling bombast of
bragging blank verse" or "the spacious volubility of a
drumming decasyllabon". This describes Marlowe's blank
verse rather than Wordsworth's:

> ‡Then shall my native city, Samarcanda,
> And crystal waves of fresh Jaertis' stream,
> The pride and beauty of her princely seat,
> Be famous through the furthest continents,
> For there my palace-royal shall be placed,
> Whose shining turrets shall dismay the heavens,
> And cast the fame of Ilion's tower to hell.

Yet there seems to me a more than merely contemporary
reference in Nash's objection. Blank verse does tend to
emphasise what it says, to lay emphasis on the meaning. It

---

* IV, Sc. III, 24.
† *The Real Rhythm in English Poetry*, chapter i.
‡ *Tamburlaine*, IV, Sc. IV.

lends itself to both rhetoric and didacticism in a way that the heroic couplet does not. In it Wordsworth and Milton may preach to us with impunity:

> *This spiritual Love acts not nor can exist
> Without Imagination, which, in truth,
> Is but another name for absolute power
> And clearest insight, amplitude of mind,
> And Reason in her most exalted mood.

Pope may not preach with impunity in his couplet:

> †'Tis not enough your counsel still be true;
> Blunt truths more mischief than nice falsehoods do;
> Men must be taught as if you taught them not,
> And things unknown propos'd as things forgot.
> Without Good-Breeding, truth is disapprov'd;
> That only makes superior sense belov'd.

The poet may use didactic or prosaic talk to make the music of blank verse, but he must not use the music of couplet form to preach or to prose. If we read by the rhyme in *Endymion*, the emphasis of the music turns the meaning into a vapour, which is at least a poetical thing to do. The eighteenth century made its couplet emphasise the meaning, not vaporise it, which is not a poetical thing to do. We resent the use of the music of poetry to sharpen the point of prose wit. Thus the heroic couplet appears bombastic to us, who think of it as it was in the eighteenth century, over-emphasising the meaning; it is our "drumming decasyllabon". Nash, who precedes Pope, and has Marlowe close to him, objects to blank verse on the same principle; it lays more stress on the meaning than the heroic couplet of poets who do not often use it to point their meaning. As a general rule, the meaning of blank verse is more outstanding than its music, since we read by the meaning in the "attention spans" of thought; whereas

* *Prelude*, xiv, 188.   † *Essay on Criticism*, 572.

the music of the rhymed couplet is more outstanding than the meaning, since we give each couplet its tonality contrast despite the meaning. Like all general rules, these are not universally applicable; just as rhyme was used in the eighteenth century to give point to the meaning, so some of our great poets have written blank verse so lovely that we cannot say our attention is rather held by the sense than charmed by the sound. Still, if my conscience told me— not that I have any such conscience—that I ought to distinguish between the particular aptitudes of the rhymed and the unrhymed "decasyllabon", I should make this distinction: Blank verse is most suited to poetry where the thought is either noble enough to carry great emphasis, or too near prose to bear vaporisation. In the heroic couplet, on the other hand, where the sense fits the rhythmical grouping, prose matter tends to sound artificial and grand emotion to strut. The rhymed couplet is best fitted for romantic or vague matter, since its music can easily create a poetic atmosphere, making a song of little things by phrasing and grouping to soften the emphasis of prose.

Rhyme, then, seems to make some difference to the inflection tune. I say makes a difference, but more probably the rhyme but gilds a difference already there. The poet starts with his tune, and the tune decides where the rhymes come. We cannot sufficiently emphasise the difference in the two ways of looking at this—the poet's point of view and the reader's—since when talking of causes and effects we are very apt to get into a tangle. It is more usual to take the poem as given, and study the effect on the reader. From this point of view rhyme may be very important in determining cadence, certainly more important than I have said. From the creator's point of view, rhyme has no place in determining the cadence. The poet starts with the cadence and may not bother about his rhymes, being sometimes less conscious of them than his readers.

Rhyme is a very beautiful and a very essential part of some poetry, but trivial as an element in the composition of the poem, getting small consideration and still less respect from some of our greatest poets. It is significant that the author of the most musical of all rhymed poems should refer to rhyme as:

*no necessary Adjunct or true Ornament of Poem or good Verse, in longer Works especially, but the Invention of a barbarous Age, to set off wretched matter and lame Meeter.

Nor is Campion inconsistent in preaching the despite of rhyme and practising its perfection. For rhyme may help the reader to catch the poet's melody, and yet have no place in the formation of that melody. It communicates the cadence to the reader rather than determines it for the poet.

* *Paradise Lost*, Preface.

BOOK II

MEANING

CHAPTER I

MEANING IN GENERAL

SOME time ago we differentiated speech from song by saying that speech was vocal sound used to convey meaning, song vocal sound used to relieve feeling. On this definition poetry comes nearer to song than to speech. This is true; poetry resembles music rather than speech, its subjective inspiration, intention, impulse, or whatever we call it, being more akin to that of the musical composer than to the motive of the man of prose, the impression it makes on the reader more like the impression made by music, and its material more purely musical and made for its own sake. The sounds of poetry and music differ less than on first thoughts we suppose. Poetry is almost one branch of music. A tune sung to a *vocalise* and a tuneful reading of poetry differ less in sound than a drum and a flute. But though they proceed from the same instrument, music and poetry might yet differ in subjective effect. Music by its very nature, because it does not use the material of prose, may appear more abstract, more ethereal, less definite than poetry. Although words are but music adapted to signify facts, they seem to become mere labels by the change, thus working in us differently from music, or, since they refer by name to definite things, they seem to stamp their picture, impress their meaning and de-limit the confines of their significance more precisely than music. Thus an idea has grown up that poetry, using words with a dictionary reference, conveys definite meanings, while music, having no defined words, does not give definite meanings, and therefore that the meanings of poetry and music are necessarily of different sorts. I shall try to show that this is a mistake, that the response to poetry varies as much with the individual as it does to music, that to some hearers music conveys meanings as definite and pictures as distinct as poetry does, while for some readers poetry can create the same sort of emotional, imaginative experience as music. For here also we come round to that obstinate, stone-wall fact, the different reading, the individual impression. This impassable barrier defends us now. It holds as well for poetry as for music, and not more for one than for the other. If there are a hundred different ways of hearing music, there are possibly a hundred different ways of reading poetry, but possibly not ninety-nine or a hundred and one different ways.

By "meaning" I do not refer to the prose reference of that word. In its prose significance neither poetry nor music need have any meaning; they may be merely beautiful experiences. Nor do I use the word to refer to the aesthetic *value* of the arts, for that is another problem—one which I am content to let each reader answer in his own way. I shall not say that the meaning of poetry and music is to give us a richer spiritual life, to open a fresh door on the divine, though I believe this is their meaning; nor shall I deny that poetry and music must have an ethical, or a religious, or a pleasurable value, though I believe one of these is not an essential to art. Here I am not concerned with the sublimities but with the prosaic meanings of music and poetry, with their meaning where it appears furthest apart, as revealed in their form. I discuss the subsidiary "meanings" of the arts rather than their significance to humanity, their dictionary meanings more than meaning in its context, though I shall discuss that too. Indeed, in this chapter I shall rarely talk to the appreciative portion of an artistic reader's mind, but with an almost scientific coldness I shall compare the languages of the two arts, and show how they resemble one another, and how they can give the same sorts of meaning. The question I discuss is a prosaic man's question, and I shall discuss it after the manner of prosaic men, the idea I wish to shatter that which considers music a language of the spirit and denies that poetry also is a language of the spirit.

An aesthetic "meaning" is the whole content of the mind as filled by the thing that gives meaning, the meaning of a sonata or of a poem being everything the mind felt or saw or thought under their guidance, every consciousness modified or induced by them. When we listen to music we may be aware of sitting on a hard bench in a large hall, or when we read poetry, of holding a book in our hand or of reading the print of a poem, but these consciousnesses do not form part of the meaning of the sonata or the poem. We grasp their fullest meaning when we forget the bench and the hall, the book and the print, and our minds stand full of what the music or poem has put there. Certainly only when we become unaware that our eyes trace a printed line, or of the environment and instruments of music, can a poem and a sonata mean something so similar in texture that if the meaning of one of them could fill our minds without an objective agent we should not be able to say whether it came from music or poetry.

Since the language of poetry uses words, we must see how words work in us. The scientific and the artistic brain respond to words differently.* Galton† discovered that most scientists have no power of mental imagery; they do not recollect things in pictures and cannot summon a

* *American Journal of Psychology*, vol. xxviii, Murphy, "Literary *versus* Scientific Types".

† *Inquiries into the Human Faculty and its Development*, pp. 85-7.

mental image of, say, their breakfast table; also* that the power of visualising is higher in women than in men, and goes, too, a little in families and also possibly in races. If we talk to a scientist in pictorial metaphors we soon realise this. Such metaphors can neither illustrate a point of view nor clear up a difficulty; they are merely irrelevant, and wholly unrelated to fact. We might think it impossible that anyone could read Keats's line about "sweet-peas, on tiptoe for a flight" and have no image of the sweet-pea, but a scientist of the deepest dye thinks it foolish to talk of a sweet-pea being on tiptoe for a flight, an incomprehensible or a stupid way of talking. On being urged to admit the bare accuracy of this description, one of them replies: "No, I can *not* see how a sweet-pea looks like a bird." After further explanation he admits that the shape of a sweet-pea resembles that of a resting butterfly, but objects that its stalk is an essential part of the sweet-pea; in short, a sweet-pea is not a butterfly, so why talk as if it were. Nor is this picture blindness confined to scientists. People who habitually think in the abstract often lose the power of visualising what they read.† We cannot, therefore, assume that all readers of poetry see its pictures. They may get nothing more from descriptive poetry than a knowledge of what is said and a sense of the music and form. One supposes such readers derive their pleasure from technical excellencies in poetry rather than from the emotional or imagin-

* *Inquiries into the Human Faculty and its Development*, p. 99.

† Myers, *A Textbook of Experimental Psychology*, p. 151, says: "We 'fix' imagery in our memory by verbal symbols. Thus we remember a shade by recollecting that the original colour was 'bright', 'rather dull' or 'very dark'.

"The more cultured the individual the more he comes to rely on words, especially abstract words, rather than on the imagery of concrete objects. The individual sometimes almost completely loses the more elementary forms of visual, auditory and other imagery."

Possibly the "culture" referred to is a scientific or philosophical training.

ative content. The things and thoughts of poetry cannot seem as definite as facts to them; words are not even labels or pointers, only "abstract words", unless they remain susceptible to music.

The purely musical reader makes another type, uninterested in the things the poet says and absolutely innocent of visual imagery. The rhythm of poetry excites him, and the sweetness of its sounds entrances him, but so far from caring what the poem means, he does not miss much when it is sheer nonsense as long as he is wrapped away in a flush of lovely sound. I think Swinburne delights many with this delight, and Shakespeare, too, occasionally moves us vaguely to sublimity by passages which say nothing very definite, give us no sense of picture, and yet sound full of meaning to our musical imagination. Often when Shelley is away on his giddy, aerial triumph, he carries us with him in a musical turmoil meaning nothing, save that to those with visual imagery the words throw up vast pictures.

A reader both insensible to the music of words and with no sense of imagery does not get what we should call a characteristically poetic effect from poetry. What sort of pleasure he gets I have no conception, unless in poetry voicing strong or common emotions such as love, and setting forth comfortable or inspiring moral truths. But we need not worry about him since he is outside our sphere, poetry, if he reads it, certainly not being a music to him.

The more usual reader of poetry, the characteristically literary one, has both a picture imagination and a sense of music. The ideal reader must be sensitive to words over their whole poetic range, and respond to poetry musically, emotionally, imaginatively and in other ways besides. His psychology is the most interesting and relevant, and though it has never been collated, the evidence of such readers lies waiting in the work of our more sensitive literary critics.

Meantime in the *American Journal of Psychology** we learn that Mr. Bagley has experimented to discover how words work in us. He says that words evoke verbal and visual imagery, and sometimes other sense imagery. His method was to read a sentence without any context to his "subjects", who reported what they got from it. Some of their responses are curious and not very relevant to us.† "We did not see the train approaching" was given.‡ One "subject" reacted: "Were they run over?" To "His death must be reported to the authorities" another reacted: "Yes, death and birth registrations are compulsory." Such responses would not normally occur in reading. A sentence read without any context is quite unlike one read in a context. Sentences without any reference have really no meaning. "His death must be reported to the authorities" is a string of nonsense made up of meaningful words in strict grammatical relation. We make what meaning we can from it; one "subject" docketed it in the correct pigeon-hole—"Yes, deaths and births must be registered"; if he had overheard the statement in a bus he would have responded differently; differently again if he read it in another context. A context limits the possible reactions of the reader. Give me one word, "It", and I give back at once: "Very small child", but we must not therefore infer that "It" in a context gives me a suppressed reference like this. In "It is raining", "raining" is the only word that gives me a picture, although to many even this would give no image; they would note the fact

* ·Vol. xii.

† Vol. xii, p. 119: "Particular parts of a context are often visualized as printed, or heard out separately ('auditized'). . . . Observers of the auditory type tend to hear the word spelled out or pronounced very distinctly, observers of the visual type . . . to see it printed."

‡ *Ibid.*, p. 116.

without any mental vision, just as when I read in an elementary chemistry that oxygen and hydrogen make water, I note the fact and have no image at all. In: "It is raining in irregular drops", "irregular drops" holds the picture; I see not rain but raindrops coming irregularly.

The whole purpose of literature is to control our reactions to words. A "good style" grips the attention and forces us to react in the right way. But however perfect the style, it cannot altogether control the reaction of the reader, who is an individual accustomed reacting in an individual way. Words may paint a definite picture and paint the minutest details with care, yet the picture will be definitely different for each reader, even more in the minutest details than in the general impression. The history of criticism is a history of modes of reaction. How humorous we think some of Johnson's well-worn *dicta* about the Elizabethan poets; it amuses us to compare his response to *Paradise Lost* with our own. Not the poem but the reader has changed. The notorious first reviews of Shelley, Keats or Wordsworth show a different reaction from ours. Only when we are educated up to appreciating the great poets, or frightened into it, do the reports of our reaction to them come out alike.

Words often raise misassociations in us. "Pollution of the ballot is the curse of democracy" was given in one of Bagley's experiments,* and a "subject" visualised "muddy water". This sort of irrelevant association is common among poets. It leads Shakespeare into many a curious maze. The Homeric simile indulges it. We can see the fire of Milton's imagination spreading from irrelevant suggestions in *Paradise Lost* (I, 591):

> His form had yet not lost
> All her Original *brightness*, nor appear'd
> Less than Arch Angel ruined, and the excess

* p. 121.

Of Glory *obscured*: As when the Sun new risen

.   .   .   .   .   .

Shorn of his Beams, or, from behind the Moon,
   etc.

Or a few lines further on:

             Cruel his eye, but cast
Signs of remorse and passion, to behold
The fellows of his crime . . . condemn'd

.   .   .   .   .   .

. . . and from Eternal Splendors flung
For his revolt, yet faithful how they stood,
Their glory *withered*. As when Heaven's Fire
Hath scath'd the Forest Oaks, or Mountain Pines,
   etc.

Or (line 761):

            All access was thronged, the Gates
And Porches wide, but chief the spaceous Hall

.   .   .   .   .   .

Thick swarmed, both on the ground and in the air,
Brusht with the hiss of russling wings. As bees
In spring time,
   etc.

"Brightness", "obscured", "withered" and "swarmed" suggest to the poet the same sort of irrelevant pictures as "pollution" suggested to the "subject" of the experiment.

Bagley concludes, and naturally enough, that there is no such thing as imageless apperception.* His "subjects" had to make images in self-defence against sentences which really meant nothing. As far as I can gather from a style too scientific to let its meaning ever blossom, he would say that we cannot understand a word unless we already know the fact it stands for, that words are pointers representing things, and bring the image of the thing they represent to

* p. 126.

mind. It is as if our mind were a cup.* When we hear the word "theatre", the cup, our mind, empties itself—he says we adapt or readjust it—and fills itself with the "mood", to use his own word, suggested by "Theatre". He calls the full cup a "mental system", and says:† "In fact, experience might be considered a . . . panorama of mental systems." I can only guess the meaning of his next sentence. I think it means that since the mind's cup can hold but one "mood" at a time, an economical mind, instead of emptying and refilling itself at every word, mixes its drinks and takes a mixed "mood". At all events, he continues:

And so it is not surprising that we now find . . . a verbal idea coming to represent a complex mental system, and reproducing in a condensed form all the essential conditions of a given environment.

The school to which this sort of philosophy belongs assumes that all things are concrete. The supporters of "imageless thought" know that many things are not concrete; our senses have never come in contact with them. We cannot have an image of a thing which is purely abstract. When we refer to "the spirit of the Elizabethan age", we talk about an abstraction and can understand it apart from any latent idea of angels or any other imageable thing. We may say: "Pope's writings are not in the spirit of the Elizabethan age", and anyone who has read Pope and knows a little about the Elizabethans will understand us and without an image, while anyone who visualised a volume of Pope or a picture of Queen Elizabeth would have misunderstood us. One who has not read Pope and knows little of the Elizabethans will not understand, and may in his effort to make something of the sentence, react concrete images, but it does not follow that no one can

* Bagley is not responsible for this unscientific metaphor.
† p. 128.

understand without having an image. Those who think there is no imageless thought believe that when we speak or think abstractly like this we compress our images of Pope's volume of writing, and Queen Elizabeth's large frill, and perhaps a picture of Sir Philip Sidney spreading his new coat over a puddle, or Drake playing at bowls, or the *Globe*, or the *Mermaid Tavern*, and all the concrete things these words can conjure up—we compress them into one complex "mental system"; and the complexity of it, rather than the complete absence of concreteness about it, makes us imagine we have an abstract idea. But when we say: "Pope's writings are not in the spirit of the Elizabethan age", we do not mean any of these concrete things; we do not even mean that Pope's style differs from Shakespeare's, or that Pope was bad-tempered and the Elizabethans generous-hearted. The nearest synonym for "spirit" is not "mind" or "mental processes", but the abstract thing, the mystic thing we mean by "soul". The fact we call the "spirit of the Elizabethan age" was never a concrete thing; it always was an abstract fact.

From his remarks about imageless thought Bagley develops his description of *meaning*. It is a good one. He notices that words give different associations in different contexts and yet retain the same dictionary significance; "play" may signify a drama, taking tricks at whist, hitting a ball over a net, yet the dictionary meaning of "play" does not change. To turn his explanation into easily understood English we must alter our metaphor a little, and consider the "mood" out of its cup. We fill the cup of our mind with a theatre "play", and empty it over a table in a dark room; we flash the electric torch of our consciousness on to the spilt "mood", and the light focuses on one part of it; this is the significant part of the meaning; but round about, the "mood" fades into the darkness, where the fringe or margin of the meaning is. For whist "play" the "mood" is

perhaps the same as for theatre "play", but the torch
focuses on a different part; what was illuminated in theatre
"play" is now in the darkness.

All meaningful things fill the mind with a "mood" in
a dark room, and a jet of light shines on it; everything
within the circle of light is within our consciousness, but
in the shadows lurk half-conscious portions of the meaning.
We may develop the idea further. Two listeners may hear
the same piece of music; one notices its form and the way
the themes develop; he listens to each note as a note, each
chord as a chord, and includes a vision of the players in his
impression; the other cares nothing for the form of the
music, his eyes hardly see the players, he is rapt away
in an emotional thrill, yet the *meaning* of the music may
be the same for both. If we examine their "mood" and the
light cast on it in the dark room of their mind, we find that
what the torch of one lights up is in the darkness of the
other's mind. The light on the one's mind focuses on the
design of the music and the actual sounds, but the emotional meaning of the music lies in the shadows; the torch
of the other's focuses on the emotion of the music, but
the actual sounds and the form of the music lurk in the
shadows. The music means the same for both listeners
though its light is focused on different places. And so in
poetry, the prosaic meaning may linger in the shadows of
the poetical reader's mind, the mystery on the fringe of the
prosaic reader's.

The dictionary is interested in the marginal meanings of
words, literature in the focal. For literary purposes, and
therefore for our purpose, words have no precise meaning;
it varies with the jet of light thrown on their "mood". And
more, words are in themselves alive, not dead; they are not
labels, but living personalities with varying moods and
perversities and amiabilities like ourselves. Some of them
have descended from an ancient aristocracy and bear them-

selves with an air of antiquity, others are young and upstart
and perky. You never know what any of them will do next;
it is no use trying to define their meaning. Even in its
marginal meaning "play" does not always mean the same
thing. Settle their precise significance to-day, and when
to-morrow's sun shines on your nicely catalogued chrysalis,
behold it has turned into a butterfly and escaped you. Not
much wonder that *The New English Dictionary* supplies
debating societies with such mirth. You can no more define
the meaning of a living word than you can define John
Smith:

JOHN SMITH, *irresponsible youth in flannels* (*derivation
unknown*).

Ten years hence he would not be recognised for it; we
must have a new dictionary:

JOHN SMITH, *overworked medical practitioner*.

"Sad" once meant happy, satisfied, fed. To be fed in days
of strenuous effort was to be happy; alas, "to be fed" now
means to be pampered. Words change their meaning gradually, not all of a sudden; they grow old as John Smith
does, minute by minute, and if they have a past, that past
shines from them and is felt in the present. "Sad" still has
a feeling of *satis* in it, fed full; it is a fat, dull, immobile sort
of sorrow, different from the sorrow of "misery", which is
lean and ravenous. Such a concrete, definite thing as a
balustrade was once the pomegranate bloom growing beneath a Mediterranean sun, and some suggestion of the
eastern blossom still lingers in its music. Who will tell us
the meaning of "fair"? It has all sorts of associations, re-
flecting the light from a million facets; you have only to
turn it round to see one meaning shimmering into the next.
We cannot define it in:

> Fair as a star, when only one
> Is shining in the sky.

How much of the meaning comes from its association with
womanly loveliness, how much from its connotation of
clear-weather loveliness, how much from its original sense
of brightness, and does not some glimmer come from
"fair" meaning frank, open, just? It describes at one
moment two such different things as a woman and a star;
it can hardly be a label. In fact "fair" by itself has no
meaning; it has not yet come to life. In this poem it is the
word into which the simile concentrates itself. Within its
embrace "fair" holds the clear evening hue of the lonely
sky and one shining star, and this makes half the meaning;
but the picture of the sky and the star runs back into
"fair", where it meets the meaning that has come from
our idea of Wordsworth's Lucy; two gametes join and
form one zygote, and "fair" is a living word.

Poets use words not as pointers indicating their meaning but as things with life potential in them. A poem is not
a catalogue of impressions, not a lot of symbols standing
for something, a book describing something. The meaning
of a poem is not something else but itself, and that self is
not the sum of the meaning of all the words, but the blend
and fusion of them. In the alchemy of poetry the words
form not a mechanical but a chemical mixture. For the
poets work magic on words and turn them into something
different from the words of prose. Prose has a way of
directing our minds precisely, because that is its aim; but
the poet does not wish to direct us precisely even to facts
of the imagination; he wishes to escape definition and
definable things, to dematerialise, not to materialise vision,
using words to recreate unenshrinable things, not to en-
tomb them. Poetry is in its essence vague, a wandering
cloud, a mist on the mountain, loosening our stability and
undermining our certainties rather than securing us in
them. In the brutalities of every day we use words as slaves
and treat them without consideration; they have to do all

the dirty work that someone must do, but this does not mean that their origin is ignoble. Because work has hardened their hands their nature is not any less god-like. Poetry is not more concrete than music because its material has washed dishes and darned stockings, nor more firmly bound to earth because it uses mountains instead of pedal notes, and plays on sunsets and seas instead of on strings, or blows through violet and rose and not through flute and oboe.

Just as we think the meaning of words or of poetry more definite than it is, so we exaggerate the indefiniteness of music. Music may make us see pictures of the imagination as definite and detailed as those of poetry, and is peculiarly fitted to imitate the prose world. We can make a cock crow or a donkey bray more realistically in music than in words. And apart from its pictures and onomatopoesis, music is the most emotional language we have.* Excite or move uncontrolled people and they sing. We already quoted Aristoxenus telling that the Greeks avoided taking their "intervals" in the singing jump when speaking, "unless . . . forced at times by reason of emotion to resort to this type of movement."

Music can convey its meaning in many ways. Its language is as easily analysed as poetry's and not so very unlike. Melody is intrinsically meaningful, as Spencer explains, and many of the best tunes are possibly unconscious echoes from the inflections of speech. We cannot mistake the tune of complaint in the Londonderry air. A tune gives

* Any music is not necessarily more emotional than any poetry. One provincial company of players had the want of taste to bring in music where the emotion of *Antony and Cleopatra* got intense, and the temperature of the emotion dropped with an almost physical shudder. Had the music been of the same dignity and intensity as the poetry, it would have heightened the effect. As it was, it merely pointed its insignificance. This company used the same sort of music in *Twelfth Night*, where it was not so out of place, and indeed rather effective, sublimating rather than degrading the emotion.

us a feeling of "something said",* of being a "specific mental act",† a "form of thought"† or language. It relies on our sense of tonality; and tonality is meaningful. Some notes in the scale have a greater sense of repose than others; the tonic (*do*) usually gives us a sense of rest and the leading note of restlessness; accidentals, too, have their own sensation; the way the notes are arranged in melody controls our feelings. We feel that some tunes are joyful, even humorous, others solemn, some jubilant, others depressed. Each tune has a definite atmosphere, being vulgar or exotic, calm or disturbed or remote and so on, just as any poem.‡ Harmonies, too, have definite atmospheres. Each chord has its own sensation, and just as the meaning of a word changes with its context, so do harmonies. They are as meaningful to the emotions as the colours of a picture or the associations of words. And as our sense of tonality takes meanings from tunes and harmonies, a change of tonality is meaningful; a new mode means a new mood, and a new key a change of altitude, a shifting of the emotional centre of gravity. All these effects are elements

* Gurney, *The Power of Sound*, p. 125.
† Wallace, *The Threshold of Music*, pp. 200-202.
‡ Gehring, *The Basis of Musical Pleasure*, p. 137, says that:

gives an impression of "great stability, firmness, quiet strength, and confidence.... To account for this we note that E flat, the point of rest, occurs on each strong beat, that the melody departs from it up, then down, then up further and finally settles down on it again." I have paraphrased his remarks a little. All the notes are, of course, on the tonic chord. For a contrast, he quotes from Raff's *Lenore* Symphony:

"The movement from which this theme is taken represents the departure of the lover to war. Hence its roving character, the tonic is avoided; it occurs only on unaccented notes."

in the language of music, as words are elements in the language of poetry.

The *tempo* and rhythms of music are hardly less definite in their suggestions than tonality. Nearly all ordinary mortals sensitive to musical impression feel that music speaks to their emotions. The analytic musician, who thinks of music as a thing of designs in sound with no emotional connotation, possibly inhibits his emotional response to leave his intellect a clearer view. Many philosophers of music (if we may use the phrase) from Aristotle onwards find that music has its roots in the emotions. Mr. Britan writes:

> *The stream of consciousness is one of the most variable streams in the world, and one of its marked characteristics is its ever-changing rate of flow; now it is hurrying on with all speed to some emotional climax, now it moves leisurely with no distinct end in view, and now laboriously, and all but stops because of the obstacles that impede its chosen path. . . . Now since this ever-changing rate of movement is one of the fundamental attributes of consciousness, those factors which signify it—and speech and musical sound are included under this head—will have a strong effect upon the mind. Thus the tempo with which a composition is rendered will exert a strong impressive suggestive emotional influence over consciousness. . . . The secret of music's power over the emotions *lies in the fact that the symbolism of music conforms so closely to the dynamics of the emotional consciousness. . . .* This is what Aristotle means when he says music more than any art imitates the inner activity of the soul†. . . . The secret of the emotional value of literature lies in its power of accurate representation of those conditions which in real life would bring such an emotional reaction. In music the

---

* *The Philosophy of Music*, pp. 161-75.

† Helmholtz also quotes from Aristotle: "Why do rhythms and melodies which are composed of sound resemble the feelings; while this is not the case for tastes, colours or smells? Can it be because they are motions as actions are also motions?" Ellis's translation, p. 385.

same power is gained by duplicating in musical sound the dynamic qualities of the various emotions.

Dr. Reimann, in his *Catechism of Musical Aesthetics*,* says:

I have already indicated the general foundation of those relations between movements of tone and movements of the soul, namely, the fact that increasing pitch, strength, and rate of movement have the significance of positive forms of movement, of coming forward, of a more energetic manifestation of the will, and that the contrary has the meaning of negative development, . . . every increase of emotion raises our voice without our knowing it, that with every increase of excitement we speak not only more loudly, but also more quickly, and that when we become calmer again the pitch of our voice becomes lower, its strength reduced, its quickness less rapid. The total effects of the various combinations of these factors are, accordingly, movements of the soul corresponding exactly to these movements that are experienced in affections like longing, joy, sadness, anger, fright, fear, *etc.*

Gehring† says the workings of music parallel those of the mind in the following ways, among others:

Both are moving things never still; "ideas succeed one another, tone follows tone."

Both are composed of simultaneous members, "music spreading out into a network of themes and voices, mind unfolding into a spectrum of thoughts and feeling."

Both have differences of intensity, loudness and softness. Some people's thoughts progress at a heavy *largo* rate, others trip along in merry *allegros*. We have mental *ritenutos* and *accelerandos*.

He cannot find any analogy between mind and music in melody, but Spencer has supplied us with this.

Timbre or harmony are like colours of association in the mind. Harmony gives a characteristic background to a note of the melody, changes its meaning somewhat, and

* Bewerunge's translation, p. 16.
† *The Basis of Musical Pleasure*, pp. 94-111.

"imparts direction and significance" to it. It corresponds to the fringe of thought.

Counterpoint is like parallel trains of thought; "sustained or recurring notes in the bass" correspond to thoughts which keep "thumping away in the background of the mind."

"Interlinking of successive chords is analogous to the connection of ideas."

Codas are like the mind "condensing its previous activities, or like a novel or a drama bringing all the chief characters together at the end."

Music, he concludes, works precisely as the mind does; without obstacles it moves the mind along as it likes to be moved, hence the pleasure it gives us. Dr. Williams* quotes the very irregular rhythm at the opening of the slow movement of the *Sonata Pathétique*, and says it gives a feeling of deep, introspective thought:

Raymond† provides another sort of illustration:

Wagner seems to be exceedingly fond of ending an upward movement that is expressive, as all such movements are, of anticipation, indecision or questioning, with a downward movement, containing a minor cadence, of, as often, an unresolved seventh. This downward movement, in as much as it is supposed to contain the conclusion or answer to the upward movement ... suggests, in such cases, that there is no satisfactory conclusion, decision, or answer to the feeling embodied in the preceding upward movement. Hence, the arrangement of tones represents the extreme of disappointment. ... Here is the expression of Sieglinde's compassionate yearning for Siegfried in the *Walkure*.

* *The Rhythm of Modern Music*, p. 96.
† *Music as a Representative Art*, p. 289.

Bach, among other composers, certainly associated his themes with emotions in some such way. Moreover we feel this sort of thing in bad music as well as in good, becoming very conscious of it in songs where the musical meaning clashes with that of the words. It explains the tide of applause that bursts after the music hall *prima donna* has finished on her highest note. The lift to such a climax of pitch excites the emotions and upsets the mental equilibrium; it is like turning an airy somersault. No wonder the unwonted exhilaration should spend itself in applause; music could not communicate its intention more unequivocally.

Music can imitate not only the emotions but the sounds of life more closely than any other art. Indeed some believe that it originated in this sort of imitation rather than in the Aristotelian. Gardiner, in his *Music of Nature*,* gives an attractive list, from which come these:

HAYDN, Quartet 38—Barking of a dog.

HAYDN, Quartet 76—Braying of an ass.

HANDEL—Laughter.

MOZART, Overture to *The Magic Flute*—The scolding of a woman.

* *The Music of Nature*, pp. 199, 202.

† *Ibid.*, pp. 194-6. Of these, Raymond, *Rhythm and Harmony in Poetry and Music*, pp. 318-20, says: "Very likely some of the above

HAYDN, Quartet 58—The tone of a mother fondling her child.

BEETHOVEN, 3rd Trio, Op. 9—Moan of sorrow and pain.

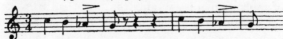

BEETHOVEN, C minor Symphony—Children frightening one another.

woo, woo, woo, woo   woo, woo, woo, woo

Music can very easily represent movements. "Hopping, violent bouncing, soft clinging, running, stopping, and all the thousandfold graduated and intermixing possibilities"* are easily represented by music. Daniel Webb, in his prosaic eighteenth-century way, says:

† Handel seldom fails to ascend with the word *rise*, and descend with the word *fall*. Purcell goes still further, and accompanies every idea of *roundness* with an endless *rotation* of notes. But what shall we say to that musician who disgraces the poet by realising his metaphors, and, in downright earnest, makes the fields laugh, and the vallies sing. In music, it is better to have no ideas at all than to have false ones, and it will be safer to trust to the simple

---

appearances of imitation are merely coincidences. Others, perhaps, are strains that had been heard by the composer and retained in memory, and were afterwards used without any definite notion of the source from which they were derived. . . . Most musicians, however, though quick to detect the appropriateness of different movements for different sentiments, have difficulty in explaining the reasons for their preferences."

Such onomatopoeia are like words which were originally onomatopoeic but whose mimetic origin we have forgotten.

* Reimann, *Catechism of Musical Expression*, p. 53.

† *Observations on the Correspondence between Music and Poetry*, p. 143.

effects of impression than to the idle conceits of forced imitation.

In our attempts to reduce music into an union with descriptive poetry, we shall do well to consider that music can no otherwise imitate any particular sound, than by becoming the thing it imitates.

Quite so; yet why music should not become a laughing field, or a singing valley, is difficult to see. Our greatest musicians paint like this; the Elizabethans rarely miss an opportunity of indulging in this sort of fancy; some opera composers turn the action and imaginings of the libretto so faithfully into music that we feel as if the visible action on the stage were an insubstantial emanation from the music, the picture of our imagination taking objective form. *Don Giovanni* among operas does this for me. Bach can give us a pastoral sensation by a subtle realism. Even on the piano, where all effect of orchestral colouring is lost, some of his pastoral passages have a pastoral atmosphere, due to something shepherd-like in the melodies. Macdowell's seascapes reproduce the atmosphere of the seashore in some subtle way.

There are as many ways of listening to music as of reading poetry. Mr. Weld* collected evidence, and divides listeners into four types—the analytic, intellectual type whose enjoyment is neither emotional nor imaginative, but consists in perceiving the form and structure of the music; this listener tends to be "coldly critical": the emotional listener who does not necessarily see pictures or notice the formal structure of music: the "motor type" of listener who wants to sing or whistle to the music and beat time: and the imaginative listener who sees pictures, and has day dreams, reveries, or "thought processes" foreign to the music on the focus of his consciousness with the music on the fringe.

* *American Journal of Psychology*, vol. xxiii, pp. 295, 300-301, "The Psychology of Musical Enjoyment".

The imagination of the listener who sees pictures moves closely in sympathy with the music. The pictures imagined by one of his "subjects" altered with each phrase of the music, and when the phrase repeated, the picture repeated too.* This kind of listener† "is . . . passive . . . and . . . relatively uncritical towards both the work of the performer and composer", surrendering himself to the will of the music, letting it make its own impression, in contrast with the analytic listener who, with his mind alive and alert, concentrates "a high degree of attention" on the music.

The four types are not exclusive. An imaginative listener may become analytic, and presumably an analytic mind may sometimes listen imaginatively or emotionally. But the more interesting part of the psychology is to know how far imaginative listeners see the same picture, how far emotional listeners feel the same emotion. In Weld's researches‡ a programme piece was played without its programme or its title. None of the audience got the programme precisely right, though some of them got the direct mimicry. It was a hunting scene; one listener saw a circus and heard dogs barking and bells ringing and shouting voices, others got woodland and dogs, or a menagerie and dogs, *etc.* Raymond§ tells of similar experiments where the "pictures and emotions" aroused in different listeners were often remarkably alike. But perhaps the most interesting example is the oft-quoted one from Bosanquet's *History of Aesthetics*:‖

Schumann's *In der Nacht* used to summon up before my imagination the picture of the moon struggling through the clouds in a windy night—emerging and disappearing by turns; then for a while reigning "apparent queen" amid

* p. 256. † p. 296. ‡ pp. 274-7.
§ *Rhythm and Harmony in Poetry and Music*, pp. 306-9.
‖ Appendix II, written by J. D. Rogers. Raymond quotes this on p. 303.

white fleecy clouds, which are not sufficient to intercept its light. During two moments even this silken veil is withdrawn, only to be succeeded by a bank of black clouds, for a long time impenetrable, at last penetrated at intervals a little more irregular and with a brightness a little wilder and more meteoric than before; finally—the light is put out and quenched by the storm.

I learnt some years afterwards that Schumann also associated this piece with a picture, the idea of which occurred to him after he had written the entire set of *Fantasiestücke* to which it belongs. It was a picture portraying the story of Hero and Leander; his picture is not incompatible with mine. In his, the clouds correspond to the waves, the moon to a swimmer, buried and stifled in their troughs or flashing and calling out from their crests. Where the moon triumphs in my story, in his there is a love scene on the shore, accompanied by the distant rippling of waves; it seems almost as though

> The billows of cloud that around thee roll
> Shall sleep in the light of a wondrous day.

But no; there comes the plunge back into waves blacker than before—tossings to and fro—cries from the swimmer and from the shore—and finally "night wraps up every thing".

The music meant the same thing to the writer of this as it did to the composer, only he saw the meaning in a metaphor. The real meaning of the music was neither the swimming Leander nor the struggling moon, but the something behind both, that they have in common. We find the same sort of thing in the psychology of poetry. I should imagine no two readers would take the same meaning from:

> It is a beauteous evening, calm and free,
> The holy time is quiet as a Nun
> Breathless with adoration.

One will see an evening landscape and no nun, another

the nun breathless with adoration and no landscape, another landscape and nun, while another may feel the calm, quiet spell of breathless adoration without any picture. Some readers may get neither picture nor emotion, and but realise that the line is an "iambic pentameter" with no rhyme, or more likely they would recognise it as the beginning of a sonnet they know very well. My picture at this moment includes quiet hills, Scotch ones with heather, a vagrant cloud, the onset of twilight, ripe corn uncut, "dykes" and wire fences round the fields, and over all the breathless expectant hush one feels when night gathers day to sleep in the silence of the hills; the nun is but a spirit, her grey cloak the gathering dusk, her adoration the breathless air. The details of this cannot have been in Wordsworth's picture; I should be surprised if they are in anyone else's, yet we should not say they are not included in the meaning of the poem. The real meaning is neither the evening nor the nun, but the feeling behind both the evening and the nun. The picture which rises unbid and unencouraged to my mind is my way of getting the significance of that meaning, just as the evening which prompted Wordsworth to write was but the concrete fact which suggested that meaning.

Poetry is as "absolute" as music; for we cannot chain the meanings of a poem down to one definite peg any more than we can confine the meaning of a piece of music. Music may be absolute in two ways. We may enjoy it as absolute music. And so may we enjoy poetry not as meaning anything, but as a succession of beautiful sounds or impressions. And music may be written absolutely, the composer not meaning anything by his music, merely putting together sounds beautiful in themselves. But in music written absolutely, if melody is meaningful, our sense of tonality one of the most fundamental facts in our emotional composition, and modes and keys dependent on different moods, how can an imaginative or emotional listener feel the music absolutely? Such music, although written absolutely, has an emotional or imaginative meaning. The musician weaves his melodies together in a dispassionate and abstractly artistic mood as if he were threading beads, but the beads he works with have meanings. Yet I should be surprised if music is often written absolutely. Some composers certainly mean something when they write, and use music as a sort of language. And "absolute" composers are not necessarily introspective or aware of the individuality of the temperament which influences their melodies, and they must be in some sort of mood when the ideas for their music come to them; their inspiration must come from somewhere that is not mere hard work or skill with no meaning. Wishing probably to damp the sentimentality usually associated with believers in inspiration, some writers point out such things as that a sonata may take six months to write, and ask if we are to imagine the composer in one mood for six months. But the ideas for a work, the creative nucleus, that part of artistic production beyond the control of the artist, is a different thing from the working out of the inspiration. The creative nucleus of a sonata that takes six months to write need not take as long as half an hour to unfold itself. We might expect Beethoven, if anyone, to write absolutely. According to Mr Ernest Newman,* Beethoven "told one of his friends that he had always a picture in his mind when composing". He is also reported† to have said that music must speak "from the heart to the heart"—a statement an artist of almost any *genre* might make of his art, but not the sort of statement we should expect from an absolute creator. But perhaps all the talk about absolute music we become so tired of indicates not music with absolutely nothing in it, but music

* *Musical Studies,* p. 133.
† Antcliffe, *The Nature of Music,* p. 178.

whose meaning is absolutely expressed within itself, that needs no further elucidating. Mendelssohn said:

*What any music I like expresses for me is not *thoughts too indefinite* to clothe in words, but too definite. If you asked me what I thought on the occasion in question, I say, the song itself precisely as it stands.

If this is the real meaning of "absolute music" we can equally well talk of absolute poetry. We cannot explain what poetry means, certainly not what the best poetry means, and not because it is too indefinite, but because it is too definite to put into other words; it means precisely what it says, and will not paraphrase or translate. People often bothered Tennyson wanting to know what certain passages in his poems meant. When asked to explain: "God made himself an awful rose of dawn," in the *Vision of Sin*,

†He replied that the power of explaining such concentrated expressions of the imagination was very different from that of writing them.

‡The Bishop of Ripon (Boyd Carpenter) once asked him whether they were right who interpreted the three Queens who accompanied King Arthur on his last voyage as Faith, Hope and Charity. He answered: "They are right, and they are not right. They mean that and they do not. They are three of the noblest of women. They are also those three Graces, but they are much more. I hate to be tied down to say, "*This* means *that*", because the thought within the image is much more than any one interpretation."

As for the many meanings of the poem [Hallam Tennyson continues] my father would affirm, "Poetry is like shot-silk with many glancing colours. Every reader

* Quoted from E. Gurney, *The Power of Sound*, p. 357.
† Hallam Tennyson's *Memoir*, vol. ii, p. 475.
‡ *Ibid.*, vol. ii, p. 127.

must find his own interpretation according to his ability, and according to his sympathy with the poet."

The analogy holds for music. It does not follow that the music has no meaning because its writer could not symbolise that meaning in a picture or put it into words. The musician puts the things behind poetry into music, the poet puts the things behind music into words. Both poetry and music spring from the same hidden well, but find their way out by different channels. We take as much of their meaning as we can and in the manner in which we can.

One might show the kinship between music and poetry in yet another way. They play upon the same psychology and illustrate each other readily. Francis Thompson talks of passages in *The Opium Eater* and in *Paradise Lost* as "contrapuntal", and although neither prose nor verse can be contrapuntal we know what he means. *The Opium Eater* and *Paradise Lost* give us the same full, vigorous sense of vitality through and through, of aliveness in every part. "Symphonic" is a favourite with *littérateurs* of to-day, although a poem can no more be symphonic than contrapuntal. But comparisons can be close enough to the facts to be analogies rather than metaphors.* We can easily show how Shakespeare's plays fit the same psychology as music. They have something corresponding to the *leitmotiv* of opera. Liddell† notices how the rhythms suit the characters; he compares Othello's:

> Most potent, grave, and reverend signiors,
> My very noble and approved good masters,
> That I have ta'en away this old man's daughter,
> It is most true: true I have married her;
> The very head and front of my offending
> Hath this extent, no more.

* See Appendix.
† *An Introduction to the Study of Poetry*, pp. 134-6.

He compares this straightforward, manly defence in direct, forward-flowing rhythm with Iago's:

> I do beseech you,
> Though I perchance am vicious in my guess—
> As, I confess, it is my nature's plague
> To spy into abuses, and oft my jealousy
> Shapes faults that are not—that your wisdom yet,
> *etc.*

It is also interesting [he* tells us] to note how associations that are rather intellectual than emotional unconsciously fix for themselves a peculiar rhythm-series in Shakspere. There is no finer illustration of this than one which appears in *Hamlet* almost in the form of a recurring rhythm-theme. The tragedy has long been recognised to be one of ineffectual purpose. . . .

This ineffectual purpose works itself into the tragedy in the form of an oft-recurring rhythm-series which reflects it. This rhythm-series is made up of a long, full, rising wave, followed by a short rising wave which either hangs in the air with an impulse considerably lower than that of the high impulse of the first wave, or reaches this low point with effort and falls away helplessly in an unstressed impulse. The series is la la′a la la″ la, "The rest is silence," or la la′a la la″ la la′ la″, "Abuses me to damn me," or simply la la′a la, "A scullion." Some of these are:

> "Devoutly to be wish-ed."
> "And lose the name of action."
> "And all for nothing."
> "And so I am revenged."
> "O nymph, in thy orisons
> Be all my sins remember'd."
> "O help him, you sweet heavens."
> "O heavenly powers, restore him."
> "O, I die; Horatio."

Saintsbury† finds some such use of characteristic rhythms

---

* *An Introduction to the Study of Poetry*, pp. 293-4.

† *History of English Prosody*, vol. ii, p. 41. He does not give his facts this interpretation.

in *Macbeth*. The thanes speak in what he calls the "gasp line, unmodulated and unsymphonised". In Goneril and Regan's speeches we miss the abundance of trisyllabic feet which characterises Lear's verse.*

And not in rhythm alone do we see a parallel to the *leit-motiv* of opera. Goneril's talk is thick, fat, cumbrous and heavy; Lear's music is lighter and brighter. The individual tones of their voices sound from the written page. The difference is readily heard but more difficult to describe:

GONERIL, I, Sc. IV.

Inform her full of my particular fear;
And thereto add such reasons of your own
As may compact it more. Get you gone,
And hasten your return. [*Exit* Oswald.] No, no, my
    lord,
This milky gentleness and course of yours
Though I condemn not, yet, under pardon,
You are much more attask'd for want of wisdom
Than prais'd for harmful mildness.

I, Sc. I.

You see how full of changes his age is; the observation we have made of it hath not been little: he always loved our sister most; and with what poor judgment he hath now cast her off appears too grossly.

LEAR, I, Sc. IV.

Let me not stay a jot for dinner: go, get it ready. How now! what art thou? . . . Follow me; thou shalt serve me: if I like thee no worse after dinner, I will not part from thee yet. Dinner, ho! dinner! . . .

Detested kite! thou liest:
My train are men of choice and rarest parts,
That all particulars of duty know,
And in the most exact regard support
The worships of their name.

* *History of English Prosody*, vol. ii, p. 44.

GONERIL, IV, Sc. II.

> Milk-liver'd man!
> That bear'st a cheek for blows, a head for wrongs:
> Who hast not in thy brows an eye discerning
> Thine honour from thy suffering; that not know'st
> Fools do those villains pity who are punish'd
> Ere they have done their mischief.

LEAR, V, Sc. III.

> No, no, no, no! Come, let's away to prison:
> We two alone will sing like birds i' the cage:
> When thou dost ask me blessing, I'll kneel down,
> And ask of thee forgiveness: so we'll live,
> And pray, and sing, and tell old tales, and laugh
> At gilded butterflies.

We need not point out the difference in the rhythms. Goneril's consonants echo brutally:

> In*f*orm him *f*ull of my particular *f*ear.
> Who *b*ears a cheek for *b*lows.
> Fools do those villains *p*ity who are *p*unished.

How inartistic is the double assonance of:

> You see how full of ch*anges* his *age is*.

The heavy vowels of "how full" are reversed in "poor judgment", and further modified into "too grossly". Lear's vowel and consonant music varies more subtly, and his echoes are not so crude. In, "Let me not stay a jot for dinner", "not" and "jot" rhyme, and *t* comes crisply from the sentence like electric sparks from a tramcar on a frosty morning, but the repetitions are not pounded out. "Pity", "punished", "inform", "full", "fears", have heavy accents. The accents on "let", "stay" and "jot" are lighter. In, "Go, get it ready", "get" has a soft accent, and so the alliteration is weakened. "How now! what art thou?" has vivid enough rhymes and deep enough vowels, but something excitable in the inflection keeps the pitch high and clarifies the quality of the vowels. The echoes come gently in the last passage we quoted, soft colours intertwining: "away" echoes in "alone" and "cage", "prison" in "sing", "birds" in "blessing" and "butterflies", "ask me blessing" with "ask of thee forgiveness", "pray" in "tales", and "tales" in "tell", "laugh", "gilded", and so on.

We have seen that the impulse of the poet and the musical composer can be the same, poetry and music even rising simultaneously in him. Now let us hammer in some old nails which we left loose, one being the difference between artistic and prose *expression*. The prose-writer, characteristically, wants to express something, or his feelings about something. If we do not understand him we say his thought is not clear, he has not expressed himself. His object is to convey his meaning, one meaning; our object in reading him to get his meaning, each of us the same meaning. If we each take a different meaning from his writing, he might as well not have written. Prose can be artistic as utilitarian things can be artistic, but the art of writing perfectly has more affinities with the art of making a perfect table than with the art of poetry. Although they both use words, prose is only dimly related to poetry. Neither the poet nor the musician, writing characteristically, wish to convey anything: both the reader and the listener wish to have something conveyed. I should suppose no creator knows why he creates, though some have theories about their impulses. It may be they are possessed of a demon. Or perhaps the principle that makes amateur carpenters operates in them, idle hands and a certain craftsman skill. Or more likely they differ from ordinary men in having the umbrella of their mind, which should shelter them from the rain and dew of the intangible universe from which our incarnation shuts us off, turned the wrong way up. Their first purpose in creating is to empty the umbrella, a secondary purpose to wash away a little of the dust from the parched, prosaic world of fact. What makes their work valuable to us appears to our hooded minds its primary purpose; we think the object of art is to convey this spiritual dew. But the artist does not want to express anything, but to recreate; his art is not a legal document of his inspiration, but the nearest model he can make. Poetry and music are not pipes carrying this dew from creator to appreciator; they are outside both creator and appreciator, lakes formed by the rain from one, into which the other would plunge himself. The creator is not directly concerned with the fate of his work; he does not address himself to an audience as the man of prose does. Poetry and music are not means of communication between their creators and ourselves, but things in themselves, just as the sun, a mountain, or a daisy are things in themselves. We feel the touch of the creator's personality in his poems or his music just as we feel the creator's touch in the sun, a mountain, or a daisy, but not otherwise.

The work of critics might be easier, aesthetics certainly would, and the judgments of reviewers more important, if the object of poets and musicians were to convey one meaning. But I can see no other advantage in each reader taking the same meaning from a poem. Different interpretations make no real obstacle to aesthetics. It is not as if we were talking of facts like rhythm or inflection tunes. There is some reason in looking for the ideally correct interpretation of the rhythm or the inflection tune of a poem; and it may be worth while trying to find this. But to desire that we should all feel alike about things in artistic appreciation, to wish that literary criticism could become a science, is against all nature. We do not wish all men to fall in love with the same woman; and yet if human nature were logical, if it were true to the best within itself, educated in real discrimination and capable of the finest appreciation, this is what would happen. In the ideal world of criticism all men could marry the ideal woman, but even if the practical difficulties were solved for the real world, still all men would not marry her; it is impossible that their individuality could be so wiped out as to admit of their all loving her. We could not hope to persuade everyone that nicely salted porridge is the only wholesome and appetising diet, that only wrong training and want of experience—not to mention English methods of cooking—make the degenerates of this earth think otherwise. If tastes differ about porridge, how much more likely that they will differ about poetry. And not only do tastes differ; our individuality often determines the nature of what we taste. The lily has formed the text of more than one moral exhortation; it preaches an aesthetic sermon too. The tiger variety emits a fulsome and nauseous smell to some nostrils, to others a sweet fragrance. It is not that one loves and another hates the same scent. The lily emits two scents; some of us have breathed both of its sweet and of its sour. The *Prelude* makes a lovely fragrance when I breathe it, to some it breathes sourly. The *Dunciad* may sparkle and wink to some with a dazzling brilliance; to me it is an ugly fester. Even if we wished, we could never eliminate the personal from artistic appreciation. Our nostrils alone determine our impression of the tiger-lily's virtue, one sense only. Each one of our senses may have its say in the impression we get from a poem. And poetry is not a matter of hearing and seeing and smelling and tasting and touching alone. No two men have the same sort of intelligence, of intellect, the same readiness in emotional response, the same sensitiveness of imagination; each one is different in the orderliness and untidiness of his mind, in its pliabilities and rigidities, in the degree and in the spheres of his intolerances, in sense of humour, and in patience. The impression the *Prelude* and the *Dunciad* make on us involves almost our whole personality; individual differences count rather more than less in determining the meaning of a poem.

Wagner, Tennyson, and possibly others, have said that music begins where words leave off. This has been taken to mean that poetry and music are incompatible. It affords a good battle-cry for those who think that poetry cannot be set to music, that music cannot hope to succeed in illustrating poetry, having methods totally different. Wagner obviously did not mean this; nor did Tennyson. They meant that poetry is a semicircle, and music begins at the diameter enclosing it and adds the complement of the circle; that there is no gap between poetry and music and nothing superfluous, that they fit exactly, even that one is incomplete without the other. Yet the most formidable supporter of the opinion that music should not meddle with poetry has a poet-laureate's authority. But it is all a matter of false logic. They reason thus. We have but to look at what Musician A has done with Poet B's work to see that music is unfit to interpret poetry. Musician A is a competent musician; he has done his best, yet the structure of his music, though a good musical structure, disagrees with the structure of the poem. But the quarrel between musician and poet is a personal one—the annoyance of Poet B when Musician A has spoilt his work, misrepresented the spirit of it, not to say the rhythm or anything as concrete; he concludes, therefore, that Musician A's failure results from some inherent incompatibility in music. But how foolish! Poet C can no more write poetry like Poet B's than Musician A could write music like him. It is not that music differs essentially from poetry, but that Musician A differs essentially from Poet B.

Mr. Bridges* states the reasons for his quarrel very definitely.

* *Ode on Commemoration of Purcell*, Preface.

1. He says that repetitions are not part of poetry's form and that they are almost inevitable in music.

Why should we leave out of account our ballads or quasi-ballad poetry?

2. He says that repetitions strengthen the feeling in music and weaken it in poetry.

But what about:

> To-morrow, and to-morrow, and to-morrow,
> Creeps in this petty pace from day to day?

The last "to-morrow" is the most emotional. Nor are repetitions inevitable in music, except in certain forms like the sonata; no one expects instrumental forms to resemble poetic forms; they were developed precisely to stand without the support of words. Bridges possibly dislikes the repetition of the same words in different "parts", as in madrigal form. But this is not to say that music must have repetitions, only that repetitions sound very beautiful in music. Moreover, the strengthening of the musical emotion by such repetitions strengthens the emotion of the words too; for when music and poetry join they are not two things but one; the poetry becomes apotheosized into music.

3. He objects that music emphasises the meaning of poetry.

It need not. Why must it? Music may not only weaken but destroy the meaning.

4. Also: "[Music] can do nothing with parentheses or dependent clauses."

But music can always beautify poetry by following the inflection, even the inflection of dependent clauses and parentheses.

The repetitions of music disturb Mr. Strangeways too.* He notices that Goethe's words do not follow the emotional movement of Schubert's spinning-wheel. "The poet",

* *Essays of the English Association*, vol. vii, pp. 45-7.

he says, "can cumulate his thought but not the actual sound." The musician here seems "to be misreading the poem." This is probably true; I said the quarrel was a personal one. But a repeated tune need not have the same words, so long as the words are equally appropriate; the poet can cumulate his emotion to the accumulating sound of the music. Poetry can even conform to such an essentially instrumental music as that of the spinning-wheel. I recollect no instance of its doing so, but a well-known Scottish poet, well known in Aberdeenshire at least, Skinner of Linshart, wrote words to music as essentially instrumental, recurring like the spinning-wheel with speed and monotony and perhaps even with a drone. He wrote words to the reel of Tullochgorum. The tune is repeated for six verses, of which these are the first two :

> Come gie's a sang, Montgomery cry'd,
> And lay your disputes all aside,
> What signifies't for folks to chide
>   For what's been done before them?
> Let Whig and Tory all agree,
>   Whig and Tory, Whig and Tory,
> Let Whig and Tory all agree
>   To drop their Whigmigmorum.*
> Let Whig and Tory all agree,
> To spend this night in mirth and glee,
> And cheerfu' sing alang wi' me,
>   The reel o' Tullochgorum.
>
> O Tullochgorum's my delight,
> It gars us a' in ane unite,
> And ony sumph that keeps up spite
>   In conscience I abhor him.
> For blithe and cheery we's be a',
>   Blithe and cheery, blithe and cheery,
> Blithe and cheery we's be a'
>   And mak' a happy quorum.

* An obsolete dance.

For blithe and cheery we's be a',
As lang's we hae a breath to draw,
And dance till we be like to fa',
    The reel o' Tullochgorum.

The reel goes thus, the words following it closely, almost syllable for note; what discrepancies we can discover may be due to my taking the wrong version, for Scottish reels, like folk-songs, are not stereotyped in one set tune, and printed versions differ as much as those carried in the mind :

The English reader will find this all wrong for his inflections. Skinner relies on Scottish intonations, and excited ones at that.

CHAPTER II

OUR ALPHABET

Music exists by itself; it has no need of poetry, and if every human language were to perish, it would be none the less the most poetic, the grandest and the freest of all the arts.—Berlioz.

A musical alphabet of the emotions. . . . It is possible to conceive that such an alphabet might leave abundant scope for originality, and yet be comparatively intelligible.* There is a natural, inarticulated language of the emotions employed by all of us. What reason is there in nature to suppose otherwise than that all its elements might be comprehended and tabulated with sufficient definiteness in a few score of carefully related forms of sound? As it is, even now, every really great composer recognises the existence of this language and unconsciously applies its principles. Why should they not be formulated so that all men could know them? Why should not the psychological correspondences of music be unfolded with as much definiteness as those of elocution, to which in their elements they are analogous?—Raymond, *Rhythm and Harmony in Poetry and Music.*

The answer to Raymond's question is: because it would do music harm. Art abhors nothing more than the formulated material and the stereotyped process; these are for manufacturers. But he has looked at music with the eye of imagination and seen things as they were early in the human dawn. There was a time when mankind had nothing but music out of which to develop a definite speech. Our alphabet is an adaptation of music. The arts still love to keep up the connection. After they became officially

* This sentence I have cut and altered a little.

separated, poetry and music still grew side by side, suffer-
ing the same shocks and flourishing in the same fair
weather. Elizabethan poets have the same sense of music
as Elizabethan musicians, eighteenth-century poets as
eighteenth-century musicians. A description of one of
their arts almost does for the other. Pope, although a
different sort of man from Handel,* is not unlike him, both
having, compared with the Elizabethans, a restricted sense
of rhythm, writing in equal bars with smooth and solid
cadences. Neither poetry nor music can exist by itself;
each has need of the other; if one of them perished, the
other would die of loneliness.

Let us tidy up the musical facts about our alphabet and
get them clear. Every sound is caused by some movement,
which has raised vibrations in the air; these vibrations
travel into our ears and give us the sensation of sound.
Pure tones, such as we hear in tuning-forks, come from
regular oscillations, noises from irregular vibrations. *The
pitch of a note depends on the number of vibrations per
second—the faster the vibration, the higher being the pitch.*
Sound very rarely comes in the form of pure tones. A musical note is a conglomerate, or rather a blend of pure tones.
If we play middle C on the piano, the pure tones sounding
are C itself, which we call the fundamental, and its

harmonics, that is . The fundamental,
or lowest pure tone, determines the pitch of a note, and
the partials, or harmonics, or overtones, as the other pure
tones are called, determine the quality of the note. Notes
played on the violin have commonly more partials than

* Although born in the same year as Handel (1685), Bach is comparable with Milton, rather culminating the old style than practising
the new. The comparison between Handel and Pope is relevant, since
Handel wrote in England for the English and in the English style.

those played on a flute, hence their different *timbre*. We can see an analogy to what happens in the ear when we hear, if we sing into the front of an open grand piano with the loud pedal on. The air communicates the vibrations from our throat to the wires of the piano, which pick these vibrations up and sing us back our note, each tone resounding on its own wire. The basilar membrane in our ears acts something like that. Helmholtz, who first discovered this, discovered also that vowels depend for their characteristic quality on the presence of characteristic partials, just as the tones of the flute or violin do. He tells us* that if we sing the *a* of "father" into an open grand piano, the piano will sound the same *a*, while if we sing the *oe* of "toe" it will sound that vowel. And indeed we can hear the piano changing its partials for the new vowel if we sing *a* and then *oe* on the same note. After hearing the piano analyse them, we can detect the characteristic partials of vowels for ourselves.

In 1878 *Nature*† had a notice of a phonograph experiment by Mr. C. R. Cross and Dr. C. J. Blake. The vowels *ou* and *ō* were spoken into a phonograph, each four times, while the cylinder rotated one revolution per second. On rotating the disc of the gramophone which reproduced them, at the same rate the experimenters reproduced the vowels correctly; but when they increased the speed to two revolutions per second, *ou* became indistinct, and *ō* came out as a very clear *ĕ*. At a half revolution per second these became *au* and *ou*. The vowel *ō* was sung into a phonograph rotating at different speeds. When reproduced on the gramophone at a uniform rate, the slow rate record returned the vowel as *au*, changing to *ō*, *ë* and *ĕ* as the rate increased, and falling to *ĕ* again as the velocity slackened a little. The vowel *ä* was spoken while the cylinder made one

---

* *The Sensations of Tone*, Ellis's translation, p. 104.
† For May 23rd.

revolution per second; reproduced at a half revolution per
second it came out as *au*, changing to *ä* when the rate was
increased to one revolution, and at three revolutions per
second it became *ĭ*. The vowel *ō* was spoken several times
in succession, the rate of the cylinder being gradually
accelerated. When reproduced at a uniform slow rate the
sound came out *au* and *ou*, and at a uniform fast rate *ĕ*
and *ĭ*.

By means of scientific analysis and measurement Mr.
Miller has determined the pitch of the characterising
partials of vowels. He tells us about his method of analysing vowels, and how he checked his results, in *The Science
of Musical Sounds*, which is too mathematical to be easily
understood. He took phonograph records of sung vowels,
analysed them into their constituent pure tones, and
checked the results by synthesizing these pure tones. In
this way he was able to produce such words as "ma-ma",
"pa-pa", by sounding an array of pipes emitting pure
tones, so confirming Helmholtz's theory about vowels. As
proved by Miller,* the facts stand thus. Each vowel has
its own characteristic pitch. When we sing a vowel to any
note, our vocal cord sounds the given fundamental and
its harmonics; the resonating cavities in the mouth, nose,
and head reinforce the harmonic nearest the characteristic pitch of the vowel till it resounds louder not only
than any of the other harmonics, but louder than even the
fundamental itself. Thus† if the vowel *a* of *father* is intoned
on , a pitch with 154 vibrations per second,
the sixth partial—(6 × 154 = 924 vibrations per second)
—is the loudest. If the same vowel is intoned on

---

* Chapters vii and viii, which an unmathematical mind may
understand.
  † *Ibid.*, p. 260.

, a pitch with 462 vibrations per second, the

second partial — $(2 \times 462 = 924)$ —is loudest.

Some vowels have two areas of reinforced resonance, two characterising pitches. We may tabulate the results thus:

* SINGLE-NOTE VOWELS.		DOUBLE-NOTE VOWELS.	
Vowel.	Characteristic pitch.	Vowel.	Characteristic pitches.
a in father	c. 922–1100 per sec.	*a* in mat	c. 800 & 1843 per sec.
au in maw	c. 732 per sec.	*e* in met	c. 691 & 1953 ,,
o in mow	c. 461 ,,	*a* in mate	c. 488 & 2461 ,,
oo in gloom	c. 326 ,,	*i* in meet	c. 308 & 3100 ,,

Or in musical notation:

oo in gloom	*o* in mow	*au* in maw	*a* in father	*a* in mat	*e* in met	*e* in mate	*i* in meet

Miller says that we cannot intone any vowel on a note higher than its characteristic pitch. This is not so; it is difficult but not impossible. The *oo* of *gloom* can be sung

at least as high as . Helmholtz's theory can stand

this contradiction, the proofs are so strong; but there must be some explanation to reconcile them. We notice that the characterising pitches of vowels sound very different

or unrelated. is not a harmonic of ,

nor of ; they are not a bit like each

other. Vowels rely on our sense of absolute pitch; we can hear the difference between *a* and *o* because we recognise

* The whispered vowels are a little higher.

their characteristic pitches as characteristic. While anyone with absolute pitch may never confuse "d" and "e", he may find it difficult to distinguish "d" from its octave, the note most nearly related to it.* The fifth is the interval next nearly related; those with a feeble yet natural sense of absolute pitch, if they have not been trained, more often mistake a note for its fifth than for its second. The fourth comes next in kinship, then the major third and major sixth. None of the vowels have characteristic pitches as nearly related as these, except where one has a double pitch. Perhaps the reinforcing of the octave or the fifth above the characteristic pitch of a vowel may come near enough to give the character of the vowel. But this is matter for experiment, not for speculation. Miller also tells us that we may whisper a vowel without its fundamental or vocal tone, but must sound the partial which characterises it, and that the *a* of *father* is the easiest vowel. Indeed *a* is the father of all the vowels. Perhaps we derive our sense of musical pitch from it. At all events, in identifying vowels we depend on our sense of absolute pitch. They are pure musical notes, resulting from our musical sense and probably training it.

Miller experimented on sung vowels. Dr. Scripture has done most work on spoken ones. He differs from the accepted, one might almost say, proved theory, in believing the characterising pitch to be fixed absolutely, independently of the fundamental. According to the accepted theory, the vocal cord sings the fundamental with its harmonics, and the resonating cavities in mouth, nose and head augment the harmonic nearest the characteristic pitch. Scripture thinks† that the air which sets the vocal chords vibrating to sound the fundamental and its harmonics sets the resonant cavities vibrating with their own periodicity,

---

* Myers, *A Textbook of Experimental Psychology*, p. 50.
† *Researches in Experimental Phonetics*, p. 111.

that is to say at their characteristic pitch, independently of the fundamental or its harmonics. His reasons for thinking so are too technical for me to understand, so I must accept the orthodox verdict against him, although, since he suffers the fate of all heretics, I had much rather agree with him. But we can all understand so much: if his theory were right, vowels would make sometimes harmonies, sometimes discords, as the fundamental happened to be in harmonic relation with their fixed pitch or not; our ears side with orthodoxy. We recollect that the spoken fundamental never rests for one moment, continuously flying up and down the ladder of sound. The problem concerns the relation of this flying fundamental to the characteristic pitches of vowels. If Scripture is right, then the music of poetry forms a harmonious interplay of inflection tune and vowel music—a two-part song as it were; if Miller is right, the inflection tune is a single melody, the vowel music determining the quality of its notes and the harmony being only incipient*—a slight though real difference, resulting partly because Miller investigates intoned vowels, Scripture spoken ones. In sung vowels the fundamental being given, limits the characterising pitch to one of its harmonics. In the spoken vowel the characterising pitch may determine or at least influence the fundamental. The low vowel of *doom*, *gloom* tends to induce a low inflection; in the stanza quoted on page 154 from Spenser's *February Eclogue*, the high pitch of the vowel of "sere" lends itself to a high inflection, though the lower of its characteristic pitches is only a semitone from that of *gloom*.

Consonants have been studied in the same sort of way as vowels, and attempts made to discover their characteristic pitches, but with less success. They tend to the class *noise* rather than to the class *note*, though the difference

---

* Gehring, *The Basis of Musical Pleasure*, p. 98, says: "Timbre is incipient harmony, harmony is developed timbre."

between a noise and a musical discord is only one of
degree; the tones constituting them are not harmonic, and
this makes them difficult to analyse. Their quality depends
partly on their overtones, but also on their different attack.
There are many varieties of consonant, and we probably
ought not to lump them all in one category against vowels;
s differs as much from *m* as from *a*. We group them on
different principles: *b*, *d*, *g* in one lot, *p*, *t*, *k* in another,
f, *th*, *h* in another, *m*, *n*, *ng* in another; or *p*, *b*, *f* in one
group, *d*, *t*, *dh* in another, *g*, *k*, *ch* in another. For *p*, *t*, *k*,
b, *d*, *g*, *f*, *th*, *h* the mouth may have almost the same shape;
p and *b* are articulated by a lip action, *t* and *d* by action
of the tongue on the front teeth, *k* and *g* by the throat, *f* by
the breath blowing between the teeth and the lower lip,
th by the breath blowing between the tongue and the upper
teeth, *h* by the breath blowing straight from the throat
through the open mouth. The names usually given to the
groupings of consonants seem to me misleading; *t*, *d*, *th*
are not so much dental consonants as tongue ones. The
real dentals are *s* and *z*, *s* being formed by the breath
pressing through the almost close teeth, *z* being an *s* with
vocal tone. We commonly distinguish *b*, *d* and *g* from *p*, *t*
and *k* by saying that they are voiced. But *b*, *d* and *g* need
not necessarily be voiced; they whisper as well as *p*, *t*, *k*;
b, *d*, *g* whisper with a pout, *p*, *t*, *k* with a smile.

Written consonants are only generalisations, classifica-
tions. Ever so many varieties of *t* or *d* or *k* obtain. Our
alphabet is a live part of us, and its letters related in more
than mere likeness; they grow out of each other. Grimm
showed how, in the history of languages, *p* changes to *b*,
b to *f*, *t* to *d*, and *d* to *th*, so that what was once *pater*
becomes *father*, and so on. Changes like these do not come
suddenly. Vowel changes are supposed to become percep-
tible only in three generations. *B* does not emerge from *p*
as a butterfly from its chrysalis; it grows gradually out of

b and into *p* through many intervening sounds for which we have no distinctive letters, *b* and *p* being generic symbols for many different species of *p*s and *b*s. All letters are related in this way. The history of languages shows *p* and *t*, *t* and *k*, *b* and *d*, *d* and *g*, *f* and *th*, *th* and *h*, *g* and *c*, *c* and *h* related, as *p* and *b* are. *Qu*, *v*, *f* and *w* are brothers; Latin *quod* is our *what* (really pronounced *hwot*) and Aberdeenshire Scots' *fat*. We often pronounce *cl* in *clean* as *tlean*. *Ch* is related on one side to *k* and on the other to *j*. The English *church* is the Scottish *kirk*, and in Scotland *James* is often pronounced *Chames*. Even *l* and *m* have affinities.* We articulate the trilled consonants *l* and *r* with the mouth shaped as for *t*, but

† for *r* the sides [of the tongue] remain fixed while the point is released and allowed to vibrate, and for *l* the point remains fixed while the sides are released, and their margins allowed to tremble.

The *r* of Latin *purpur* turns into the *l* of *purple*. Both *l* and *r*, being soft, pliant and vowel-like, when vocalised become really vowels with a consonant trill; and indeed they often prove their vowel-like nature by dropping the trill and becoming vowels outright. They sometimes‡ "register" themselves on phonograph records exactly like a vowel; and we may hear *r* becoming *a* any day in England, while in Scots the vowel of *ball* and *all* has swallowed both *l*s and become *ba'* and *a'*. *M*, *n* and *w* also resemble vowels. They too may lose their consonant variation, retaining only the vocal tone. Aberdeenshire, which is proud of its distinction in these and other respects, claims to rival Italy in its vowels, and in proof of this preserves the following conversation about a jumper, or some such garment:

---

* Scripture, *Elements of Experimental Phonetics*, p. 44.

† Ellis, *Speech in Song*, p. 124.

‡ Scripture, "Inscriptions of Speech" (reprint from *Volta Review*, July 1920).

Question: Oo?
Answer: Ai, oo.
Question: A oo?
Answer: Ai, a oo.
Question: A ae oo?
Answer: Ai, a ae oo.
which, being translated, means:
Question: Wool?
Answer: Yes (ay), wool.
Question: All wool?
Answer: Yes, all wool.
Question: All one or ene [kind of] wool?
Answer: Yes, all one wool.

The nearest vowel to *m, n, ng* is *u.* "The humming tone heard when singing with closed mouth is nearest to *u.*"*

Vowels divide themselves into families, some closely related, some distantly, just as consonants do, and for the same reasons; we articulate some with a similarly shaped mouth, others sound alike. The *i* of *meet* is more like the *a* of *nay* when it is not diphthongised than the *e* of *met*, the *a* of *nay* more like the *e* of *met* than the *a* of *hat*, the vowel of *hat* is more like that of *father* than that of *awe*, which again is related on the further side with the vowel of *gloom*. In articulating *meet, nay, met, hat, father*, we have come a gradual progress from the front of the mouth to the back, and from a shut to an open mouth; and the pitch of characteristic resonance has come down the scale. As we proceed from *father* through *awe* to *gloom*, the articulation continues its progress backward, but the mouth shuts again, only with a pout instead of a smile, the same ground being covered in the progress from *father* to *gloom* as from *father* to *meet*. The vowels of *gloom* and *meet* are near relatives, since we articulate both in the very

* Helmholtz, *The Sensations of Tone*, p. 169.

front of the mouth, and the lower of the characteristic pitches of *meet* being only a semitone from the characteristic pitch of *gloom*. The vowels of *mate* and *owe*, *men* and *awe*, *mat* and *father* are related in the same sort of way. Just as

$$\begin{array}{l} \longleftrightarrow \\ \uparrow \text{p, t, k,} \\ \vert \text{ b, d, g,} \\ \downarrow \text{f, th, h,} \end{array}$$

merge into each other horizontally as well as vertically, so do the vowels tabulated on page 208; *p* cannot turn into *k* or *f* save through *t* and *b*; *d* may become *t*, *th*, *g* or *b* directly; we do not require other letters to express the intermediary sounds. The ear determines the relationship as well as the mouth, and has the last say in the matter. It decides that *gloom* resembles *awe* more than *sweet*, that *sweet* resembles *met* rather than *gloom*. But this is only a contemporary judgment. The vowel of *gloom* was not always nearer *awe* than *sweet*. Lowland Scots, which developed from Northern Old English, pronounces *good* with a rounded *oe*, something like French *œuf* (spelling it *guid*); Aberdeenshire Scots pronounces it with the *i* of *sweet* (spelling it *gweed*). This must mean that at one time the *oo* of *gloom* was more like the *ee* of *sweet* than it is now. To us *f* perhaps sounds nearer to *th* than to *b*, but when the *f* of *frater* was becoming the *b* of *brother*, *f* must have sounded nearer *b* than *th*. It must also have been nearer in the mouth, for we ought not to talk as if the sound of a letter and the action of the mouth in articulating it were really separate things. The sound depends on the shape and action of the mouth, throat and resonating cavities. Any sound related in the mouth must be related to the ear. The aural and the oral relationship is identical.

That we can divide consonants into families, and that some mix well and others badly, has often been noted.

Lanier* points out how some recur easily—"lal, lal, lal"—
others with difficulty—"bag, bag, bag", or "Shouldst
stand still", and† that consonants related through having
"nearly the same adjustment of the vocal organs" like
d, t, th, p, b, v, and *g, c, k,* have similar tone colour. We
can use this to explain the music of poetry in one of two
ways. Lanier thinks of letters as colours, *timbres,* with
different tone qualities. He would explain the music of
"lal, lal, lal" by saying the tone colours blend, while the
colours of "bag, bag, bag" do not blend. To show how
dull, verse written in monochrome may be, he quotes:

‡'Tis May-day gay: wide-smiling skies shine bright,
Through whose true blue cuckoos do woo anew
The tender spring.

Omond records another freak, a verse without a sibilant:

§No, not the eye of tender blue,
    Though, Mary, 'twere the tint of thine,
    Or breathing lip of glowing hue
    Might bid the opening bud repine,
    Had long enthrall'd my mind.

For contrast we might give:

The soughing breeze sweeps hushing through the trees.

In *Frater Ave Atque Vale,* Tennyson uses the colour of
l, m, n, r, and particularly of the vowel of "glow", to give
a liquid effect:

Row us out from Desenzano, to your Sirmione row!
So they row'd, and there we landed—"O venusta Sirmio!"
There to me thro' all the groves of olive in the summer
    glow,

* *The Science of English Verse,* p. 305.
† *Ibid.,* p. 306.   ‡ *Ibid.,* p. 302.
§ Written by Thelwall, quoted in *English Metrists in the 18th and
19th Centuries,* p. 99.

There beneath the Roman ruin where the purple flowers
  grow,
Came that "Ave atque Vale" of the Poet's hopeless woe,
Tenderest of Roman poets nineteen-hundred years ago,
"Frater Ave atque Vale"—as we wander'd to and fro
Gazing at the Lydian laughter of the Garda Lake below
Sweet Catullus's all-but-island, olive-silvery Sirmio!

All musical poetry blends the colour of its words, the
blend being of the Persian-carpet sort, not that of colours
mixed on the palette; the mixture is in our impression.
But Raymond would call "lal, lal, lal" chords, each "lal"
being a blend in fact, like a chord in music, not a succession of sounds.* I do not suppose many people could
believe that we pronounce the letters of a syllable simultaneously, but we can easily show that we do not. We distinguish *but* from *tub*; Raymond might object: "Yes, *but* is
in the first position of the chord, *tub* is an inverted *but*."
Phonograph records show that in reality we do not pronounce the letters of a syllable simultaneously; in an experiment of Fleming Jenkin and J. A. Ewing,† a phonograph record reproduced backwards on the gramophone
came out right, the sound *ab* reproduced backwards becoming *ba*, *noshaeesossa* becoming *association*. In a much-
inflected syllable we hear the inflection moving under the
letters; when *yes* is spoken slowly, with a rising inflection
on the *y* and a falling thereafter, we hear the *y* on a higher
note than the *s*. If *s* and *y* form harmonies, they do so with
the pitch their inflection traverses, not with each other.

Raymond is always interesting and on the track of something good. When the letters in a poetic context are nearly
related, have a similar tone colour, he calls the effect a
"consonance";‡ a context of unrelated letters he calls
"dissonance"§—a rather loose way of using musical

* *Rhythm and Harmony in Poetry and Music*, p. 170.
† *Nature*, March 28th, 1878.
‡ p. 156.   § p. 159.

terms. This "consonance" or progress of poetry through
related letters has, he tells us, an analogy in music:

*In passing from one chord to another, the ear, in order
to preserve the unity of effect, requires† the presence in
both chords of an identical note, and that, when, through
the second chord, the music enters a different key, it re-
quires† what sometimes is, in a sense, an arbitrary introduction into the first chord of a note legitimate only to
the second. . . . In this passage from Milton, notice how
the like sounds of *f, b, s* or *w* and of the *p* as altered to the *b*
are thus introduced into the other series coming before
and after them, and introduced in such a way as to
separate them from the series to which, as like sounds,
they belong. Notice, also, that as a result the sounds of the
whole passage are so blended together as to produce a
general effect of unity, in exact analogy with that which is
done by methods of modulation, as the term is understood,
in music:
                                        The air
*Floats as they pass, fanned with unnumbered plumes.
From branch to branch the smaller birds with song
Solaced the woods and spread their painted wings.*

Stevenson‡ gives a good example from *Antony and Cleopatra*:

The BaRge she sat iN, like a BURNished throne
BURNt on the water; the PooP was Beaten gold,
PURPle the sails, and so PERFUMèd, that
The wiNds were lovesick with them.

It may [he says] be asked why I have put the F of per-
fumed in capitals; and I reply, because this change from
P to F is the completion of that from B to P already so
adroitly carried out. Indeed the whole passage is a monument of curious ingenuity: and it seems scarce worth while
to indicate the subsidiary *s, l* and *w*.

* p. 160.   † As a matter of fact this is wrong.
  ‡ *Technical Elements of Style*, Pentland Ed., p. 285.

To return to Raymond:

*What has been said implies that there are two applications of this method of *phonetic gradation*. The first causes each of a series of sounds to differ from the one nearest it in a like degree. The second causes it to differ by a movement of the organs in a like direction. Of the two, the second is the more important, and it is worthy of notice that the same is true of these methods as applied to the use of musical scales. Gradation performs a more important office in guiding the general direction of the voice upward or downward than in leading it upward or downward by regular degrees.

What he means by this I do not know, but quote, hoping the fault is only mine. He appears to mean something interesting by it. Perhaps we find examples of his musical gradation in the opening bar of the Welsh tune commonly called *The Ash Grove* —a more simple way of progressing than by what he calls "degrees", *do, re, mi, fa, so*; or perhaps he means that gradations of tones and semitones form scales, not a succession of regular degrees, *i.e.* all tones or all semitones. I am utterly at a loss for what corresponds to these in "poetic phonetic gradation", unless he would say that *th, t* and *d* differ "in a like degree", *i.e.* are different though all pronounced forward in the mouth, while a movement of the mouth in a like direction, *i.e.* forwards, makes the difference between *a, e* and *i*; but if he means this, the musical analogy does not seem very relevant. And he soon goes off into an imagined likeness between the arts. He says of:

> Who, rowing hard against the stream,
> Saw distant gates of Eden gleam,
> And did not dream it was a dream.
> (*The Two Voices*.)

* p. 164.

*The *was* in the last line prepares for the closing of the series of gradations in very much the same way as the discord of the seventh that precedes the last note of a musical melody.

In the interest of greater precision we might read "may precede" for "precedes", "notes" for "note" and "harmony" for "melody". He can write as well as think loosely, though he is not the sort of thinker we should overlook. Despite his horrid habit of landing in the ditch, he often catches sight of the hare no one else can see; and though he cannot always relate them to facts, his ideas are interesting and original. This is characteristic of him; again and again we find him in new shoes, tripping on laces he has neglected to tie. He tells us that in poetry each syllable is a chord, like a chord in music, and that these poetic chords *modulate* as he says chords modulate in music, and, though he is wrong about the facts of both poetry and music, and very loose in the analogy, yet he has got hold of a fact which very few writers have noticed. He points out that the letter sounds of poetry form a sort of "key", or atmosphere of a certain colour, and that the change from one "key" or colour to another is often made through mutually related sounds. This, it seems to me, is a valuable suggestion. I wish he had stated it without the musical analogy, which, strictly speaking, is only a metaphor; and a musical metaphor is the one sort of metaphor we may not use when treating of the relationship between music and poetry. The analogy is not precise enough. If it were, we should have a giddy time in poetry, to say the least of it, modulating every third bar or so. Then how many letters should we allot to each key, and which? Presumably, in his example from Milton, *p*, *f*, *a* and *u* form the characterising notes of one key, *b*, *a* and *s* of another, *w* and *sp* of the third, the other letters being either negligible or common to all three.

* p. 165.

How many keys can poetry have, and does anything prevent p, f, a, u, w, sp, b and s etc. from combining in innumerable ways to form innumerable keys? Can we say that y never occurs in certain keys, or y and z never occur together, or is poetry as fond of chromatics as of modulation? The whole thing is too vague and vaporous to have an analogy in the keys of music. We may say of Thelwall's verse without an s, that s is not in its key, or that Lanier in his freak verse makes the change from key to key too abruptly. But this is a precious way of talking, and tells us nothing more than that Thelwall's verse has no sibilant, and that Lanier's vowel music is crude and monotonous, changing its colour in sudden jerks, or, to use Raymond's word, has no vowel gradation. We gain nothing by the musical analogy; it clouds the meaning. In his last example, from Tennyson, what right has Raymond to call *was* a dominant seventh? On his own showing it is rather a chord from the "key" of the second line than in this key; or is it the dominant seventh of this key and the tonic seventh of the last? But when are we to stop conjecturing? How shall we decide where we cross the border into nonsense? We have no litmus paper to distinguish the alkaline of our fancy from the bite of fact. Besides, anyone who disagrees with Raymond may nearly always confound him by his own examples. I think he has no satisfactory illustration of "dissonance". He* gives this:

> What! keep a week away? seven days and nights?
> Eight score eight hours? and lovers' absent hours,
> More tedious than the dial eight score times?
> *Othello*, III, Sc. IV.

Presumably he refers only to consonants, though he may conceivably think the vowels "dissonant" too. After all, if "keep a week away?" has "dissonant" consonants, why

* pp. 142, 159.

not "dissonant" vowels? I can recollect no "dissonant" passages in literature, though there may be some. When I try to write a sentence without either phonetic gradation or echo of any sort, I become annoyed before I solve the riddle. Poetry undoubtedly has phonetic gradation; but with letters so closely related, and with a relationship so interwoven, melting into the memory of each other so easily, it is difficult to find in our literature a sentence to illustrate this "dissonance". Perhaps we should find it in the writings of blind deaf-mutes, whose words, as Mr. Wallace* tells us, are nearly ideographs, not things implying sound; or perhaps not there, for words themselves were formed by our sense of music. English almost inevitably sounds melodious to English ears. It is significant that we do not decline even the second person singular of our verbs in some such form as "sangslb thou" or "thou comegtm". We hardly realise how musical we are, till we begin to imagine how unmusical we might be.

Let us analyse one of Raymond's examples of "*Abruptness as distinguished from gradation*":

†The following might be termed an artistic abruptness intended to represent the sense:

> Though the yesty waves
> Confound and swallow navigation up;
> Though bladed corn be lodg'd, and trees blown down;
> Though castles topple on their warders' heads;
> Though palaces and pyramids do slope
> Their heads to their foundations; though the treasure
> Of nature's germens tumble all together,
> Even till destruction sicken—answer me
> To what I ask you.

> *Macbeth*, IV, Sc. 1.

This is an interesting illustration. An abrupt break does occur at "answer me" in the second last line. "answer me

* *The Musical Faculty*, pp. 98-100.   † p. 166.

To what I ask you" is in a different colouring from the rest of the sentence. But this is not the abruptness he appears to indicate. Raymond's way of working appeals to poetical people, because he seems to rely more on his subjective impressions than on a punctilious observation of facts; we can say with some satisfaction: "Well, anyway he's not a scientist!" He appears to have chosen this passage because it gave him a sensation of abruptness, not because he computed the number of related sounds like a counting machine, and found the number small. Now the sensation of tumultuousness, or abruptness, depends not on the stringing together of unrelated sounds, but on the quality of the related sounds used. The gradation is only a little more subtle than that in his extract from Milton illustrating gradation. We can explain the musical effect thus: "yesty waves" gives the sound of choppy water, *ye* being a sharp, barking sound, and *st* cutting the vowel up with a spitting noise; "wave" suggests its meaning almost onomatopoeically. "Confound" and "swallow" have sea-sounding vowels; the *w*s and *l*s of "swallow" are liquid, water sounds; *sw* echoes *st* of "yesty", the *s* being liquefied in *w* instead of terminated in *t*. "Navigation" sounds hard; if we may be a little fanciful, and please let us, the *n*s and *g* sound like water knocking against a ship. "Up" stops us with a jerk. In the next line, in spite of its change of scene, "bladed" echoes "waves", "corn" "confound", "lodged" "swallow" and "confound", "down" "confound". "Trees blown down" imitates the buffets of a gusty wind; the "bladed", "blown" alliteration is a rough one. The sound of "bladed" *modulates* or rather grades into that of "lodged" and "blown" by a heavy gradation. The consonants are related: *t* and *d*, *r* and *l*, *wn* in "blown" and "down". In the next line "castles" echoes "corn", "trees" and "yesty"; the *d* of the preceding line appears now as *t*, changing

again through *th* to *d*; the *b*s have turned into the *p*
of "topple", which links them to the alliteration of the
next line; "warder" echoes "swallow" and "waves"; *c*,
p, *t*, and *d* and *s* close on some other consonant, make
hard noisy sounds—"castles", "warders", "heads". The
next line emphasises *p* and *s*, "palaces" and "pyramids"
do slope, while *l* and *r* still continue. In the succeeding
line we find "heads" again; "foundations" recompounds
the closing syllables of "confound" and "navigation";
"treasure" echoes "trees" and "yesty". In the next
line "nature" has the vowel of "bladed" and "palace" and
the ending of "treasure"; *t* is emphasised; "tumble" is a
mutation of "topple"; "germens" reflects "treasure" and
"pyramids"; "together" has affinities with "germens". In
the line after that, "till" joins the *t* and *l* sounds which,
with their relatives *d*, *p*, *b* and *r*, give character to the
whole passage; "destruction" emphasises *d*, *t*, *r*; *s* and *k*
in "sicken" are distant relatives of *t*. The vowel colours
change abruptly in "answer me To what I ask you",
though "answer" and "ask" have the consonants of
"sicken" and *w* has some feeling of *y* in it, not that
either is a strong consonant in this context. "Though"
binds the whole passage together in sound as well as
grammatically.

This analysis is anything but close; we have by no
means exaggerated the interrelatedness of the vowel and
consonant sounds. And these echoes are not incidental;
they count. The redistribution of the same sounds in new
patterns makes its effect as part of the beauty. Indeed,
combined with the inflection tunes, this subtle interweaving of sounds in all degrees of relationship makes half
the music we hear in poetry. Just as we can analyse any
given rhythm but not find rules for its composition, so we
may analyse any piece of well-sounding verse but cannot find rules for its composition. Each individual poet

requires a separate code of laws for his letter music as well as for his rhythms. The rules which Wordsworth's sounds obey differ from those obeyed by Milton's, and still more do Milton's laws differ from Spenser's.

The study of phonetics helps to explain the music of poetry in yet another way. When we read nothing but the best poetry, we begin to feel as if, words being such tuneful things, to write untuneful poetry were impossible. The miracle seems a commonplace. But very great poets some-times write mistuned poetry, giving us the uncomfortable feeling of music rendered out of tune. We located the out-of-tuneness of one of Yeats's poems in the inflection melody;* but what makes the inflection flat? The words form the only tangible things in the poetry books; it looks as if the letter music influenced the inflection tune. Vowels, as we already said, perhaps influence the inflection to come on those notes which will give a related fundamental to their characteristic pitch; they may do more than this, possibly giving us a sense of scale. To illustrate some point Ellis† strung these words together:

pit, pet, pat, pot, put.

They go down a scale, a ladder of sound, from "pit" to "put", rung upon rung. Experiment shows that the partials which characterise their vowels go down like that; but not only these partials, the notes of the fundamental, or inflection, come down the scale too. As I say them they

descend by semitones:  . Our

pit, pet, pat, pot, put.

sense of the high characterising pitch of "pit" keeps the fundamental high, or, more likely, the shaping of the mouth to resonate the high partial makes a relatively

* p. 58.   † *The Alphabet of Nature*, p. 63.

highly pitched inflection the easier. At all events, vowels
may determine or influence the inflections of speech.

Consonants probably influence vowels and through
them the inflection. Perhaps one has no right to give
personal observations as facts on ground which science
can investigate. But science has not yet investigated,* and
it is more difficult to analyse by machinery than by ear.
Hardly anyone has "tackled" or even asked the question:
"What influence have consonants on the pitch of vowels?"
A study of sound changes in language shows how consonants alter the vowels and the vowels change the consonants. More than this, a vowel may affect not only its preceding consonant but the vowel before that.† The vowel
i tends, or at one period in the past, tended to raise the
pitch of the preceding vowel; hence *Cam* and *Cambridge*.
But we do not need to go to history to find vowels influ-
encing their consonants. There is really no such thing
as an unattached consonant, a *t*, a *b* or an *m*. We
cannot articulate *t* or *b* or *m* without a ghost vowel.
If we articulate *t* with the mouth in the *a* shape, the
rudiments of the *a* vowel sound too; if in the shape for
u, there is a ghost *u*; and the mouth must be in some
shape when we articulate *t*; *t* is not so much a sound
as a method of attacking a sound. In articulating English
words we shape our mouth to form the vowel, then strike

* M. Rousselot (quoted by Scripture, *Elements of Experimental
Phonetics*, p. 483, from *Les modifications phonétiques du langage*) discovered among other things that in French:

1. An isolated vowel has no fixed pitch for the "cord tone".

2. The cord tone of consonants is usually higher than for vowels.

3. "Generally, the approximation of a vowel and a consonant raises
the pitch of the consonant and lowers that of the vowel."

In America (*ibid.*, p. 42):

"The short vowels in *an, en, etc.*, alter their tones as they are about
to change into the following consonants."

† Besides the proof of this given by the history of language changes,
experiments in phonetics show it (*ibid.*, p. 122).

the consonant, and the shape of the mouth alters the sound of the consonant. The *t*s of "tatter", "tot", "tent" all differ, the *b*s of "bat", "bot", "bent", the *d*s of "dash", "dot", "dent", the *p*s of "pat", "pot", "pent", the *g*s of "get" and "got", the *c*s of "came", "come", "Kent". We hear a difference between the *m*s of "man" and "men", the *f*s of "father" and "fool". Letters are only the approximate symbols for the sounds of words. Here is one benefit of our eccentric spelling, which, like most eccentricities, is logical from its own point of view; it throws the symbolic nature of our alphabet into relief.

We know that birds do not articulate letters, yet we can spell their song, just as we spell poetry:

> *Swee! Swee! Swee! Swee!
> Zweé-o! Zweé-o! Zweé-o! Zweé-o!
> Sis'-is-is Sweé! Sis'-is-is-Sweé!
> Joo! Joo! Joo! Joo!
> Jeé-o! Jeé-o! Sis'sy-sejoó!
> Jit', jit, jit', jit, jit, jit! Dzoó!
> Zeé! Wee, weé, wee! Sis'-is-is-Sweé!
> Sweé-o, Sweé! Sweé-o, Sweé!
> Sweé, swee, sweé, swee, sweé, swee! Sweé!

Anyone who has not merely heard but listened to the lark can recognise his song from this transcription, especially in the sound of "Swee" or "Zwee", yet no one would think of saying that it is compounded of $s + w + ee$. The lapwing does not really say "peeweet", nor the cat "meouw". And our speech no more resembles our letters than "peeweet" resembles the call of the lapwing. We have to be educated into interpreting the sounds of our speech as letters, and some of us remember what a difficult job it was. If we had not been taught to spell, we should never have thought words were made up of letters. A letter is not a sound, merely a hieroglyphic. A word being one

* Garstang, *Songs of the Birds*, p. 49.

continuous though changing sound, it is not surprising that consonants influence their vowels, and vowels their consonants; they are part of each other.* And just as the vowels determine the quality of the consonants, so the consonants determine the precise pitch of the vowels. Thus it seems to me that the *a* of "fair", "praise", "blame" goes down in pitch from "fair" to "blame", that the *a* of "pray" has a lower pitch than that of "praise"; *s* keeps the pitch up; *m*, as in "blame", lowers it. The pitch of the vowel in "blaze" is nearer to that of "praise" than to that of "blame", yet it is not precisely that of "praise". "Ma" has a lower note than "mam" or "man"; "man" is higher than "mam".The *e* of "yet" is higher than that of "well"; *y* or *t* keeps the pitch up, *w* or *l* lowers it—the pitch of American "wall" has come down a lot. "Queen" has a lower *ee* than "clean"; *qu* brings the pitch down, *cl* keeps it up.

We can relate this study to poetry the more easily since it explains some of the mismanaged music of the poets. Sir Arthur Quiller Couch, talking about the Horatian "falling close" in Marvell, quotes:

> Nor called the gods, with vulgar spite,
> To vindicate his helpless right;
>   But bowed his comely head
>   Down, as upon a bed.

and gives the explanation of it:

†with its shrill, spitting, "spite"—and the sharp *i* and *s* concentrating on the labial *p*—lowered at once and dupli-

---

* Scripture, *Researches in Experimental Phonetics*, pp. 42-3, says of letters: "Not only must we say that every individual sound changes from beginning to end, but we must assert that each one develops out of the preceding sound and into the following one. In speech there is a flow of sound which cannot truthfully be represented by any spelling; there are no well-defined limits between neighbouring sounds —not only because the limits are vague, but also because there are no independent sounds to be limited. . . . Speech is a fusion and not an agglomeration." † *Studies in Literature*, p. 66.

cated as by echo in the thinner *i* and softer sibilant *v* (sp*i*te to v*i*vid)—followed by the quiet:

> But bowed his comely head
> Down . . .
> (mark the full *o*s)
> Down, as upon a bed.

Then he objects that the final rhyme spoils it. It does; the comparatively high pitch of *e* brings us up again when we ought to have faded away. Cowley uses the combination "So though" in *Awake, awake my lyre*, and Donne in the *Obsequies of Lord Harrington*—one would hardly have believed it of Donne. The *s* of "so" probably affects the vowel *o* very little; *th* of "though" damps the tone of *o*, slackens the vibrations, flattens or lowers the pitch till "though" is out of tune with "so". "So though" irritates us; after the clearer and more beautiful note is struck in "So", we feel as if "though" were the same note botched; the pitch has slipped and gone flat. "Though" is not always out of tune. In "although" we have no brilliant, insistent, clearly determined note to contrast with the deadened sound that follows, but a gliding, slurring, accommodating *al*, and we are not horrified as if by a hideous blunder.

> * To the deep, to the deep,
> Down, down!

does not sound in tune. *Th* has pulled "the" down to the sound "th'" pronounced with the ghost *e*, not the full *e* sound of *thee*. "To th' market" or "to th' room" make a melodious enough progression, but when we combine *th'* with "deep", whose *p* keeps the pitch of the vowel very high, the words sound out of tune with each other. The slightly flattened "th'" vowel and the slightly sharpened "deep" make the interval just too large. Then "deep"

---

* Shelley, *Prometheus Unbound*, II (3), 54.

followed by "down" sounds out of tune again. When we change:

> To th' deep, to th' deep,
> Down, down!

to:

> To thee dee, to thee dee,
> Dow, dow!

the intervals come right. It is interesting that although

> . . . deep,
>
> Down . . .

makes an unpleasant sound, "deep down in th' earth" does not offend us. "Down" following close on "deep" does away with the *staccato* finish of the *p*; the *d* following so closely lowers the pitch in the same way as "bridge" heightened the vowel of "cam". That Shelley's ear for pitch was not always precise does not necessarily mean that, like Yeats, he has no ear for tune. His inflection tunes, as far as I have noticed, are at least inoffensive; but neither is his ear for pitch delicate, nor his taste in sound fine. He has a sense of the music of words, but no nice discrimination in it.

> *The tumult of thy mighty harmonies
> Will take from both a deep, autumnal tone,
> Sweet though in sadness.

"Deep autumnal tone" sounds a mighty music, and surely ought not to lead us to a lump of sugar like "sweet". This is not exactly out of tune, but gives us a feeling of no relationship, as if we had put our foot in a hole and pitched headlong. The out-of-tuneness of vowels lies in the pitch of their characterising partials, their quality is wrong. But these false qualities may communicate their falseness to the inflection. A reproduction of the phonograph record

* *Ode to the West Wind.*

given by Scripture in his "Inscriptions of Speech"* suggests this. "Whale" (*hwale*) pronounced with its *h* appears to have a lower fundamental than "wail"; *h* like *th* tends to lower the pitch of the vowel.

Except for some of the second person singulars of our verbs, I think English, used properly, has no really unmelodious words, and perhaps few that, if properly mauled, cannot become unmusical. We hardly realise that when we write prose we are really writing music. But besides being more or less grammatical, clear, expressive, delightful in idea or imagery, to give pleasure, even mere prose must be tuneful. Words, being musical sounds, jar on our sense of music when compounded unmusically.

* *Volta Review*, July 1920. My inference from the reproduction of a record taken on a revolving drum.

CHAPTER III

HOW THE MEANING USES THE MUSIC OF WORDS

WE have shown that words are musical sounds adapted to convey meaning, but the meaning is the prior thing; and we should put the problem of relating sense and sound in the form: "How does the meaning express itself in the sound?" rather than: "How does the sound express the meaning?" Possibly the most ancient and certainly the most primitive and the most universally intelligible language is a gesture one. Although in cultured society this method has gone out, or is used only partially and exceptionally, we can understand how vitally significant gestures once were, and indeed still are, not only in conveying meaning but in relieving feeling, if we notice the effect of "wrong" gestures in the surviving gesture arts, as we might call them—sculpture, dancing, acting, and the painting of living things. Thus owing to a "wrong" posture in the well-known picture called *The Angelus*, what was meant presumably for religious emotion has come out superficial sentiment. The theme is not necessarily sentimental, nor are the feelings of the figures, supposing them alive, necessarily superficial, but their attitude outrages our sense of significant gesture. Every action or posture we see in life is not an expressive gesture revealing feeling. *The Angelus posture*, though copied from life, makes a conventional sign, not a spontaneous movement translating emotion into action. It is in absolute contradiction; the figures stand

231

with bent heads. The standing religious attitude results from exalted feeling. A congregation rises to sing by a natural and spontaneous act; we do not say "Hallelujah" with eyes on the ground. On the other hand, a religious feeling that casts down the eyes should cast down the body too. The figures in the picture should kneel at least, and they would kneel in matter-of-fact reality if the ground were not damp. Here is a miserable conceding of the soul's expression to the prose of a damp world. Such a static gesture strikes us as "wrong" only less than the absurd attitude of those angels of peace or hope which used to come from Germany and fly over our cities on picture post-cards. They suffered from a misplaced centre of gravity. If one could but draw!

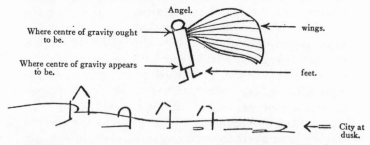

We feel at once that there is something wrong with angels like this, even if we have studied neither dynamics nor the flight of birds. It takes some time for a brain incapable of translating vision into line to locate the error, to discover that if you give an angel the wings of a sea-gull you must give it the flight of a sea-gull too—but the disturbed, unconvinced sensation is there from the beginning. We may not locate the error in *The Angelus*, but we get the sense of superficial sentiment almost at once. We, who no longer point at the things we indicate, still remain so sensitive to the meaning of gestures that a contradiction in gesture expression upsets the balance of our emotions no less inevitably than a dynamic absurdity like a wrong attitude in an angel.

Some students of language trace the origin of speech to vocal gesture. The sounds we represent by letters involve actions or posturings of the lips, tongue, jaws, vocal cords and lungs; and these make the gestures of speech. Edward Tylor in *Primitive Culture* tells how certain Brazilian tribes make

*the words "wood-go" serve to say, "I will go into the wood", by pointing the mouth like a snout in the direction meant . . . such expression by feature itself acts as a formative power in vocal language. . . . The bodily attitude brought on by a particular state of mind affects the position of the organs of speech, both the internal larynx, *etc.*, and the external features whose change can be watched by the mere looker-on.

The letters are gestures. Language originates in exclamation, in vocal action resulting from feeling.

One of the marks of gesture language is its universality, a gesture meaning the same thing to the Tahitian native as to us; a striking thing about vocal gestures likewise is their universality.

†The sound *m'm, m'n*, made with the lips closed, is the obvious expression of the man who tries to speak, but cannot. Even the deaf-and-dumb child makes this noise to show that he is dumb.

We spell this noise "mum"; the Tahitian word meaning to be silent resembles this sound. We are also told that:

‡there is a remarkable tendency among the most distant and various languages of the world . . . to use vowel sounds, with soft or hard breathing, to express "yes" and . . . nasal consonants to express "no". . . . It is an old

---

* pp. 149-50.   † Vol. i, p. 168.
‡ p. 175, order of sentences changed.

suggestion that the primitive sound of such words as *non* is a nasal interjection of doubt or dissent.

We use this nasal gesture to give a doubting or undecided assent, "m'yes". Then* "ma-ma" and "pa-pa" mean the same thing all the world over, save that our "ma" may be someone else's "pa" and *vice versa*, or the letters may be reversed and "ap" or sometimes "at" or "ta" mean father and "am" or "na" mother.

†The languages of the lower races use *pu* = evil smell. The Zulu remarks that "the meat says pu" . . . Timorese has *poop* = putrid.

We use the same gesture to "poo-poo" things. The Zulu's disgust has turned into our contemptuous disregard. On the other hand, the natives of the New Hebrides hiss their approval, the Veddas of Ceylon their disapproval.‡ Some audiences in this country stamp their assent, others their dissent.

Similar to exclamatory, involuntary gestures and as universal are imitative ones.

§In remote and most different languages we find such forms as *pu, puf, bu, buf, fu, fuf*, meaning *puffing, fuffing* or *blowing*. Natives call a gun *pu* from the puff of smoke.

M. Taine, who studied the origin of language in the child, not in the primitive race, notices a gesture between the exclamatory and the imitative—"ham", used by a tiny child meaning something to eat, or I want to eat.

‖On listening [he says] attentively and attempting to reproduce it, we perceive that it is the *natural vocal gesture* of a person snapping up anything.

* pp. 202-4.   † p. 179.   ‡ p. 178.
§ p. 184 paraphrased.
‖ Quoted from *Mind*, vol. ii, p. 256, in a review of M. Taine's *Acquisition of Language by Children*.

In his *Observations on the Correspondence between Poetry and Music*, Daniel Webb says:

*Some imitations act with the united powers of sound and motion as—sob, gulp, clap, thump, bounce, burst; in others, the organs of speech seem to undergo the very operation specified, as may be experienced in some of the examples already given, and still more forcibly, perhaps, in the words—grind, screw, lisp, yawn.

And Guest:

†If the mere sound of the words *hiss* and *bah* recall the cry of the animal, so may the muscular action, which the organs exert in pronouncing the words *struggle, wrestle,* call up in the mind the play of muscle and sinew.

We might add to these indefinitely. Some of them, however, are not strictly speaking either exclamatory or directly imitative. They involve what we might call analogy gestures. Wedgwood, in *The Origin of Language*, quotes Augustine thus:

‡But because there are things which do not sound, with these the similitude of touch comes into play, so that if the things are soft or rough to the touch, they are fitted with names that by the nature of the letters are felt as soft or rough to the ear. Thus the word *lene*, soft, itself sounds soft to the ear. . . . As honey is sweet to the taste, so the name, *mel*, is felt as soft by the ear . . . *Lana*, wool, and *vepres*, briars, affect the ear in accordance with the way in which the things signified are felt by touch.

He then says§ that since *b, d, g, p, t,* and *k* "stop the emission of the breath"‖ we employ them

§to signify a movement abruptly checked as . . . *jag, jog, jig, dag, dig, stagger, job, jib, rug, tug . . . zigzag.*

* p. 64.   † *History of English Rhythms*, p. 17.
‡ p. 107.   § pp. 109-10.
‖ Quoted from Müller.

Notice, he continues,* the difference in meaning between
tot, titter, tottle, or the difference a vowel can make to this
sort of gesture analogy:

†trap	trip.
sup	sip.
top	tip.
nab	nib.

‡The consciousness of forcing the voice through a
narrow opening in the pronunciation of the sound *ee*
leads to the use of syllables like *peep, keek, teet,* [*teeny-
weeny*].

§A ringing or prolonged sound is commonly represented by a syllable ending with one of the liquids *l, m, n,
ng, r.*

He compares *squeak* and *squeal* or *clap, rap, rat-tat-tat*
with *knell, boom, din, ring, clang.* Then, high-pitched
sounds like *ee* represent near events, low-pitched sounds
events far off:

‖The device [says Tylor] of conveying different ideas
of distance by the use of a graduated scale of vowels seems
to me one of great philological interest, from the suggestive
hint it gives of the proceedings of the language-makers in
most distant regions of the world, working out in various
ways similar ingenious contrivance of expression by sound.
A typical series is the:

Javan:	*iki* =this (close by);
	ika =that (at some distance);
	iku =that (furthest off). . . .
Malagasy:	*ao* =there (at a short distance);
	eo =there (at a shorter distance);
	io =there (close at hand);
	atsy =there (not far off);
	etsy =there (nearer);
	itsy =this or these. . . .

Canarese: *ivanu* = this;
              uvanu = that (intermediate);
              avanu = that.
Tamil: *î* = this; *a* = that.
Rajmahali: *îh* = this; *âh* = that.
Dhimal: *isho, ita* = here; *usho, uta* = there . . .
Abchasian: *abri* = this; *ubri* = that.
Ossetic: *am* = here; *um* = there.
Magyar: *ez* = this; *az* = that.
Zulu: *apa* = here; *apo* = there.
  lesi, leso, lesiya = this, that, that (in the distance);
  abu, abo, abuya = this, that, that (in the distance).

[In some languages the meaning is reversed.]

Yoruba: *na* = this; *ni* = that.
Fernandian: *olo* = this; *ole* = that.
Tumale: *re* = this; *ri* = that;
              ngi = I; *ngo* = thou; *ngu* = he.
Sapatin: *kina* = here; *kuna* = there.

*He quotes Max Müller to show how vowels may express difference of sex:

Finnic: *ukko* = old man; *akka* = old woman.
Mangu: *ama* = father;   *eme* = mother.
Carib: *baba* = father;   *bibi* = mother.

I should say the terminations of the Latin declensions were built on some such plan, *a* being the feminine vowel:

Masculine.	Feminine.	Neuter.
unus	una	unum.
unum	unam	unum.
uni	unae	uni, *etc.*

and the same in the plural. So we have:

	hic	haec	hoc.
	hunc	hanc	hoc, *etc.*
or	is	ea	id, *etc.*
or	qui	quae	quod, *etc.*

* p. 201.

French shows the same thing in *la*, *le*, *etc.* We preserve the distinction for distance in *this*, *that*, and *these*, *those*. Possibly the *ablaut* of our strong verbs results from this:

sing	sang	sung.
drive	drove.	
see	saw.	
be	was.	

—a high vowel for the present, a low for the past, and a still lower for the finished past; and so it is in all the Aryan tongues, although many of the old forms have died out in English.

This remoter sort of imitative gesture is perhaps the most important and certainly the most interesting of them all, this parallel between the world in our experience and the sounds we make—our speech a mirror in sound of the universe. We need hardly dwell on the onomatopoeic power of words—it is obvious; but we may spend a little time considering them as actions. When we hear or read a word, the sound sensation we get includes the feeling of the word in the mouth as well as its music in the ear.* Passages of Swinburne's poetry, where *s* and the vowel of *sweet* dominate, make us feel almost as if we were eating sugar; the words feel sweet in our mouths; the sounds are sweet to taste rather than to hear. But normally we do not notice verbal gesticulations though we feel their significance, just as, though we may feel its insignificance, we may not think of the *Angelus* attitude as a static gesture. We call words like *warble* and *trill* onomatopoeic, when they really imitate not so much by onomatopoesis as by the trilling gesture of the tongue on the *r*s and *ll*s. *Tumble* is a vocal gesture giving us a different feeling from *fall*, which in a sense is a continuous motion like *flow* where the breath starts with easy egress in *f* and flows through the liquid *l* into the continuing vowel, or in *fall* through the vowel to

* Wundt, *Principles of Physiological Psychology*, p. 310.

the *l*. A *tumble* is a *turn*ing over descent, the vocal action
turns over but not as it does in *churn*, where the trilling *r*
lends itself to a continued turning. If we *st*op before we
tumble, then we *stumble*; the sibilant arrest*s* the fall. In
wallow the sounds turn, but without the firmness of those
in *tumble*; we wallow in s*l*ime and tumble on something
ha*rd*, and churn *r*ound and *r*ound. Then *wield* runs with a
certain gathering-up laboriousness through its easy though
accumulating liquids* to *d*, where the action ends de-
cisively, finishe*d*. In *heave* the effort comes first, and the
wave or wallow motion after. *Weave* differs from *wave* in
a higher, narrower vowel, as if the waving action were
being directed through narrow holes. The finished article
is a *web*, which differs from *weave* as *wollop* from *wallow*,
in its decisive, finished, achieved ending. *Ending* likewise
has a continuing *ring*, different from the end of end*ed*. Or
again, we make a *bubble* with our lips, and *gargle* in our
throat.

The vocal gestures represented in our *abc* came naturally, or rather inevitably, to have characteristic atmospheres
about them. The sound we write *hist* (it should really have
no vowel) is an arresting exclamation, *st* has the meaning
of *st*opping *sh*ort, of *st*and*ing on something firm, or of
*st*aying indefinitely, *etc*. according to the sounds that follow.
The sound we write *hush* (pronounced without the vowel)
makes a quietening gesture. It communicates softness and
has the feeling of something s*l*uggish or squa*sh*y; hence
crush—different from *crunch*, where the bones remain hard
to the end, *slush*, *mush*, *mash*, and so on. At the beginning
of a word *sh* feels different. We say *shoo* to drive hens out
of the garden; hence perhaps *shoot*. It may mean other
things too, *shore*, *shoal*, *shiver*, but we feel a latent affinity
in them all. *C* initially, especially with *l* or *r*, gives us a
*cl*ear, *cl*ean, *cr*ystal, *cr*ysolite, *c*ut effect. Mr. Loane, writing

---

* Using "liquid" metaphorically, not as a technical phonetic term.

to the *Times Literary Supplement*,* says it has a *c*ursing, threatening sound, among his examples being *clove*, *clarion*, *clang*, *cloud*; but the cursing *c* resembles the cutting one, certainly in *clove*, *clang*, *clarion*, *cloud*; a *curse* has a sharper edge than a *damn*; it hits out with a knife, not with a bludgeon. While the bad temper of civilised man resorts only to cutting or heavy sounds, a more brutal wrath *snaps* or *snarls*; *sna* draws the lips back from the teeth as a dog's lips *curl* when he snaps or snarls; whereas *snap* ends the action with a sudden closure, as of the child who said "ham" for food, *r* and *l* prolong it in *growl*ing trills. *Sneeze* and *snuff*, too, are imitative gestures. Trilled *r*, especially with a *u* or *o* vowel, gives a *horrid*, *rough* effect; we have *hurricane*, *rude*, *crude*, *rugged*, *rock*. *F* breathing through the lips and teeth is the consonant for *flight*, *fast*, *fleet*, *fish*, *forth*, or lightly blown things such as *fluff*, or *f*rail or *f*eeble things. *M* is expressive as a considering consonant in *mean* and *moot*, a heavy one in *more*, *much*, *smudge*, *masculine* (cf. *feminine* with its lighter consonants and higher vowels), and is directly onomatopoeic in *moan*. Loane says it is soft, and gives *mater*, *mulier*, *melior*. Perhaps this comes from its bleating sound, as in *mercy* and *me*. *N* is not quite so heavy or so soft, but more final and decisive, as in *near*, *neat*, *nought*, *no*. Final stopped consonants curtail the sound, cu*t* it shor*t*, as we already noticed; *soot* and *smut* aligh*t* or sto*p*; on the same principle *p* turns *flow* into *flop*; *t* is often a *little*, *tot*, *tiny* sound and can be very *p*erjin*k* as in *tip-toe*; *tut* relieves a light feeling of arrested effort, and is not final like *dud*. *D* makes a *d*oughty gesture, a *d*readful soun*d* suitable to *d*ungeons or *dudgeon*. Loane noticed this, and gives among others *decision* (*decided* is more so), *despair* and *dread*, or this from Swinburne:

> Leap into lustrous life and laugh and shine,
> And darken into swift and dim decline.

* September 12th, 1918.

*Loane calls *p* contemptuous, and quotes "a poor, paltry prelate, proud of petty popularity, and perpetually preaching to petticoats." *P*, like *d* and *b*, can also be energetic and muscular. *Proud*, *popular*, and perhaps *prelate* are not always contemptuous, though possibly always haughty. In *purple*, *pompous*, *pulpous* it has a full round richness. Then we notice the bigness of *b*. With a liquid or an oily vowel it *boils* or *bubbles*; with a stopped ending it makes a *blob* or, more liquidly, a *blobule*. Hence too, *bloom*. Saintsbury, who disapproves of looking at words in this way, refers to the statement that the *oo* sound of *gloom* is

†peculiarly adapted to express horror, solemnity, awe, . . slowness of motion, darkness, and extreme or oppressive size,

and turns to *bloom*, which in addition starts off on our big rounded consonant, and ends with the ending of *boom*, and says "Does it?" Yes, of course it does. Although it sounds no knell, *bloom* is yet first brother to *gloom* and *doom*; add but an *in'* and see. It gesticulates a big bubble instead of a big catastrophe or a big depression, the bloom of a rose being a full *b*lown *b*eauty ready to *b*urst. The word suits the rose, but is too *fool* (commonly spelt "full") for cherry or apple *blossom*; they need a diminutive with lighter vowels and bright *ss* to separate the heavy consonants— a lot of little blooms. A bloom can never be either *f*eeble or *f*rail, even *blossom* being too cu*m*brous for wood-sorrel. We must have *flower* for the sorrel, which is delicately formed as if by a whisper of the wind. *Bloom*, *blossom*, *flower*, though in their way synonyms, have different atmospheres, different shades of meaning, due to the different colouring of their sound. *Beauty*, *lovely*, and *pretty* form another trio distinguished in the same way, beauty being a bigger thing

* *Times Literary Supplement*, August 22nd, 1918. Incidentally, his study of the meaning of letters is very good.
† *History of English Prosody*, vol. iii, p. 495.

than loveliness, which is a little frail, though a sound to *l*inger over; and prettiness, with its stopped consonants and high vowel, being distinct from both in a certain li*tt*leness. But we must not run such comparisons too closely. If we have many sorts of *b*, then we must have many meanings for *b*. Yet just as all *b*s sound like each other, so their meanings are similar. The clenched fist which a clergyman bangs on the pulpit in the out-of-the-way fastnesses of religion means something different from the clenched fist he shakes at the boy who has raided his orchard, yet they have a similar atmosphere; a clenched fist expresses something different from an open hand; it means intensity of some sort, even if it be an intense control. Nor must we dogmatise too much on the distinction between analogy gestures and direct onomatopoeia. *Splash* is onomatopoeic; *dash*, not so unlike a *splash*, an exclamatory or an analogy gesture; we cannot put all sound imitations so easily in one or the other category—*murmuring*, for instance. Even Bacon makes no distinction between them:

There is found a similitude between the sound that is made by inanimate bodies, or by animate bodies that have no voice articulate, and divers letters of articulate voices; and commonly men have given such names to those sounds as do allude unto the articulate letters; as trembling of water hath resemblance to the letter *l* [cf. the *gurgling* of a brook, or *light*], quenching of hot metals to the letter *z*, snarling of dogs with the letter *r*, the noise of screech-owls with the letter *sh*, voice of cats with the diphthong *eu* . . ., sounds of strings with the diphthong *ng*.

We do not know whether vocal gesture or direct onomatopoeia is the older or more primitive. Tylor finds both in the primitive languages he studied. Words arising by direct onomatopoeia are understood almost as universally as those which originate as vocal gestures. *The cock, pro-

* *Primitive Culture*, vol. i, p. 187.

nounced *kok* in English, is *quiquiriqui* in the Spanish nursery, *koklo, akoka, kuku, etc.* in other tongues; and our hens, as Tylor notices, *cackle*. He* associates *crack* with *kra-kra*, which in Dahomian means the watchman's rattle, with Peruvian *ccallani* meaning to break, *ccatatani* to gnash the teeth, and *ccaccaccahay* a thunderstorm. The associations of our *crack* have got smaller since Shakespeare's time; we should not now think of originating the expression "the crack of doom". In †Maori, *pata* means *patter*; primitive Australian has *pat-patin* = *pitpattering*, and so on.

It was inevitable that language should arise in these ways. ‡Even bird-speech may be just such a combination of natural vocal gesture and onomatopoeia. The easiest way to tell a tale is to act it; and the mouth, when it is clever enough, acts or represents our experiences, "imitating" both emotions and sounds. As the human mind grows, languages develop by ways which have nothing whatever to do with either imitation or gesture, depending rather on intellectual associations. Intellectual ways of making words contribute more to the bulk of our dictionaries than primitive methods, but not therefore more to the spoken or written language. We have a feeling for the meaning of sounds, an elementary sense that the sound of words reflects their meaning, and this feeling forms a vital part in our recognition of the meaning. Mrs. Malaprop has this sense too, only rather crudely; she remains insensitive to minute shades of difference, mauling her mother-tongue through sheer indelicacy. Even when words have not arisen by onomatopoeia or from vocal gesture, the vocal gesture which pronounces them colours their meaning, and through this colouring sometimes alters it. Or if the gesture does not influence the meaning, then the meaning

* pp. 191-92.
† Witchell, *The Zoologist*, 1890, "The Evolution of Bird Song".

will influence the gesture. Tylor says we tend to make words

* conform their sound to the sense. *E.g. waddle* is from Latin *vado*, to go. So *stamp* is from the root *sta* = stand. *Step* really = *foot*, from the same root.

In these, the appropriate gesture of the root words, the gesture of *vado* and of *sta*, is merely modified in the derivative. *Sta* was originally a vocal gesture, and *step* and *stamp* only particularise it further. But the same thing happens to words not originally onomatopoeic, or imitative. Max Müller noticed† that *squirrel*, though expressive of its meaning, did not originate imitatively, deriving from *skiuros* = shady tail, and that Sanskrit *mârgâra* = cat has nothing to do with purring, and means the animal that is always cleaning itself. *Squirrel* came through old French *escurel*, from low Latin *scurellus*, a diminutive of Latin *sciurus*, the same word as Greek *skiouros*, from *skia* = shade and *oura* = tail; but though the squirrel got the name from its shady tail, the gesture of that name, *skia-oura*, was somehow expressive of the squirrel, and this expressiveness possibly helped in the naming, just as an alliteration may determine a nickname appropriate in other ways. In Scotland we call the millipede "Maggie-mony-legs", *Maggie* to alliterate with *mony*; had our idiom been French, and *legs-mony* were the usual order of the words, we should probably have chosen "Lizzie-legs-mony". The expressive sound of *mârgâra* or *skia-oura* possibly helped the original description to become the permanent name, for we need not suppose that cleanliness was the only striking attribute of the cat, or its shady tail of the squirrel. The squirrel might have been called, and perhaps was called, the nut-cracker, the tree-weasel, the bright-eyed one, the leaf-imp, and the cat, the little tiger, the spitting one, the mouse-

---

* pp. 194-5.　　† *The Science of Language*, vol. i, pp. 505-6.

killer, the purring animal. But *skia-oura* for Greek and *mârgâra* for Sanskrit, or *cat* for us, had the quality of survival, being expressive. Latin *sciurus* was not expressive enough, so *scurellus* ousted it. *Cat*, though expressive, sounds too catty for the cat-lover, our more affectionate gesture for the domestic pet being *puss*, perhaps because it combines *purr* and a spit. On the other hand, we say "a stray cat", not a "stray puss". In this way our feeling for the fitness of words to express sense still influences our language, checking inexpressive derivation and encouraging expressive. It was the mother of language, and, like all parents, gives up its authority reluctantly. At all events, there is, as Earle* put it, "running through a great part of human speech, a remarkable chime of sound with sense." In everyday talk which is fully alive we use words for their sounds, and invent slang on the same principle.

†Take [says Wedgwood] an instance from the first novel that comes to hand:

"Then came a light *pattering* of feet, the *flutter* of a muslin dress, the *resonant bang* of a heavy door; and the *prettiest* woman I had ever seen in my life came *tripping* along the churchyard path."

We might add to Wedgwood's underlined words perhaps "first", "light", "heavy", "had", "seen", "path", and even "take", "an", "from", "comes", "came", "hand", "muslin" despite its intellectual derivation, "door", "woman", "life" with its frail and fleeting consonants. Indeed, in every word of this sentence the gesture may have helped the meaning.

No one is more aware of the correspondence of sense and sound than the poet, and no poet makes fuller use of this knowledge than Milton. "Through each high

---

* *Philology of the English Tongue*, p. 625.
† *The Origin of Language*, p. 130.

street"* shows what *h* may do, especially when two come together.

> Clashed on their sounding shields the din of war,
> Hurling defiance toward the vault of Heaven.
>
> (*P. L.* i, 668-9.)

The sound imitates the meaning in close detail—"Clashed", "sounding", "shields", "din", "war". The *cl*, *sh*s, *d*s, and *n*s of this noisy line take, as it were, direction in the *H* of "Hurling", which trills into *ing*, debouching on "defiance", directed by the *t* of "toward" (*t* being a pointing consonant, as in *to*, or its brother *th* in *there*, *this*, *that*) to the hollow and vast reverberation of the "vault of Heaven". But we cannot quote the whole of *Paradise Lost*, nor will the reader have forgotten Spenser's "sea-shouldering whales" or "Eftsoones they heard a most melodious sound", nor how Tennyson can sound like the sea and water lapping on cliffs. We would not illustrate the obvious, but for the pleasure of dwelling on a pleasant theme.

English lends itself to this subtle imitation of the sense by the sound, having few declensional or conjugational endings to distract from the characteristic sound of the words themselves.

> Abortive as the first-born bloom of spring
> Nipt with the lagging rear of winter's frost.
>
> (*Samson*, 1577.)

"Abortiva as firsta borna blooma springis" may not detract much from the expressiveness of the line, though it substitutes *a* for the sounding letter in place of *b*; but "nipt" and "frost" would lose all their expressiveness if we had to say "niptata frostae". The Latin way is clumsy and inert compared with our own crisp "nipt" and "frost".

---

* *Samson Agonistes*, for further illustration from which and from the *Eve of St. Agnes* see *The Real Rhythm in English Poetry*, by the present writer.

The much-derided monosyllable allows a more varied music than the classical tongues can indulge. If *frost* must always have an *a* attached to it, we cannot use it in a context where *a* is not wanted; it is as if we had always to strike E in music when we want to use C. And besides allowing more variety they make poetry neat, delicate, dainty, in a way no richly declined or conjugated language can ever hope to be. We often hear English abused as unmusical, and are told that other than musical considerations mould our language, our deplorable monosyllabic vocabulary being attributed to an abrupt, slipshod way of snipping off endings and running syllables together. It is a libel. We snip off endings and run syllables together with a sense of music, with an English impatience of the slovenly or clumsy. Cumbrous conjugational terminations are ugly, too ugly for everyday use; we cannot bear such monstrous noises on our lips every minute, and when our poets use an archaic survival such as the 2nd personal singular they commonly prefer bad grammar to impossible sound. This lament over our lost endings comes of our mediæval drilling in Latin; we are still under the rule of pedagogues dead centuries ago. No one considers our music inferior to that of the Russians or Germans. We thank our stars for having no *Londoniviskis* and sorrow over our escape from *Cantabrigiensis*.

We hear the same "grouse"—expressive word—about our consonants. English lacks the loveliness of the Italian liquid. English is too brisk to be beautiful. But when Milton, who was afraid of no consonant, writes:

> Smoothing the rugged brow of night,
> Not trickt and frounc't as she was wont,
> Rocking winds,

his music is not only more expressive because of the rugged consonants, but more beautiful.

> There let the pealing Organ blow,
> To the full voiced Quire below,
> In Service high, and Anthems clear.

This liquid and vowel music would be less lovely if it were not for the rougher sounds, the *s*-like sounds of "Service", "Anthems", the cut of "clear", or the *r*s in "Quire" and "Organ".* A purely vowel and liquid music is too oily for our native taste. Perhaps the music of Tennyson's *Frater Ave atque Vale* comes as near as our poetry can to the Italian ideal. How pleasantly do lines like, "There to me through all the groves", with the rasp of its *r*s,* stand out from the oily music; here is something to hold on to, grit to prevent us sprawling on the slipperiness. The pleasure this line gives shows that we really prefer the clean sounds of our own language to the more inert unctuousness of a tongue unlike our own. When it has a consonantal music poetry sparkles like a mountain rill dancing over sharp rocks and shining pebbles; in comparison the liquid music makes but a muddy river slipping between forget-me-nots. Flowering water weeds are not so natively pleasing to us as a dancing rill. It would be sad indeed were it otherwise, for all our poets love their consonants; even *s* is not despised of any of the great ones save Tennyson; it reminds Milton neither of geese nor of serpents. Not even when the final *s* meets the initial *s* does he squirm:†

> ‡His goary visage down the stream was sent,
> Down the swift Hebrus to the Lesbian shore.

Thus does water whisper among the reeds as it slips towards the roaring gulf of sea-sounding "shore". I do not know why it should ever have been said, and yet it has,

* If we articulate the "r"!

† This is the only *s* Mr. Lamborn dislikes (*Rudiments of Criticism*, p. 37): "The truth is that esses only hiss when a terminal *s* clashes with an initial one."

‡ I have not distinguished between *z* and *s* in these illustrations.

that Milton avoids *ss*. He was not a timid man. When he
has an *s* meaning, so to speak, he never hesitates to write
an *s* sound. *Lycidas* is full of *ss*, perhaps because the name
itself has two, though more probably *s* sounds there for
sighing and the noise of streams. In *Comus*, both the song
to Sabrina and Sabrina's song have this sound of the
sedges:

> Sabrina fair,
> Listen where thou art sitting
> Under the glassie, cool, translucent wave,
> In twisted braids of Lillies knitting
> The loose train of thy amber-dropping hair,
> Listen for dear honour's sake,
> Goddess of the silver lake,
> Listen and save.

And so on.

> By Thetis tinsel-slipper'd feet,
> And the Songs of Sirens sweet.

A little further on we have:

> Where young Adonis oft reposes,
>
> .   .   .   .   .
>
> In slumber soft, and on the ground
> Sadly sits th' Assyrian Queen.

Turn back the pages at random and we fall on:

> And fell Charybdis murmur'd soft applause:
> Yet they in pleasing slumber lull'd the sense,
> And in sweet madness robbed it of it self.

Or "Such sober certainty". "Narcissus" is not too hissing
for him: he writes "likest thy Narcissus". Line 132 has
"Stygian darkness spets her thickest gloom". Line 108:

> And Advice with scrupulous head,
> Strict Age, and sowre Severity,
> With their grave Saws in slumber ly.

Line 80:
> Swift as the Sparkle of a glancing Star.

Indeed, he begins the poem with this sound of song:

> Before the starry threshold of Joves Court
> My mansion is, where these immortal shapes
> Of bright aëreal Spirits live insphear'd
> In Regions milde of calm and serene Ayr,
> Above the smoke and stir of this dim spot,
> Which men call Earth.

L'Allegro can sooth us with *s* music:

> By whispering Winde*s s*oon lulled asleep;

as Satan can hiss in it:

> The Serpent subtl'st Beast of all the field
> (*P. L.* vii, 495),

while in the *Nativity Ode* final *s* touches initial *s* one dozen times. So pleased is Milton with the music of "In variou*s s*tyle" (*P. L.* v, 146) that he repeats it immediately:

> In various style, for neither various style.

Spenser no more avoids *ss* meeting thus sweetly than Milton. He gives us:

> Oft soust in swelling Tethy*s s*altish teare (1, iii, 31)

Opening Book I of *The Faerie Queene* at random I found these between two leaves:

Canto 6.

> (7). Her shrill outcryes and shrieke*s s*o loud did bray,
>
>   .   .   .   .   .   .
>
> Whiles old Sylvanu*s s*lept in shady arber sownd.
> (8). Who when they heard that pitteou*s s*trained voice,
> (10). And every tender part for feare doe*s s*hake:
> (11). And read her sorrow in her count'nan*ce s*ad;
> (12). But still twixt feare and hope amazd doe*s s*it,

(13). Their hart*s* *s*he ghesseth by their humble guise,
(14). And aged limbs on Cypres*s*e *s*tadle stout
(15). Far off he wonders, what them make*s* *s*o glad,
(16). And old Sylvanu*s* *s*elfe bethinkes not,
(18). But all the Satyre*s* *s*corne their woody kind.
(21). A Satyre*s* *s*onne yborne in forrest wyld.

One line from Shakespeare will show he did not avoid meeting *ss*—"The courtier's, soldier's, scholar's eye, tongue, sword". We could easily add to these lists others from Shakespeare, Wordsworth, Coleridge, Keats, and Shelley; indeed Coleridge is the only one who does not carry *s* about with him wherever his name goes. *S*, so far from being unlovely, may be one of the sweetest and softest of consonants. We cannot have music or song, or star, or sky, or silver seas, or whispers, breezes, or shade, or sunshine, or spring showers, roses, streams, or even solitude, silence, slumber, or sleep without the sound of *s*. Like the tone of the violin it will bear repeating for a long time without cloying. The Mu*s*es, so far from disdaining this sibilant, turn *poetry* into *poesie* when they wish to be especially melodious. Even Tennyson was not afraid to write a poem on Ulysses. He, ungrateful, was indebted to this consonant for his music more than once.

Our language has no ugly sound from *a* to *z*; English sounds can offend only when used offensively, and no sound is so beautiful that a bad use of it will not sound hideous.

> Still by the shore Alp mutely mused,
> And wooed the freshness Night diffused,

wrote Byron in *The Siege of Corinth*. "Alp mutely mused"! It is a cow's rumination. How ugly it makes "wooed" and "diffused"! These horrid sounds result not from any ugliness inherent in the sound *mu*, but from Byron's ugly use of it. Shelley writes: "Most musical of mourners", making the alliteration emphasise the vowel gradation, as poets commonly do:

One of those heavenly *d*ays that cannot *d*ie. (*Nutting*.)

By misuse *s* may sound unmusical. Tennyson objects to:

And freedom broadens slowly down.

He wrote not this, but:

And freedom slowly broadens down.

The second version may be the better. Yet we cannot improve on

His goary visage down the stream was sent.

His goary visage sent was down the stream

is not an improvement.

Nearly all my friends say to me: "Do you like Swinburne?—but *of course*, being so keen on the music of poetry, you must. His lack of meaning won't trouble you." So sure are they, that I hardly ever dare own that I cannot appreciate Swinburne. I feel troubled when his poetry is empty of meaning, and am not sure that the trouble is not partly a musical one. We ought not really to distinguish between the sense and the sound of a poem. Nothing makes music so easily as meaning. When writing nonsense Swinburne cut himself off from one of the most lovely melody makers. Our attention flags; reading him requires too much effort,* I think because the inflection tune has not enough vitality; certainly the sounds do not grip everyone. Conversely, nothing is so apt to give meaning as the sound of words; we can hardly prevent it, the ear being so sensitive to the meaning of sound.† Mr. Lamborn gives a striking example of this sensitiveness in children:

* I know this is not so for his admirers. I think they are either carried on by the rhythm, wound up by it into a pleasant fever, or soothed by the silky or furry feel of the words.

† Wundt says in his *Principles of Physiological Psychology*, p. 312: "A heard word first of all arouses a feeling for its meaning, before the

*Those who have not made such experiments will be astonished by children's intuitive insight into the meaning of mere sound—unless they happen to have really loved a dog. I lately heard a "Greats" man read a passage of Homer to some boys of twelve, who knew no language but their own; they listened breathlessly and then told him that there had been a challenge, a fight, and a song of triumph —which was really the "substance" of the passage. He then read some lines of Vergil, and they said "it was a cavalry charge"; *passer mortuus est* of Catullus, and they suggested that "some one was speaking of a dead child". Ages before articulate speech existed emotion was expressed and communicated in sound, and in poetry it is still so communicated, apart from the mere dictionary meaning of the words used.

I once asked a boy the meaning suggested by the sound of "Tendebantque manus ripae ulterioris amore", and he said he thought it was a part of the psalm that tells how by the waters of Babylon they sat down and wept.

So the music of poetry can hardly help conveying meaning. When we begin to *notice* that poetry has no meaning, this usually means that the sounds are not properly related, they have not the relation of sense. If the mere music of poetry is strong enough it will weave, if not meaning, then an atmosphere of meaning. The music of poetry is not a compound of two things, sound and meaning, but one thing, meaningful sound.

No parody can shake this truth.

> And so no force, however great,
>   Can strain a cord, however fine,
>   Into a horizontal line
> That shall be absolutely straight.

---

meaning itself has come clearly to consciousness. This order of events obtains more especially in the case of unfamiliar or entirely unknown words."

"Nonsense in grammatical form sounds half rational." (James, *Principles of Psychology*, p. 264.)

* *Rudiments of Criticism*, pp. 19-20.

Now, you may say, what has its tune to do with the feeling of *In Memoriam*? A very great deal. This parody is funny; it makes us smile. But why should it be funny? Neither the truth stated, nor the tune, have anything humorous in them. The humour consists in their incongruity. So far from disproving the close connection between the *In Memoriam* feeling and its music, the parody proves their essential congruity, by showing how ludicrous, how unfitting the tune sounds, set to a mathematical meaning. Moreover we should never notice the incongruity if this very stanza occurred in one of the philosophising passages of *In Memoriam*, and we read it half asleep. The stanza would have the right tune, therefore the right mood, and the tune and the mood would colour the meaning of the words to the right shade. Then our homophones! That one sound should mean two things is ridiculous—hence the joke of a pun. The pun is funny because it guys an eccentricity. But poetry would "dwine" and perish away if homophones abounded sufficiently to destroy our sense of meaning in sound. Shakespeare and Donne may fuse a double meaning in one word and dazzle without startling us too much by the shock, but this is taking liberties with poetry. Repetitions of the same sound do not disturb the music of poetry.

Never, never, never, never, never,

makes one of the most heartrending lines in all Shakespeare, because Lear means the same thing every time. We may say, "See! see!" or "The sea! the sea!" but not, as Mr. Bridges points out,* "I see the sea's untrampled floor." This jars. It alarms Bridges, who spreads a frightening array of homophones before us. Fortunately, however, "egg", to incite, rarely comes into the same context as the hen's "egg", and if it did, would add to the humour.

* S.P.E. Tract, No. II, *English Homophones*.

Though the ready-made departments of large shops stock
more than one frock of the same design, we are very seldom
outraged by meeting our least-loved neighbour in the same
frock as ourselves. The really dangerous homophones are
those innocent-looking words we should never suspect.
Cowley blunders into a terrible hole in *Awake, awake, my
Lyre*:

> Weak Lyre! thy virtue sure
> Is useless here, since thou art only found
>   To cure, but not to wound,
> And she to wound, but not to cure,
>   *Too* weak *too* wilt thou prove
>   My passion *to* remove;
> Physic *to* other ills, thou'rt nourishment to love.

In three lines one insignificant sound has four meanings.

Perhaps our dislike of identical rhymes results partly
because of this sensitiveness to homophones, but not altogether, since it is a late development. An identical rhyme
makes us feel as if we were not out of the bit; it makes
poetry stagnant. Hence Tennyson's repetition of "land"
to rhyme with "land" in the *Lotos-Eaters*. He says of it:

*The *strand* was, I think, my first reading, but the no-
rhyme of *land* was lazier.

Occurring in a more vigorous context an identical rhyme
bounds back like a tennis-ball forever beaten against a
wall. It can be effective:

TO CUPID.

> Fly to her heart, hover about her heart,
> With dainty kisses mollifie her heart,
> Pierce with thine arrows her obdurate heart,
> With sweet allurements ever move her heart;

* Note in the Eversley Edition, vol. i, p. 372. I quote from an
article by Mr. W. C. A. Ker, *The Times Literary Supplement*, Jan.
24, 1918.

At midday and at midnight touch her heart,
Be lurking closely, nestle about her heart;
With power (thou art a God) command her heart,
Kindle thy coales of love about her heart,
Yea ever unto thyself transforme her heart.
Ah, she must love, be sure thou have her heart,
And I must dye if thou have not her heart.
Thy bed (if thou rest well) must be her heart:
He hath the best part sure that hath the heart;
What have I not, if I have but her heart?

Says Griffin, of the sixteenth century: "And one may imagine that Cupid, with gay wings all in a flutter, is hovering just at his ear, like a humming-bird poised over a flower-bell, ready to dart off on his errand as soon as he may."*

---

* Both the sonnet and Griffin's observation are quoted from Sidney Lanier, *The Science of English Verse*, p. 304.

CHAPTER IV

HOW THE MUSIC OF POETRY MAY GUIDE THE MEANING

FEW sounds we hear die without an echo in the vaults of our mind; having got into these chambers they try to find a way out. After a concert, tags of tune sound in our memory, or more curious, months later, when we have forgotten all about them, strains of music come singing into mind. After the Greek play acted in Cambridge in 1921 a whole college rang with the *motifs* of Agamemnon and the Furies. These died. Suddenly, and for no apparent reason, some weeks later the music of Agamemnon and the Furies disturbed the peace once more. Next year Dr. Rootham's opera was performed and the tune of *The Two Sisters* sounded up and down the corridors. This died. But suddenly, and for no apparent reason, some weeks later the tune of *The Two Sisters* echoed once more in the minds and on the lips of everyone. We took the melody into our minds, and after caressing it for a bit, let it go; when it had nosed its way silently like a cat all over its new domain, it sat up and begged to be taken note of. If a word I never came across before catches hold of my imagination, I go about thinking of it till my mind can remain hung up on that string no longer; then I forget it. Next time I take my pen, though on the most unlikely topic, up comes my late fancy, the very word to express the meaning. An old-fashioned or at least a teacher's rule for good writing forbids the repeating of a word on the same page or paragraph, I forget which. The rule is necessary, for we shall almost certainly break it. In a letter I must use the word "meantime", not at all a ubiquitous friend, but on reading my letter I find three "meantime"s and the last two unnecessary. Next Sunday I must use "at any rate" in another letter, and on reading it find three "at any rate"s, and the last two unnecessary; perhaps I look for "meantime", but it is not there. For coherent thought we must have coherent sound, but whether our thought is coherent or not, repetitions and repeated repetitions link together the sounds we think in.

Our minds retain sounds for a long time, and we love to hear a sound or tune we have half forgotten. Music is built up of repetition; simple music repeats simply and openly; more subtle forms disguise their repetitions and transform their echoes. Fugues and symphonies exploit our desire to have yet another sweet; and so does poetry. Although we may find many reasons why art should repeat (as Ruskin's that repetitions give an "impression of quietness" like a landscape reflected in calm water that is "lulling to us in its monotony"*), repetitions do not form the distinguishing delight of art, or the chief care of the artist; this is Nature's way of constructing. Everything on earth reflects something else. The whole world is literally one energy functioning variously. Whether for economy, or because the Creator had only one idea in creating, the universe has evolved by a series of disguised repetitions. When she came to make man, Nature remembered the mixture of salts she gave to the sea and repeated that mixture—the same salts and in about the same proportions. The solar system mimics in its gigantic way the system of the atom. Art

* On Turner's "Scarborough", in *The Harbours of England*. This reason, however, is probably not the right one, repetitions being peaceful only if the thing repeated is calm; the monotonous iteration in the music of *Tristan and Isolde* can harass us most distressingly. Reflections in water possibly enchant by giving a sense of remoteness.

recapitulates and repeats because it cannot very well help it, the artist's business being rather to control and arrange and modify repetitions than to form them.

Alliteration has been called* "the intensest English ornament" of prose, and rhyme is sometimes considered as artificial or exotic an ornament of verse. Though sea-anemones make the beds of the sea beautiful, and flowers adorn the surface of the earth, scientists do not think of them as frills oversewn on to the garment of the universe, and no more are the echoes of poetry frills. We ought not to talk of the flowers of poetry as if they were ornaments, perhaps tawdry ornaments. One of the most quaint mis-conceptions man ever had of the wherefore of art, results in rhyming dictionaries. Saith the editor of one of them:

†The marshalling of rhymes into columns will save the poet and the builder of verses much turning of leaves, and much searching for the word. Relieved of a purely mechanical labour, they will be the more free to dwell on the poetic thought. The editor believes that he has thus rendered a genuine, if modest, aid to that art which appeals most strongly to him.

Even the ancient Gascoigne, in *Certayne notes of Instruction concerning the making of verse or ryme in English*, makes this mistake:

‡To help you a little with ryme (which is also a plaine yong scholler's lesson) worke thus, when you have set doune your first verse, take the last worde thereof, coumpt over all the wordes of the selfe same sounde by order of the Alphabete. As for example, the laste woorde of your firste line is *care*, to ryme therwith you have *bare, clare, dare, fare, gare, hare,* and *share, mare, snare, rare, stare,* and *ware* etc. Of all these take that which best may serve your pur-pose, carrying reason with ryme: and if none of them will

* Saintsbury, *History of English Prose Rhythm*, p. 121.
† A. Loring, *The Rhymer's Lexicon*, preface, p. xxv.
‡ Haslewood Collection, pp. 7-8.

serve so, then alter the laste worde of your former verse, but yet do not willingly alter the meaning of your Invention.

What a paltry thing rhyme would be if this were the way poets worked. It would dim the glory of *The Faerie Queene*. The poet does not usually seek his rhymes and alliterations; they come unsought, sometimes unconsciously. It is natural for poets to think like this.

*"People sometimes say," said Tennyson, "how stupidly alliterative Tennyson's verse is." Why, when I spout my lines first, they come out so alliteratively that I have sometimes no end of trouble to get rid of the alliteration."

An experiment Dr. Myers† tells us of shows an interesting fact. The "subjects" were given a word, and asked to write the first word it suggested, or a sequence of words suggested one by the other. The experimenter might say "dog", and the "subject" might answer "cat", or say, "Cat, mat, bat, fat, thin, *etc.*" The results could be classified and tabulated thus:

Similarity—			Word Given.	Word in Response.
in meaning	{	co-ordination	baby	infant.
		superordination	soldier	man.
		subordination	man	soldier.
	{	contrast	peace	war.
in sound	{	in letters or syllables	port	porter.
	{	in rhyme	fight	kite.
Contiguity—				
in time	{	causal	lightning	thunder.
	{	verbal	one	two,
		or	snow	snowball.
in space			handle	lock.

‡Fatigue, influence by drugs and pathological disorders

* Hallam Tennyson's *Memoir*, vol. ii, p. 15.
† *A Textbook of Experimental Psychology*, p. 152.
‡ *Ibid.*, p. 153, paraphrased.

of the nervous system . . . tend, broadly speaking, to increase the proportion of associations by similarity in sound and decrease those in meaning.

So, thinking in rhymes is not only a natural but a relaxed, and perhaps an excited, way of thinking. Rhymes may well lead the thoughts of the poets. There is much solid argument in Leigh Hunt's joke of *Rhyme and Reason*. The whole matter of a poem may lie in its rhymes, he says:

A LOVE SONG.

grove	heart	kiss
night	prove	blest
rove	impart	bliss
delight.	love.	rest.

The rhyme guides the thought, but does not make it on Gascoigne's receipt. The sound of the emphatic word ending the line brings to mind the thought with a related sound.

*For sure in an eminent spirite whom nature hath fitted for that mystery, Ryme is no impediment to his conceite, but rather gives him wings to mount and carries him not out of his course, but as it were beyonde his power to a farre happyer flight.

Many poets have fits of Campion and despise rhyme for the nonce, shutting the door on conventional channels for echo, and indulging in intenser repetitions. In *Paradise Lost* Milton sometimes offends the too delicate ear with his jingles. Campion makes up for loss of rhyme in a more subtle way, as we shall see. Mr. Flint, one of our modern rebels against this tyranny, prefaces his poems by an abjuration of all the conventions. He rejects both metre and rhyme, and thinks we ought to get back to the funda-

* Samuel Daniel, *An Apologie for Ryme*, p. 202 (Haslewood's Collection).

mentals of poetry. Instead of rhyme he has the heavier echo of repeated words:

> And my heart aches at the thought of the millions of miles
> of space—
> The millions of millions of miles that lie between us.

> He is there, I know—I am there,
> Since every combination exists;
> He must be there, I must be there;
> I must be happy somewhere.

> He knows I say; but I mean I know,
> He knows that to-morrow will be like
> To-day and yesterday.

One would almost say the whole point of:

> He must be there, I must be there;
> I must be happy somewhere

lies in the echo. The poet cannot get away from the iteration; the demon has him by the hair.*

Flint tells us that he is no scholar and writes purely by instinct. Since rhyme and metre are artifices, part of the learnt technique of poetry, he believes we should neglect them, and write in the primitive, unstudied way. If he is as little of a scholar as he declares, then his instinct led him aright. His repetitions deal with him in precisely the primitive manner. Here is a Veddah Song from Malacca:

†The doves of Taravelzita say kuturung.
> Where the talagoya is roasted and eaten, there blew a
> wind,
> Where the memmina is roasted and eaten, there blew a
> wind,
> Where the deer is roasted and eaten, there blew a wind.

---

* Perhaps, in fairness to Mr. Flint as a poet, I should say that these quotations show him at his worst, and are quoted solely as samples of his iteration.

† Wundt, *Elements of Folk Psychology*, p. 96.

Another song from Malacca, referring to the ring-tailed
lemur, a monkey common in Malacca and called *kra*, goes
thus:

> He runs along the branches, the kra,
> He carries the fruit with him, the kra,
> He runs to and fro, the kra;
> Over the living bamboo, the kra,
> Over the dead bamboo, the kra;
> He runs along the branches, the kra,
> He leaps about and screams, the kra,
> He permits glimpses of himself, the kra,
> He show his grinning teeth, the kra.

The Maoris transport tree trunks to the coast, singing:

> Give more room,
> Joyous folk, give room for the totara,
> Joyous folk,
> Give me the mara.
>   .
>   .
> Slide on, slide on!
> Slip along, slip along!
> Joyous folk!
>   *Etc.*

And from New Mexico comes:

*All ye fluttering clouds,
All ye clouds cherish the fields,
All ye lightnings, and thunders, rainbows and cloud-
    peoples
Come and labour for us.

In such songs we notice the seeds, on the one hand, of
our stanza refrains and rhyme (*totara*, *mara*, and *the kra*),
and on the other, of the parallelism in the *Psalms*:

†O give thanks unto the Lord, for he is gracious: and his
    mercy endureth for ever.

* Wundt, *Elements of Folk Psychology.* p. 268.
† No. 136 (Prayer Book version).

O give thanks unto the God of all gods: for his mercy
  endureth for ever.
O thank the Lord of all lords: for his mercy endureth for
  ever.

.   .   .   .   .   .

Who by his excellent wisdom made the heavens: for his
  mercy endureth for ever.
Who laid out the earth above the waters: for his mercy
  endureth for ever.

Or:

*O praise the Lord of heaven: praise him in the height.
Praise him, all ye angels of his: praise him, all his host.
Praise him, sun and moon: praise him, all ye stars and
  light.
Praise him, all ye heavens: and ye waters that are above
  the heavens.
Let them praise the Name of the Lord: for he spake the
  word,
.And they were made: he commanded, and they were
  created.

The poetry of the mystery plays may have parallel repetition, rhyme, and alliteration, all three:

†I thanke the as reverent rote of oure reste,
 I thanke the as stedfast stokke for to stande,
 I thanke the as tristy tre for to treste.
 I thanke the as buxsom bough to the hande,
 I thanke the as leefe the lustiest in lande,
 I thanke the as bewteous braunche for to bere,
 I thanke the as flower that nevere is fadande,
 I thanke the as frewte that has fedde us in fere.
    I thanke the for evere,
    If they repreve me
    Now schall thei leve me!
    Thi blissinge giffe me
    And douteles I schall do my devere.

* No. 148 (Prayer Book version).
† Saintsbury, *History of English Prosody*, vol. i, p. 210.

From identical repetition comes varied repetition, the idea growing as the sounds grow. When people become less primitive, their feeling for echo becomes more subtle and their ideas less monotonous. Rhyme echoes more quietly than direct repetition, or alliteration, since there is longer between the echo. Hence in the earliest poetry we do not find rhyme unless as an exception, or identical rhymes like "the kra" of the Malaccan song. Early Welsh and Irish poetry had this kind of rhyme and may have let Europe hear the ring of it. The Romance poets sometimes repeated the same rhyme twenty or thirty times.* Teutonic, German and old English poetry had close alliteration but no rhyme. Our oldest poem, *Beowulf*, has one or two promiscuous rhymes, but they come very close to each other as if the sound could not wait long:

†siþþan ic hond and rond hebban mihte. (*Beowulf*, 656.)
   sæla and mæla; þat is soð metod. (*Beowulf*, 1612.)
   Hroðgar maðelode, hylt sceawode. (*Beowulf*, 1688.)

‡Later poems have more rhymes; more and more as time advances through *Andreas* and *Judith* up to *Byrhtnoth*, till in fact, the French influence in the eleventh century gave a push to its use. Contemporary examples of both English and French folk-song show a tendency to rhyme or assonance at the strong cadences, but these are not stereotyped and sometimes occur so irregularly that they almost seem to arrive as if by accident. The Troubadours seized on the suggestion of rhyme they found in the folk-song, which gave them their first model, and made a feature of it. From them Europe learnt to rhyme. But this native tendency to rhyme may have been helped very much by the influence of rhyme in the Roman hymns, where it arose

---

  * Guest, *History of English Rhythm*, p. 577.
  † Examples given by Schipper, *History of English Versification*, pp. 65-6.
  ‡ *Ibid.*, pp. 65-6.

by playing on the heavy declensional and conjugational endings:

*Pauper am*abilis* et vener*abilis* est ben*edictus*,
Dives in*utilis* insati*abilis* est mal*edictus*,
Qui bon*a* *negligit* et mal*a* *deligit*, intrat abys*sum*,
N*ulla* pecun*ia*, n*ulla* potent*ia* liberat ip*sum*,
Irreme*abilis*, *insati*abilis* *i*lla vor*ago*,
Hic *u*bi *mergitur*, horrida *cernitur* omn*i*s im*ago*.

Thus goes the jingle of Theodatus' *De Contemptu mundi*; from it we may see why classical Latin avoided rhyme. Its declensions and conjugations echo sufficiently without being placed to catch the emphasis. It is interesting to find that in early Hebrew poetry rhyme occurs exceptionally,

†formed by the recurrence of the same pronominal suffixes—the suffixes which in Hebrew are equivalent to our personal pronouns. Occasionally rhymes are formed on the plural terminations -im or -oth, and more rarely on the plural terminations of the verb, -un.

These rhymes result probably rather from the parallel arrangement of Hebrew poetry than deliberately for their own sake.

Although prose arose later than poetry it too has rhyme, alliteration, assonance, and iterations of all sorts.

The beauty of the contents of a phrase, or of a sentence, depends implicitly upon alliteration and upon assonance. The vowel demands to be repeated; the consonant demands to be repeated; and both cry aloud to be perpetually varied.

So says Stevenson in his *Technical Elements of Style*,‡ practising the music he describes. He quotes the following

---

* Guest, *History of English Rhythms*, p. 571. The *i italics* of the second last line are mine, the others Guest's.

† Adam Smith, *The Early Poetry of Israel*, p. 25.

‡ Pentland Ed., p. 282.

from Macaulay to show the thing done crudely, as his own essay shows it managed artistically:

Meanwhile the disorders of Kannon's Kamp went on inKreasing. He Kalled a Kouncil of war to Konsider what Kourse it would be advisable to taKe. But as soon as the Kouncil had met, a preliminary Kuestion was raised. The army was almost eKsKlusively a Highland army. The recent viKtory had been won eKsKlusively by Highland warriors. Great chie*f*s who had brought si*K*s or se*v*en hundred *f*ighting men into the *f*ield, did not think it *f*air that they should be out*v*oted by gentlemen *f*rom Ireland, and *f*rom the Low Kountries, who bore indeed King James's Kommission, and were Kalled Kolonels and Kaptains, but who were Kolonels without regiments and Kaptains without Kompanies.

He says that prose may alliterate to the eye as well as the ear.

Where an author is running the open A, deceived by the eye and our strange English spelling, he will often show a tenderness for the flat A; and that where he is running a particular consonant, he will not improbably rejoice to write it down even when it is mute and bears a different value.

When this happens the writer writes as an artist—an artificial thing to do—and moreover, allows the sign to usurp the right of the sound, thinking in the corpses of letters and not in living sounds. Stevenson is a little too conscious of his music, more conscious of it, at least, than we expect of the prose writer. The writer of prose usually concerns himself first in expressing his meaning clearly, and is interested in his style chiefly for its neatness, its power of gripping the mind, of sending its shaft home, and only secondarily with its design, the art of managing the sounds. His business is not, like the poet's, to stir the unstirred depth of echoing sound, to raise the hidden music of words and send it whirling in the wind, since he does not write with intense emotion. Still we cannot quite separate the two artistic interests. Stevenson was the artist supersensitive; but all good writers write with their ears as well as their brains; an expressive sentence always sounds musical. The music is less powerful in prose, only because the meaning is slighter. Moreover, since we read poetry passively, its echoes reverberate fully; in prose we direct our attention actively on the meaning and notice the music less readily. When we walk with vacant mind along an empty street, and a small boy in a scarlet jersey comes round the corner where the scarlet letter-box stands, we feel as if two notes were struck in sudden harmony. The echoes of poetry have this sort of effect. But in prose where the streets are crowded, and the colours move with other purposes than a spontaneous and naïve response to life, we do not notice the red jersey; the coincidence goes unheeded or appears fortuitous unless our minds are vacant and open to feel its music. Yet in prose the boy intent on his business often strikes a chord with the box intent on its. When Stevenson has in his market a booth where lemons are sold, he often brings along a yellow milk-cart, and yet we pursue our way uninterrupted, heeding no more than we heed the real colour harmonies struck daily in our streets. From the top of a tram the other week I watched a cart carrying fresh tares from the country; their luscious green had an answer from every newly painted pole along the car track, yet walking among the traffic in the street I should never have noticed this almost impressive sight.

Let us watch Stevenson matching his colours:

The genius of prose rejects the *cheville* no less emphatically than the laws of verse; and the *cheville*, I should perhaps explain to some of my readers, is any meaningless or very watered phrase employed to strike a balance in the sound.

The f(ph), p, v gradation which Stevenson likes stands out among the other echoes. He repeats it in the next sentence from p through b to f:

Pattern and argument live in each other; and it is by the brevity, clearness, charm, or emphasis of the second, that we judge the strength and fitness of the first.

He varies this strand of colour by interweaving other echoes such as "genius", "rejects", "*cheville*", the vowels of "very", "less", "emphatically", "employed" and "emphasis", and so on; perhaps "*clear*", "*charm*", "*second*" is a modified echo of the sequence "*genius*" "*rejects*", "ch*eville*". *S* runs in the background of both sentences and comes forward to dominate the opening of the next one, and recur later in two spots:

*S*tyle i*s s*ynthetic; and the arti*s*t, *s*eeking, *s*o to *s*peak, a *p*eg to *p*lait a*b*out, takes up at once two or more elements or two or more views of the su*b*ject in hand; com*b*ines, im*p*licates and contrasts them; and while, in one *s*ense, he was merely *s*eeking an occa*s*ion for the *n*ecessary k*n*ot, he will be found, in the other, to have greatly enriched the meaning, or to have tran*s*acted the work of two *s*entences in the *s*pace of one.

"Implicates" rhymes Spooner-fashion with "take"; "artist" reflects "contrast"; "transacted", which focuses the t sound and restarts the s, forms with "contrast" a double assonance and an inverted alliteration, if we may put it thus—"cont*ras*t" and "tran*sac*t", "con*tra*st" and "*tra*nsact". We need not point out all the echoes and gradations in this other sentence from the same essay:

These not only knit and knot the logical texture of the style with all the dexterity and strength of prose; they not only fill up the pattern of the verse with infinite variety and sober wit; but they give us, besides, a rare and special pleasure, by the art, comparable to that of counterpoint, with which they follow at the same time, and now contrast, and now combine, the double pattern of the texture and the verse.

An almost Euphuistic subtilty occurs in "the dex*terity* and *s*trength of *p*rose" contrasted with the "*p*a*tt*ern of the ver*s*e", *t*, *t*, *s*, *p*, turned to *p*, *t*, *t*, *s*; both come originally from "the *t*e*x*ture of the *s*tyle". He sums up this play on *t*, *s*, *p*, at the close, in "the double pattern of the texture and the verse"; "double" stands for "dexterity", "verse" and "texture" being chosen one from each of the other phrases. When the end of a sentence echoes the beginning like this, binding the meaning together in iterated sounds, our sense of finish is complete. Poets often end on echoes of the beginning to give their poems this feeling of having come round the full circle. *Lycidas* opens on "Yet once more", and has "more", "crude", "rude", and "year", "dear" for its rhymes. The last paragraph of *Lycidas* being really an epilogue, the real end begins:

> *Weep* no *more*, woful Shepherds *weep* no *more*,
> For Lycidas your sorrow is not dead.

and ends:

> Now Lycidas the Shepherds weep no more;
> Hence forth thou art the Genius of the shore,
> In thy large recompense, and shalt be good
> To all that wander in that perilous flood.

As we pause in Stevenson's essay, before he passes on to "The Rhythm of the Phrase", we may think this is all very nice, but rather trifling, merely Lyly a little less blatant; and perhaps the prose, matter-of-fact man would think that men of letters were so indeed. We go to Stevenson to learn about the technical elements of style, and come away with sounds ringing in our head—*style*, *knot*, *web* and *pattern*. Curious! This makes a mnemonic for his teaching. In following the artistry of his sounds we have been all the time on the trail of his meaning. We can no more escape these reverberations, or miss the meaning, than we can escape the reverberations or miss the meaning of some of Matthew Arnold's prose. Both writers write prose that is all sound; but the sound is all meaning too.

Art alone did not make Stevenson's echo-enchanted paragraphs; Nature did most of it for him. Somewhat fearing his subtilty and suspecting he was all the time leading me a wild-goose chase, I took the nearest commonplace prose to discover how much of it was art, how much nature. In the same volume of *The Contemporary Review** as his essay, occurs an advertisement:

About Claret

There has been during *the last few years* a *great* deal of *exaggeration* and *misconception*, mainly arising from letters and articles in the Press, by those who are almost entirely ignorant on the subject. They *exaggerate* the *quantity consumed* in this country and understate the *quantity produced*. Why, Paris alone *consumes* more *wine* than the whole of Great Britain and Ireland. It is true that *production* of *common wine* in *France has been* enormously decreased by the ravages of the phylloxera within *the last few years*, and as every person in *France consumes wine, low wines* have to be *imported* to supply the home demand. Hence the unusual circumstance of *France importing great quantities* of *common wine*. There *has* never *been* any difficulty in *procuring good pure* French *wines*, except in the very *low*est qualities. For ourselves, *owing* to the large reserves *we buy*, *we* have al*way*s *been able* to su*pply Good* Vin Ordinaire at 13s. per doz.

Good prose differs from commonplace or bad prose in having echoes more subtle or in more pleasing designs. Moreover every original writer echoes in his own way; Arnold's music differs from Stevenson's, and both from Emerson's. And this is more true of poetry, though to

* April 1885.

investigate it would make a research in itself; we can only illustrate from one or two poems.

Campion's *Rose-Cheeked Laura* is among the most wonderful examples of beautiful letter music:

> (1) Rose-cheeked Laura, come;
> Sing thou smoothly with thy beauty's
> Silent music, either other
> Sweetly gracing.

In the first line the consonants do not echo save for the *r* in "rose" and "Laura"; the second line emphasises *s* and *t* with its relative *th*; the third carries on *t*, *th* and *s*; the last gathers up the consonants into "sweetly", which has *s* and *t*, and whose *l* comes through "silent" and "smoothly" from "Laura", and "gracing" with *c* and *r* as old consonants and *ng* for new. An *s* alliteration marks the beginning of each line—"Rose", "Sing", "Silent", "Sweetly". The loveliness of the vowel music lies not so much in echo, although there are lovely echoes—"beauty's", "music"; "cheeked", "sweetly"—as in their gradations.

> Rose-cheeked Laura, come;
> o   ee   aw a ă
> Sing thou smoothly with thy beauty's
> i   au   oo   y i   ai   u y
> Silent music, either other
> ai e   u i ai ă ă ă
> Sweetly gracing.
> ee y   ay i.

Read without any consonants the vowels make a lovely chain of sound.

> (2) Lovely forms do flowe
> From concent devinely framed;
> Heaven is musič, and thy beauty's
> Birth is heavenly.

In the first two lines *l* and *f* alliterate; *r*, *m*, *n* echo in a subsidiary way. The last two lines drop this with the decided change in meaning; the sounds of "Heaven" and "music" dominate, the alliterating "beauty's Birth" being sandwiched between. The charm of the vowel music lies in its gradation.

Lovely forms do flow
ă y aw oo o

is a lovely gradation through delicate shades of an "o" colouring. The next line starts with one of them and develops away into the higher vowels:

From   concent   d e v i n e l y   framed.
aw   aw e   i *or* ee ai   y   ay e

The vowels of the last two lines grade away from "Heaven" to *u i* of "music", then from *ai* back through *u y* to "heavenly":

Heaven is music, and thy beauty's
e e i   u i , a   ai u   y *or* ee
Birth is heavenly.
e   i   e e y

(3) These dull notes we sing
    Discords need for helps to grace them,
    Only beauty purely loving
    Knows no discord.

The *s* sound colours this, with a *d* and *n* strand, and a faint *t*, *th*; *p*, *b* and *l* focus in the third line. The music centres in the vowels; the repetition of the vowel of "beauty" in "purely" and of "knows" in "no" makes an eddy whirling back on itself in the onward-flowing stream. The gradations repeat, with variations.

These dull notes⎫ is answered by ⎧ Discords need,
  ee ă o ⎭   ⎩ i aw   ee

for helps⎫ is followed by diverging vowels ⎧ to grace,
aw e ⎭   ⎩ oo ay

returning to the vowel of "helps" in "them"; this aids the half-cadence. The contrast in the "o" colouring of the emphatic vowels of

Only beauty ⎱ is inverted in ⎱ purely loving.
o y u y ⎰   ⎰ u y ă i

The vowel sequences give us a sense of completeness in themselves; they form a sort of rhythm and design of their own, and make us feel a sensation of cadence at the end of each verse. Alone, without either consonant or meaning, they give us a stanza sense. We feel this very strongly in the last verse of all:

  (4) But still moves delight,
    Like clear springs renewed by flowing,
    Ever perfect, ever in them-
     Selves eternal.

L sounds through this with t, r, n, m, etc., as subsidiary echoes. The vowels grade into each other and would form a lovely music even by themselves. The gradation of

   But still moves d e l i g h t
    ă i oo ee or i ai

is echoed with variations and inversions in

  Like clear springs r e n e w e d by flowing.
  ai ee i i or ee u ai o i

Then as if to imitate the meaning by vocal gesture we have:

    Ever perfect, ever in them-
     Selves eternal.

Beauty alone can bear the monotony of an eternity of "e"s. Binding echoes keep the music of *Rose-cheeked Laura* coherent from stanza to stanza. "Sing" sounds in all but the second verse, appearing in the last as "springs", "beauty" in all save the last verse, coupled with related sounds—

"smoothly" and "sweetly" in the first, "Lovely", "heavenly" and "devinely" in the second, "purely" in the third.
These with their rhythm and the *ly* ending stamp character on the poem. Campion wrote the lyric as an example
of trochaic music; and the trochaic words form the essential character of the poem, hold the unity of its music—
"perfect", "either other", "flowing", "gracing", "Laura",
"discord", "loving". Lesser echoes also help to bind it
—*l* centring in "Laura" of verse 1, "Lovely" of verse 2,
"only", "purely", "loving" of verse 3, and "still" of verse 4.

Spenser has as great a mastery over this sort of vowel
music as Campion. The beauty of his vowels comes rather
from their melodious sequence than from echoes. Even
when he repeats a vowel we sometimes lose the echo in
the vowel sequence. Hence his rhyme stands out as the
only compelling echo in the gliding, liquid stream of
vowels, as he seems very well aware of:

> his glistring armour made
> A little glooming light, much like a shade.
> a   i le oo i   ai

He often uses alliteration to emphasise the changing
colours of his vowels:

> *S*ober he *s*eemed, and very *s*agely *s*ad,
> And to the ground his eyes were lowly bent,
> *S*imple in *s*hew, and void of malice bad.

Sometimes avoiding the heavier sort of echo within the
lines, he uses them within the stanza:

> A *little lowly* Hermitage it was,
> Down in a dale, *ha*rd by a forest's side,
> *Far* from resort of people, that did pass
> In *travel* to and fro: a *little* wide
> There was an *holy Chapel* edified.

How quiet and subdued they sound—"lowly" and "holy",

"travel" and "chapel"! Sometimes his echo comes quaintly in the same foot of the next line:

> A Gentle *Knight* was pricking on the plain,
> Yeclad in *might*y arms and silver shield,

or he may repeat a gradation in the same way:

> But *full of fire* and greedy hardiment,
> The *youthful knight* could not for ought be stay'd.

Yet he can play on one sound too:

> As gentle Shepherd in sweet eventide,

or give close assonances:

> Huge heaps of mud he leaves, wherein there breed
> Ten thousand kinds of creatures, *partly* male
> And *partly* female, of his fruitful seed;
> Such ugly monstrous shapes elsewhere may no man reed.

Though the most lovely music of poetry may lie in a sweet progress from vowel to vowel rather than in echoes, the echoing music makes the more interesting study from its connection with rhyme. We may show in various ways that poets find rhyme easy. So naturally does an echoing vowel come to end the line that the rhymes of some poets tend to assonate with each other. The *Faerie Queene* stanza has sometimes the same vowel in every one of its rhymes, as in Canto 7 of Book I, where the first stanza has:

> . . . ware,
> . . . traine,
> . . . faire,
> . . . graine,
> . . . faine,
> . . . frame,
> . . . entertaine?
> . . . Dame,
> . . . name.

For other examples of this we have the sixteenth stanza of Canto 1: "Their dam upstart, out of her den afraid", and the sixth of Canto 4: "Arrived there they passed in forth right". A great many stanzas have only two vowels to the three rhymes. And even outside the stanza the rhymes echo, one vowel often dominating for a long time. If we start with the first stanza of Canto 7 of Book I, and make a list, we get this result, where *a*, *b*, *c* represent the first, second and third rhymes of the stanza, *ababbcbcC*:

Stanza 1. *a*, *b*, *c*, all the same vowel, *train* (referred to as 1).
  ,,   2. *c* same as 1, *a* and *b* assonate with *night* (referred to as 2).
  ,,   3. *a* same as 1, *b* same as 2, *c* rhymes with *sweet* (referred to as 3).
  ,,   4. $a = 3$, $b = 1$, *c* rhymes with *dwell* (referred to as 4).
  ,,   5. *a* and $b = 1$, *c* rhymes with *grow* (referred to as 5).
  ,,   6. *a* rhymes with *glas* (referred to as 6), $b = 1$, $c = 4$.
  ,,   7. *a* and $c = 1$, *b* rhymes with *gown* (referred to as 7).
  ,,   8. *a* and $b = 2$, $c = 3$.
  ,,   9. $a = 6$, *b* and $c = 2$.
  ,,   10. $a = 2$, $c = 1$, *b* rhymes with *scorn* (referred to as 10).
  ,,   11. *b* and $c = 1$, *a* rhymes with *praunce* (referred to as 11).
  ,,   12. $b = 7$, $c = 5$, $a = 4$.
  ,,   13. $a = 10$, *b* rhymes with *fill* (referred to as 13), $c = 5$.
  ,,   14. *a* and $b = 2$, $c = 1$.
  ,,   15. $a = 6$, $b = 1$, $c = 10$.
  ,,   16. $a = 3$, $b = 2$, $c = 4$.
  ,,   17. $a = 1$, *b* rhymes with *new* (referred to as 17), $c = 6$.
  ,,   18. *a* and $c = 4$, $b = 10$.
  ,,   19. $a = 10$, $b = 3$, $c = 4$.

Stanza 20. a and $c = 1$, $b = 4$.
„   21. $a = 17$, $b = 13$, $c = 10$ (?).
„   22. a and $c = 2$, $b = 5$.
„   23. $a = 5$, $b = 2$, $c = 3$.
„   24. $a = 7$, $b = 1$, $c = 2$ or 3.

That is, we have eleven or at most twelve vowels for seventy-two rhymes, a remarkable economy and not unusual in the *Faerie Queene*. Indeed it is quite characteristic, and has, I should think, much to do with the loveliness of its music. If we read only a dozen or so stanzas of *Adonais* we feel the difference and realise how much of the *Faerie Queene* charm depends on its rhymes. Spenser will have only the most beautiful sounds to end his lines, and prefers a lovely monotony to greater variety with less beauty. He does not often* use rhymes like "burst", "first", "thirst", as Shelley does in *Adonais* (cf. line 164), or echo a word like "sepulchre" (*Adonais*, cf. line 424), preferring the diphthong "ai" of "night", or the pure vowels of "heart" or "name" with clean and crisp consonants.

Although Wordsworth's echoes differ from Spenser's, he also found rhyme easy. No one, I think, has suggested that his rhymes influence the imagery or the metaphors; which probably means that his expression easily took an echoing form. If it rarely appears to influence his thought, his rhyme may sometimes be suggested by a previous word either in the line itself or in the one before:

> She lived unk*nown*, and few could *know*
> When Lucy ceased to be;
> But she is in her grave, and, *oh*,
> The difference to me!

Then we have:

> I travelled among unknown men,
> In lands beyond the sea;
> Nor, England! did I know till then
> What love I *bore* to thee.

* He does occasionally.

The strong rhyme of the next stanza rhymes with "bore":

> 'Tis past, that melancholy dream!
> Nor will I quit thy *shore*,
> *etc.*

The Complaint of the Forsaken Indian Woman opens like this:

> Before I s*ee* another day,
> Oh let m*y* body d*ie* away!
> In sl*ee*p I heard the northern gl*ea*ms;
> The stars, they were among my dr*ea*ms;
> In rustling conflict through the sk*ie*s,
> I heard, I saw the flashes drive,
> And yet they are upon my eyes,
> And yet I am alive;
> Before I see another day,
> Oh let my body die away!

The rhymes of his *Complaint* about Coleridge's coolness show art's designing:

> There is a change—and I am p*oor*;
> Your love hath been, not long ago,
> A f*ountain* at my fond heart's d*oor*,
> Whose only business was to flow;
> And flow it did; not taking heed
> Of its own b*ounty*, or my need.
>
> What happy moments did I c*ount*!
> Blest was I then all bliss above!
> Now, for that consecrated f*ount*
> Of murmuring, sparkling, living love,
> What have I? shall I dare to tell?
> A comfortless and hidden well.
>
> A well of love—it may be deep—
> I trust it is,—and never dry:
> What matter? if the waters sleep
> In silence and obscurity.
> —Such change, and at the very d*oor*
> Of my fond heart, hath made me p*oor*.

The "count", "fount" rhyme originated in "fountain" and "bounty" of the first stanza. In the second stanza "tell" is rather an artificial than an artistic suggestion from "well". The sounds of the last stanza turn back to the first, the word which ends the first line of the poem ending the last. Wordsworth knows how to finish on the note he strikes first; he may design his rhymes more carefully than we think. The subtle difference between "door" answering "poor" in the first stanza, and the inversion "poor" answering "door" in the last, has its effect.* This close gives a feeling of inevitableness much like the ending of the verses in Elizabethan song-form poems, and yet if we look at it the thought is a rambler. There is a change and he is poor.... The fountain at his heart's door ceases to flow;... it is now only a well.... A well?... Yes, but comfortless. ... Such a change at the door of his heart has made him poor. The thought starts a fountain, becomes a well and flows on to something else in the unheeding manner of a stream; yet the music, being coherent and artistically managed, makes the thought seem coherent and artistically managed too. Here is the artist at work rather than the sheer genius.

Wordsworth's rhymes sometimes assonate as Spenser's do, but possibly not for the same reason. Spenser† rhymes on the same vowels because his fastidious ear cut down the number of vowels he could choose from, Wordsworth

---

* In the first movement of Bach's First Brandenburg Concerto we may see a parallel effect, the first bar opening:

in the solo violin and first fiddles, and the last ending:

† As far as one can generalise about Spenser.

either because his ear was sounding to that note or because
he liked his sounds to respond quickly. *I travelled among
unknown men* has eight rhymes; four of them assonate—
"sea", "seem", "feel", "concealed"; the vowel of "men"
does not differ very much from that of "surveyed"; the
remaining two, "more" and "fire", have consonantal assonance. One cannot safely generalise about Spenser's vowel
music, but on occasion he seems to avoid echoing the
vowels and especially the rhyme vowel within the line;
Wordsworth possibly seldom if ever avoided this:

The Forsaken

The p*ea*ce which others s*ee*k they find;
The heaviest storms not longest last;
Heav*en* grants ev*en* to the guiltiest mind
An amnesty for what is past;
When will my s*en*tence be rev*er*sed?
I *o*nly pray to kn*o*w the worst;
And wish, as if my heart would burst.

O w*ea*ry struggle! silent y*ea*rs
Tell s*ee*mingly no doubtful tale;
And yet they l*ea*ve it short, and f*ea*rs
And *ho*pes are strong and will prev*ai*l.
My calmest f*ai*th escapes not p*ai*n;
And, feeling that the *ho*pe is vain,
I think that he will come again.

Or again:
What heavenly sm*i*les! O Lady m*i*ne,
Through m*y* very heart they sh*i*ne;
And, if m*y* brow gives back their l*i*ght,
Do thou look gladly on the s*i*ght;
As the cl*ea*r Moon with modest pr*i*de
    Beholds her own br*i*ght b*ea*ms
Reflected from the mountain's s*i*de
    And from the headlong str*ea*ms.

The vowel of the first three rhymes echoes "smiles", and
the cadence rhyme "clear"; only in the last line does the
sound of *ai* die down.

It is well known, or at least commonly accepted, that
the echoes of Milton's blank verse come both more frequently and are further flung than those of Wordsworth's,
and that he delights in intenser and more boisterous jingles.
This impression is probably as real as we feel, though
Wordsworth is only less fond of repeating words he has
just used, likes very close echoes, and has assonances both
interlinearly and at the end of his lines:

*lustily

I dipped my oars into the silent lake,
And, as I rose upon the stroke, my boat
Went heaving through the water like a swan;
When, from behind the craggy steep till then   .
The horizon's bound, a huge peak black and huge,
As if with voluntary power instinct,
Upreared its head. I struck and struck again,
And growing still in stature the grim shape
Towered up between me and the stars, and still,
For so it seemed, with purpose of its own
And measured motion like a living thing,
Strode after me. With trembling oars I turned,
And through the silent water stole my way
Back to the covert of the willow tree;
There in her mooring-place I left my bark,—
And through the meadows homeward went, in grave
And serious mood; but after I had seen
That spectacle, for many days, my brain
Worked with a dim and undetermined sense
Of unknown modes of being; o'er my thoughts
There hung a darkness, call it solitude
Or blank desertion. No familiar shapes
Remained, no pleasant images of trees,
Of sea or sky, no colours of green fields;
But huge and mighty forms, that do not live
Like living men, moved slowly through the mind
By day, and were a trouble to my dreams.

* *Prelude*, i, 373. I have put in *italics* only the more prominent
echoes.

"Oars", "rose", "stroke" and "boat" satisfy the echo; "water" and "swan"; "when" and "then"; "heaving", "steep","peak","unreared","me","seemed" have a longer run. Here is "huge peak, black and huge" and "I struck and struck again"; "still", "grim", "still", "living", "indetermined", "it", "thing", "willow", "dim", "familiar", "solitude", "images", "live", "living", counted mechanically, give a number of echoes, but I do not know that we hear them all. The vowel of "oar" reappears in "so", "own", "motion", "strode", "oars", "stole", and is blotted out by "mooring","through","mood","do","move","through"

Typical of Milton's close echoes we have:

*Opprobrious, with his *Robe* of *r*ighteousness,

and a little further on:

*I*n glory *a*s of *o*ld, to h*i*m *a*ppeas'd
All, though *all*-kn*o*wing.

They are stronger, heavier, more sonorous than Wordsworth's. For repetitions we have:

†had levied Warr,
Warr unproclam'd.

or:

‡for I this Night,
Such night till this I never pass'd, have dream'd,
If dream'd,

with the typical Miltonic recoil back on the sense, to hammer a word. Wordsworth imitates it in softened music:

huge peak, black and huge.

Milton would have written: "huge peak, huge and black", or more likely: "peak huge, huge and black". He assonates as closely as Wordsworth:

§Such whispering w*a*k'd her, but with startl'd eye
On Adam, whom embr*a*cing, thus she sp*a*ke:

* *Paradise Lost*, Bk. x, 222. † Bk. xi, 219.
‡ Bk. v, 30-31. § Bk. v, 26-7.

*Or take Mr. Larminie's example of what he calls "unconscious" internal assonance:

> *Thus* with the *year*
> *Sea*sons re*turn*, but not to *me* re*turns*
> Day, or the *sweet* appro*ach* of *ev'n* or morn
> Or *sight* of *ver*nal *bloom*, or *sum*mer's *rose*
> Or flocks or *herds* or *hu*man face di*vine*;
> But *clouds* in*stead* and *ever dur*ing dark
> Surro*unds* me.

We cannot be sure, since no one has researched on this aspect of their poetry, but the echoes seem to persist longer in Milton than in Wordsworth, and are more emphatic and resonant. We may also say, but without being dogmatic, that though Wordsworth and Milton make music of a sweet vowel progress, the beauty of their poetry depends fully as much, if not more, on their echoes, just as we said, though not dogmatically, that Spenser's poetry depends for its charm rather on the musical sequence of his vowels than on their echoes. Though Spenser's vowels please us because they are lovely in juxtaposition, and Milton's by their repetition, the two ways of making vowels sound lovely are not exclusive, but interdependent.

Saintsbury thinks assonance unsuited to English, and says that the rhyme needs "the consonants to enforce distinct similarity of sound" in the vowels.† So we must infer that readers of English do not hear assonance distinctly. But this need not mean that assonance makes no difference, and might as well not be there. We can hardly help hearing, if only in a dim sort of way, not only vowel assonance, but that other consonant assonance favoured by Celtic and Icelandic poets.‡ None of our poets, with an exception or

---

* *Contemporary Review*, 1894, vol. i, p. 735.
† *History of English Prosody*, vol. iii, p. 539.
‡ *History of English Versification*, p. 13.

two, have ever practised consonantal or vocalic assonance avowedly or regularly, and we have neither codified rules nor any formal designs laid out for them; but they do occur all the same. Mrs. Browning knew that some of her peculiar "rhymes" like "mou*ntain*" and "dau*nting*", "fai*th*" and "dea*th*", were assonances.* But assonantal endings occur in English poetry not only as a sort of degenerate rhyme, they often sweeten our so-called unrhymed measures; and indeed, in a tongue where rhyme comes easily† and in the works of poets who have written much in rhyme, it would be surprising if assonance never marked the end of the blank-verse line. When Campion sets out to write unrhymed measures his ear is sometimes too strong for him:

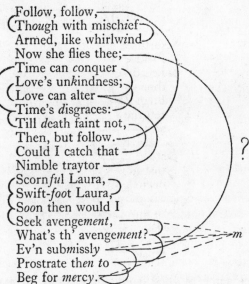

* Though Saintsbury says they are not (vol. iii, pp. 242-3).

† *i.e.* easily to most poets who use it, though not necessarily to those who are not poets.

Out of these twenty lines all save two have assonance, and one rhymes. I have marked one with a "?" because I do not think we hear the echo so far off, and because it is not a good rhyme anyway. This is all the more striking, since echoes mark the beginnings of some of the lines too.

Parts of *Paradise Lost* have assonance at the line ends. We find this even in unpromising places. (I bracket the vowel assonance on the left, the consonant on the right.)

Vowel assonance.   Consonant assonance.

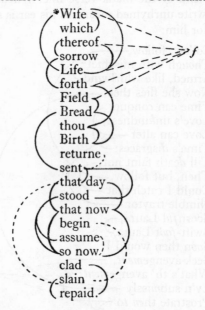

Perhaps some of these sound too faintly to make any difference, "Wife" and "which" almost certainly, even if

* *Paradise Lost*, Bk. x, 198.

we pronounce "which" without its *h*. A little further on we find a triplet:

> re*turn'd*
> re*assum'd*
> ap*peas'd*

then a couplet:

> *Earth*
> *Death*

later:

> thr*ives*
> prov*ides*

and later still:

> tr*y*
> m*ine.*

From line 280 onwards the line endings run:

at line 301:

> Bridge
> Wall
> world
> broad

lines 311-51 end:

waves
Art
Rock
track
hee
safe
bare
Adamant
made
space
Heaven
Hell
wayes
led
descried
behold
bright
stearing
rose
dear
disguise
slunk
shape
act
seconded
sought
descend
terrified
shun
wrauth
returned
Paire
plaint
understood
joy
returned
foot
hop't
dear
sight
encreased.

Assonance* for forty-one lines with only two breaks in the chain, and I think we hear them all! We certainly hear "Rock" and "track" and the vowel of "waves" whenever it occurs, though perhaps not assonances like "behold" and "bright", or "foot" and "hop't", save in a dim sort of way.

Symonds, in the course of his book on *Blank Verse*, quotes from the Elizabethan dramatists; and it was in his quotations that I first noticed this tendency to assonance in blank verse:

> †I am acquainted with sad miser*y*;
> As the tanned galley-slave is with his oar;
> Necessity makes me suffer constantl*y*,
> And custom makes it eas*y*.   (Webster.)

or:

> ‡Like to your picture in the g*a*llery,
> A deal of life in show, but none in pr*a*ctice;
> Or rather like some reverend monument,
> Whose ruins are even p*i*tied.   (Webster.)

From Jonson he quotes:

> §Here was she wont to g*o*! and here! and *h*ere!
> Just where these daisies, pinks and violets *gro*w:
> The world may find the spring by following *h*er;
> For other print her airy steps ne'er left.
> Her treading would not bend a blade of *gra*ss,
> Or shake the downy blue bell from his st*a*lk!
> But like the soft west wind she shot al*o*ng,
> And where she went, the flowers took thickest r*oo*t,
> As she had sowed them with her odorous *foo*t.

From Beaumont and Fletcher:

> ‖Fie, you have missed it here, *Antiphila*
> You are much mistaken, wench;

---

* In marking Milton's vowels, I assume them pure as they were in his day, rather than in the modern Southern English diphthongs.
† p. 48.   ‡ p. 49.   § p. 33.   ‖ p. 36.

These colours are not dull and pale enough,
To show a soul so full of mise*ry*
As this sad lady's was; do it *by me*,
Do it again by me the lost *Aspatia*,
And you shall find all true but the wild isla*nd*.
I stand upon the sea beach now, and thi*nk*
Mine arms thus, and mine hair blown with the w*ind*,
Wild as that desert, and let all *about me*
Tell that I am forsaken; do my face
(If thou hadst ever feeling of a sorrow)
Thus, thus, Antiphila, strive to make me loo*k*
Like Sorrow's monument; and the trees *about me*
Let them be dry and leafless; let the roc*ks*
Groan with continual surges, and *behind me*
Make all a desolation; look, look, wenche*s*,
A miserable life of this poor picture!

Another from *Thierry and Theodoret* shows this better:

*T<small>H</small>.   And endless parting
With all we can call ours, with all our s*weetness*,
With youth, strength, pleasure, people, time, nay r*eason*.
For in the silent grave no conversa*tion*,
No joyful tread of friends, no voice of lov*ers*,
No careful father's counsel; nothing's hea*rd*,
Nor nothing is, but all obli*vion*,
Dust, and an endless darkness, and dare you, woma*n*,
Desire this place?
O<small>RD</small>. 'Tis of all *sleeps* the *sweetest*;
Children begin it to us, strong men *seek it*,
And kings from height of all their painted glor*ies*
Fall like spent exhalations to this *c*entre.

Massinger has:

†Not far from where my father *lives, a lady*,
A neighbour *by, b*lest with as great *a beauty*
As nature *d*urst bestow without un*doing*,
Dwelt, and most happily, as I *thought then*,
And blessed the house a thousand times she dw*elt in*.
This *beauty*, in the *b*lossom of my *youth*,

When my *first fire* knew no adulterate inc*ense*,
Nor I no way to *flatter* but by *fondness*,
In all the bravery my friends *could* show *me*,
In all the faith my innocence *could* give *me*,
In the best language my *true* tongue *could tell me*,
And all the broken *s*ighs my *s*ick heart *lent me*,
I *s*ued and *s*erved. *L*ong did I *love* this *lady*,
*Long was my travail, long my tra*vel, to *win her*;
With all the duty of my *s*oul I *s*erved *her*.

Passages less assonated than Symonds' extracts occur
in the blank verse of these writers. Extracts taken at random from their plays sometimes assonate, sometimes not.
Yet on the whole we may say that their blank verse tends
to assonate, that rhyme left them this legacy. *The Duchess
of Malfi* (III, Sc. 1, lines 14-18) gives:

> place
> make
> hasten
> me
> ear

Markedly assonated passages occur in Beaumont and
Fletcher, together with passages in which assonance is
markedly absent. *Philaster* (IV, Sc. IV, lines 116-122) gives
us:

> Caesar
> men
> see
> flesh
> *w*ounds
> tears
> *w*ealth

(III. Sc. II, line 108):

> foot
> seek
> you
> beasts
> you
> hearts.

A King and no King (III, Sc. III, line 175):

> *th*is
> *th*ee
> by
> r*i*se
> d*i*e.

The Elizabethans have no monopoly of assonating blank verse. Though Wordsworth's does not fall into assonance so often as theirs, the *Prelude* (I, 191) gives us:

> *m*ind
> *m*ood
> *s*ource
> *s*tream
> heard
> l*i*ght
> *c*ourse
> t*i*me.

The Cenci (I, Sc. III, line 105) shows Shelley using assonance and rhyme:

> bou*nd*
> f*i*n*d*
> worl*d*
> *o*ut
> m*i*n*d*
> *th*in*k*
> ha*nd*
> *s*tro*k*e
> chastisement
> d*o*ub*t*
> t*e*ars
> b*e*
> nigh*ts*
> *a*ll
> *h*eard

here
feast
remain
not
again
graves
kinsman
chamberlain
justiciary
away, *or* here.

Taking Tennyson at random, we find at the beginning of *Balin and Balan*:

Lot
restored
late
call'*d*
spake
to us
throne
*s*aid
knights
*s*ide
challeng*i*ng
comes
pass
him
depart
sit
themselves
dawn
return'd
went
beheld
statuelike
down

fe*rn*
of i*t*
horse
le*ft*
tre̤e
he̤re
sa̤ke
a̤ll
proved
ca̤me
*throw*n
ha̤*ll*
wa̤rs
no̤t
throw
down
knew.

Browning, chosen at random, has towards the end of *In a Balcony*, where Norbert is speaking:

Enough! my cheek grows red, I think. Your test?

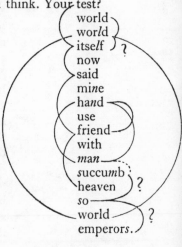

Some of these assonances are more convincing than others. It would be interesting to know how the percentage of assonances varies from author to author, and in the more lyrical blank verse compared with the less lyrical, but perhaps not interesting enough to sustain the tremendous and dull work of finding out.

If we need any proof, these assonated passages show that rhyme is a natural and indigenous growth of English lyric poetry. This is not to say that poets, and the greatest poets, never get their rhymes by force of will, or arrange them by sheer uninspired artistry. But it does mean that many poets do so think in rhyme that we can say neither that the rhyme came first nor that the thought came first, but that their thought came in rhymed form. Rhyme, therefore, being neither artificial nor sophisticated, its leading need no more be despised or set aside than the leading of any other musical element in poetry. In the next chapter we shall show the sound and sense of poetry reciprocally and inextricably dependent. Then any reader who should have ventured so far may take a glad farewell of us.

CHAPTER V

SHOWS MUSIC AND MEANING MARRIED AND AGREEING WELL

> Noise!
> Iron hoofs, iron wheels, iron din
> Of drays and trams and feet passing;
> Iron
> Beaten to a vast, mad cacophony.
>
> In vain the shrill, far cry
> Of swallows sweeping by;
> In vain the silence and the green
> Of meadows Apriline;
> In vain the clear, white rain—
> Soot; mud;
> A nation maddened with labour;
> Interminable collision of energies—
> Iron beating upon iron,
> Smoke whirling upwards,
> Speechless, impotent.
>
> In vain the shrill, far cry
> Of kittiwakes that fly
> Where the sea waves leap green,
> The meadows Apriline—
>
> Noise, iron, smoke,
> Iron, Iron, Iron.*

Mr. Sturge Moore objects to this ungrammatical accumulation of nouns and adjectives; he says the poem would

---

* Richard Aldington, quoted by Sturge Moore, *Some Soldier Poets*.

have been better without lines 1, 11, 16, 21 and 22; they give the work "the air of a translation, as though the difficulty of following a foreign idiom had overstrained the resources of the writer". But this is the wrong way of looking at such poetry. The lines he objects to "imitate" the meaning. Sense and sound are not divorced; the interjected hardness of the non-grammatical lines express their meaning:

> Noise, iron, smoke,
> Iron, Iron, Iron.

The poet could hardly express his bad temper more forcibly; and he does it as poets have expressed themselves through the centuries, with a feeling for the meaning of the sounds of words. Milton too, although he observed the proprieties of Latin grammar (we cannot always call it English), uses words because they sound like his meaning. Many readers must have watched the adventures of his echoes and alliterations in *Paradise Lost* and seen how they coincide with the meaning.* Although he probably indulged in iteration for the joy of the jingle, yet his iterated noises always "imitate" the meaning.

> †To whom the Tempter murmuring thus reply'd.
> Think not so slight of glory; therein least,
> Resembling thy great Father: he seeks glory,
> And for his glory all things made, all things
> Orders and governs, not content in Heaven
> By all his Angels glorifi'd, requires
> Glory from men, from all men good or bad,
> Wise or unwise, no difference, no exemption;
> Above all Sacrifice, or hallow'd gift
> Glory he requires, and glory he receives

* Symonds, *Blank Verse*, p. 103, says: "He confines his alliterative systems to periods of sense and metrical construction. When the period is closed, and the thought which it conveys has been expressed, the predominant letter is dropped."

† *Paradise Regained*, iii, 108-20.

> Promiscuous from all Nations, Jew, or Greek,
> Or Barbarous, nor exception hath declar'd;
> From us his foes pronounc't glory he exacts.

The contemptuous repetition of "glory", compounded with light syllables, makes Satan's snarl more bitter:

> Glory he requires and glory he receives.

> From us his foes pronounc't glory he exacts.

It has a ringing effect; we hear the formal noise of honour, bells sounding and flags going up.

> *For where no hope is left, is left no fear;
> If there be worse, the expectation more
> Of worse torments me than the feeling can.
> I would be at the worst; worst is my Port,
> .   .   .   .   .   .
> My error was my error, and my crime
> My crime;   .   .   .   .
> .   .   .   .   whether thou
> Raign or raign not; though to that gentle brow
> Willingly I could flye, and hope thy raign.

I think Milton enjoyed Satan's booming subtleties, but apart from their vigorous music, the iterated emphasis creates an impression of deceit and craft:

> My error was my error, and my crime
> My crime;

is too sophisticated to penetrate an honest brain just at once, and the hammering on the same sounds adds to our bamboozlement.

The sounds of poetry may follow the meaning more closely than this.

But how of Cawdor? The thane of Cawdor lives,

* *Ibid.*, iii, 206.

says Macbeth with an irritated emphasis on "lives". Both the rhythm and the phonetic construction of the sentence isolate "lives". The rhythm of "The thane of Cawdor" repeats that of "But how of Cawdor" exactly. "Lives" comes as a complete surprise. It stands out phonetically too, sounding almost awkwardly different from the rest of the line, which has not another l, i, v or s. Yet so spontaneous and natural is the sentence, that we forget the hundred other ways by which Shakespeare might have phrased Macbeth's objection without this feeling for the expressiveness of sounds. Poetry abounds in such subtle effects, so quiet, simple and unobtrusive that we overlook the art or the miracle which wrought them.

We should find it difficult to decide between these alternatives: The tale of *The Ancient Mariner* is told in such a natural, straightforward way that the sound of the words can have had little to do with the telling, and: *The Ancient Mariner* makes its effect so much by its wonderful music that the sound of the words must often have suggested the meaning. But these alternatives are not contradictory so much as complementary. Though for sheer music *The Ancient Mariner* is one of the most marvellous poems written, there could hardly be a better example of the indissolubility of sense from sound. The musical echoes can hardly fail to be sense echoes too. Sometimes the sense seems to suggest the music, sometimes the music the sense. This is all the more interesting when we remember that it was a work not of genius alone, not the intuitive flux of first inspiration, but a polished work. Coleridge exercised his art not only in words but in music, with a sense of design and artistry in sound. *The Ancient Mariner* has a small vocabulary; since the ballad proper, not many poems of equal length contain so few words, but not because Coleridge's vocabulary is small; the atmosphere demands the sort of music that only repeated and simple sounds will give. The poem is dominated by a few words which come again and again with an effect unlike the echoes of any other poem. The same threads weave its texture from beginning to end. We never get away from "eye"; and yet not because "eye" echoes, for it does not. We start with the "glittering eye" of the Mariner in the first stanza; it shines in lines 13 and 20. Each eye of the dying mariners is glazed in line 144, and weary in 147; eyes curse the Mariner in line 215; most horrible is the "curse in a dead man's eye" in line 260; the ghostly bodies "nor spake nor moved their eyes" in line 332; the ocean's "great bright eye" is cast up to the Moon in line 416; the dead men's eyes glitter in line 436; the ancient Mariner could not draw his eyes from theirs in 440; even the "Hermit raised his eyes" in line 562; the Mariner leaves us in the second last stanza with his eye still bright (line 618). The sound of "eye" stabs us each time because of its meaning; and this sharp meaning makes us recollect having heard the sound, thus turning "eye" into an oblique or referred echo. Such words as "sea", "sky", "ship", "sail", "sun", "moon" almost necessarily form the warp of the poem; but others like "moved" or "motion" and "moving" make a mystic woof in it. In no other context would "the *moving* moon" go up the sky; the ship is "moved onward from beneath"; the spectre ship "moved and moved", and later we hear of the ship:

> But in a minute she 'gan stir,
> With a short uneasy motion.

Towards the end we begin to notice "made" or "make" and "heard". The meaning helps to fix all these words in our memory, but the effect of their repetition is musical.

It may be worth while going through the poem, stanza by stanza, listening to its music and chronicling some of the echoes we hear. The first three verses give the colouring of

the whole, just as the first few bars often give us the whole
foundation of a Bach *Prelude*.

> (1) It is an ancient Mariner,
>   And he stoppeth one of three.
>   "By thy long grey beard and glittering eye,
>   Now wherefore stopp'st thou me?

> (2) The Bridegroom's doors are opened wide,
>   And I am next of kin;
>   *The* gue*st*s are m*et*, *the* fea*st* is s*et*:
>   May'st hear the merry din."

> (3) *H*e *h*olds *h*im with *h*is skinny *h*and,
>   "There was a ship," quoth *h*e.
>   "*H*old off! un*h*and me, grey-beard loon!"
>   Eftsoons *h*is *h*and dropt *h*e.

The second verse has the double internal rhyme characteristic of the poem: "The gue*st*s are m*et*, the fea*st* is s*et*". *H*
is a predominant colour in stanza (3); it appears occasionally at the beginning of the poem, then drops under, to
come up at the very end; I feel tempted to call it a land
motif.

> (4) *H*e *h*olds *h*im with *h*is glittering eye—
>   The Wedding-Guest *st*ood *st*ill,
>   And *l*istens *l*ike a thr*ee* y*ear*s' ch*il*d:
>   The Mariner *h*ath *h*is will.

This echoes stanza (1) and is linked to stanza (3) by "He
holds him". Does a three years' child listen differently
from a two or a four years' one? Perhaps the poet wants
the magic number; or the Wedding-Guest may "listen like
a three years' child" because he is "one of three" in stanza
(1). "The Wedding-Guest" makes one of the more prominent colours in the design of the poem. Here he "*st*ood
*st*ill"; in stanza (1) the Mariner "*st*oppeth one of three"
and is asked: "Now, wherefore *st*opp'*st* thou me?" In

stanza (5) the "Wedding-Guest" still alliterates to *s*; he "sat on a stone".

> (5) The Wedding-Guest sat on a stone:
> He cannot choose but hear;
> And thus sp*a*ke *on* that *an*cient ma*n*,
> The bright-eyed Mariner.

The "ancient" man (1) is still "the bright-eyed" (1) (4) "Mariner" (1).

> (6) "The ship was ch*eered*, the harbour cl*eared*,
> Merrily did we drop
> Below the kirk, below the hill,
> Below the lighthouse top.

This has the typical internal rhyme, and parallel iteration.

> (7) The Sun came up upon the left,
> Out of the s*ea* came h*e*!
> *And* he sh*one* b*right, and on* the *right*
> Went down into the sea.

The *s* still alliterates; "bright" is repeated from (5) and rhymed.

> (8) *H*igher and *h*igher every day,
> Till over the mast at noon—"
> The Wedding-Gu*est h*ere b*eat h*is b*reast*,
> For *h*e *h*eard the loud *b*assoon.

H alliterates; "Wedding-Guest" echoes from (5); "mast" is a *key* word of the poem; we notice it wherever it occurs. Has the bassoon any special connection with Hymen, or with weddings among the fisher folk, or is its sole musical significance here that of alliterating with "beat" and "breast" and rhyming with "noon"? The alliteration prepares us for the advent of the "bride" in the next stanza; she comes to the music of the favoured consonant *s*, and the trill of *r*—"Red as a rose is she", "rose" being rhymed in "goes".

(9) The bri*d*e *h*ath paced into the *h*all,
    Red as a *rose is s*he;
    No*dd*ing their *h*ea*d*s before *h*er goes
    The *m*erry *m*instrelsy.

"Merry" comes from stanza (6).

(10) The Wedding-Gu*est* he *beat h*is *breast*,
    Yet he cannot choose but hear;
    *And th*us sp*a*ke on *that a*ncient m*a*n
    The bright-eyed Mariner.

(10) reflects (5) almost identically, save that now he "beat his breast" as in (8) and there he "sat on a stone".

(11) "And now the *STORM-BLAST* came, and he
    Was *ty*ra*nn*ous and *str*o*ng*;
    He *struck* with his o'er*t*a*k*ing wings,
    And ch*a*sed us *s*outh al*o*ng.

The "storm" rages to *st*, *s*, *t* and *r*; gathering weight in (12) it alliterates on heavier consonants, *p*, and *b* and *d*, with a double echo in the second last line.

    With *sl*o**pp**ing ma*st*s and *dipp*ing *p*row,
    As who *p*ursue*d* with ye*ll* and *bl*o*w*
    *Still tr*e*a*ds the *s*hadow of his *f*o*e*,
    And *f*orwar*d* be*n*ds his he*a*d,
    The ship *d*r*o*ve *fast*, loud *r*o*a*red the *b*l*ast*,
    And southwar*d* aye we *fled*.

F gives the speed and *l* the water of the storm; the "o" vowel is windy; "masts" comes from (8).

(13) *And* now there came b*o*th mist and sn*o*w,
    And it grew wondrous c*o*ld:
    *And i*ce, mast-*h*igh, came flo*a*ting b*y*,
    *A*s green as emerald.

Here is "mast" again, with its twin, "mist". We still hear windy "o" sounding so "cold"ly that even the warm "a" of "emerald" gets chilly from attempting to rhyme with it. The triple internal assonance—"ice", "high", "by"— cuts us like a frosty gale; "grew" and "green" make us feel almost ill. There is a strong gradation of "grew" in "cold", g becoming c, r l, ew o.

> (14) And through the drifts the snowy clifts
> Did send a dismal sheen:
> Nor shapes of men nor beasts we ken—
> The ice was all between.

D and s sound "through" (echoing "grew") all the noise.
(15) picks up "ice" for emphasis in the typical manner, and gives us a completely onomatopoeic stanza.

> The ice was here, the ice was there,
> The ice was all around:
> It cracked and growled, and roared and howled,
> Like noises in a swound!

In (16) the "Albatross" first comes in, rhyming with "cross".

> At length did cross an Albatross,
> Thorough the fog it came;
> As if it had been a Christian soul,
> We hailed it in God's name.

> (17) It ate the food it ne'er had eat,
> And round and round it flew.
> The ice did split with a thunder-fit;
> The helmsman steered us through!

"Helmsman" gives us a good h. "It" . . . "it", "split", "did", "with", "fit" sound clearly. "Round" . . . "round" carries on the vowel of "howled" in (15) to "south" in (18).

(18) And a good south wind sprung up behind;
     The Albatross did follow,
     And every day, for food or play,
     Came to the mariner's hollo!

Here the "albatross" and the "mariner" meet. We are
beginning to notice "came".

(19) In mist or cloud, on mast or shroud,
     It perched for vespers nine;
     Whiles all the night, through fog-smoke white,
     Glimmered the white Moon-shine."

The twins, "mist" and "mast", answer each other in a line
of nothing but rhymes or assonances. Even "perched"
must have "vespers" to reflect it. The "moon-shine"
"glimmered" "white", not unlike the "bright" "glittering"
of an "eye"; the "fog" comes from (16).

(20) "God save thee, ancient Mariner!
     From the fiends, that plague thee thus!—
     Why look'st thou so?"—With my cross-bow
     I shot the ALBATROSS.

Thus Part I ends on s and th; (16) had "God"; "mariner"
and "Albatross" were in (18); "cross" and "Albatross" in
(16); "ancient" comes from (10), assonating here with
"save" and "plague", in (10) with "spake".

Part II opens with the music of stanza (7), only instead
of bright sunshine we have mist.

(1) The Sun now rose upon the right:
    Out of the sea came he,
    Still hid in mist, and on the left
    Went down into the sea.

In the first draft of this stanza the repetition was closer;
the sun still "came up" upon the right.

(2) gets its sounds from (18).

> And the good south wind still blew behind,
> But no sweet bird did follow,
> Nor any day for food or play
> Came to the mariners' hollo!

(3) gets its rhythmical construction from the storm stanza (12).

> And I had done a hellish thing,
> And it would work 'em woe:
> For all averred, I had killed the bird
> That made the breeze to blow.
> Ah wretch! said they, the bird to slay,
> That made the breeze to blow!

(4) echoes this, with "fog" and "mist" instead of the blowing breeze.

> Nor dim nor red, like God's own head,
> The glorious Sun uprist:
> Then all averred, I had killed the bird
> That brought the fog and mist.
> 'Twas right, said they, such birds to slay,
> That bring the fog and mist.

We need not point out that "fog" and "mist", and "right" and "Sun" and "God", *etc.*, are already familiar sounds. Here "made" is dropped and we find "brought" and "bring" in its place, and "breeze" and "blow" for "mist".

> (5) The fair breeze blew, the white foam flew,
> The furrow followed free:
> We were the first that ever burst
> Into that silent sea.

This is one of the loveliest *imitation* effects in the poem— "The furrow followed free", with *f* for fleetness and trilling *r*s and *l*s for water. The last line too, compared with the second last, reflects the sense. "Breeze", "blew", "white" and "sea" are old sounds keeping the continuity.

(6) comes a thud.

> *Down dropt the* bree*ze*, *the* sails *dropt down,*
> *'*Twas *sad as sad* coul*d* be;
> And we *did* sp*eak* only to *break*
> The silence of the sea!

After the thud comes the "silence of the sea", with the *s*s placed to parallel those of "sad . . . sad" and with "breeze" and "sails", *s* alliterating for sadness and stillness. Perhaps I ought to say that I do not chronicle eye rhymes like "speak" and "break", although Coleridge has one or two in the poem; here he may have written the words for their consonant assonance, and also for the echo by gradation not only of the vowels, but from the *p* of "speak" to the *b* of "break".

(7) has "sun" and "noon" and "moon" and "mast". "The sun is right above the mast."

> All in a hot and copper sky,
> The *bl*oody Su*n*, at *n*oon,
> Right up above the ma*st* did *st*and,
> No *b*igger than the Moon.

The sun is "bloody" and "bigger", the alliteration coming on the same place in each line; Coleridge often does this.

(8) makes its own monotony, "day" and "ship" being old sounds.

> *D*ay after *d*ay, *d*ay after *d*ay,
> We stuck, nor *b*reath nor motion;
> As idle as a *p*ainted ship
> Upon a *p*ainted ocean.

(9) makes a new monotony, but carries on the *d*, *b*, *p* sounds, coming down heavily at the end.

> *W*ater, *w*ater every*w*here,
> And all the *b*oards *d*i*d* shrink;
> *W*ater, *w*ater, every where,
> No*r* any *d*rop to *d*rink.

(10) Although we still have *d*, *b*, *p*, "night" and "white", "sea", "water", "green", *etc.*, a new colouring comes in with stanzas (10) and (11).

> (10) The v̧ery *d*eep *d*i*d* r͡o*t*: O Chr͡is*t*!
> That ${}$ver *th*is should be!
> Yea, *s*l*i*my thing**s** did craw*l* with *l*egs
> Upon the *s*limy *s*ea.

> (11) Ab*out*, ab*out*, in **r**eel and **r***out*
> The **d**eath-f**i**res **d**anced at n*i*ght;
> The **w**ater, *l*ike a **w**itch's oi*l*s,
> *B*urnt green, and *b*lue and white.

> (12) And some in *d*rea*m*s assuréd were
> Of the S*p*irit that *p*lagued u*s* *s*o:
> Nine *f*athom *d*ee*p* he had *f*ollowed us
> From the land of mist and snow.

"Deep", "followed" and "land of mist and snow" have already occurred. "Spirit", "dream", "nine fathom deep" and "plagued" will echo later.

> (13) echoes (6) only "*d*" is turned to *t* and *k*.
> And.every tongue, through utter drought,
> Was withered at the root;
> We could not speak, no more than if
> We had been choked with soot.

"If" makes a graded echo to "speak", the vowels being closely related, "soot" to "choked", the consonants as well as the vowels being near relatives. This sort of echo is much commoner in poetry than we should expect.

Part II, like Part I, closes on "cross" and "Albatross".

> (14) Ah! we*ll* a-day! what evi*l* *l*ooks
> Had I from o*l*d and young!
> Instead of the *cross*, the *Albatross*
> About my neck was hung.

Although hanging the Albatross on the Mariner's neck is one of the most powerfully gruesome actions in the poem, I should imagine Coleridge thought of it to get "cross" and "Albatross" into the closing stanza.

Part III makes a new start with an intrusion of "eye" and "sky", and with the form of repetition we are beginning to expect.

> (1) There **pa**ssed a weary time. Each throat
> Was **par**ched, and glazed each eye.
> A weary time! a weary time!
> How glazed each weary eye,
> When looking westward, I beheld
> A something in the sky.

> (2) At first it *see*med a little *s*peck,
> And then it *see*med a *m*ist;
> It *m*oved and *m*oved, and took at last
> A certain shape, I wist.

"Mist" and "moved" help to keep the atmosphere continuous. "Shape" is a graded echo of "certain". The first line of the next stanza sums this one up in a sort of *stretto* (a metaphorical one).

> (3) A *s*peck, a *mist*, a shape, I w*ist*!
> And still it neared and neared:
> As if it dodged a water-sprite,
> It plunged and tacked and veered.

(4) repeats "throat" from (1); "drought" goes back to II (13); "sail" is a *key* sound of the poem. The alliteration of *b* and *d* makes the stanza feel stunned.

> With throats uns*l*a*ked*, with b*l*ack *l*ips b*aked*,
> We could nor *l*augh nor wai*l*;
> Thr*ough* *u*tter drought all d*u*mb we st*ood*!
> *I* b*it* m*y* arm, *I* sucked the b*loo*d,
> And cried, A sail! a sail!

(5) repeats the first line of this.

> With throats uns*l*a*ked*, with black lips b*a*ked,
> Ag*a*pe they heard me c*a*ll:
> Gramercy! they for joy did grin,
> And *all* at once their breath drew in,
> As they were drinking *all*.

"Breath" comes from II (8).

(6) See! see! (I cried) she tacks no more!
> Hither to *w*ork us *w*ea*l*;
> *W*ithout a br*ee*ze, *w*ithout a tide,
> She steadies *w*ith upright k*ee*l!

"Breeze" comes from II (5) and (6); perhaps we hear an echo of "heard" in "hither".

(7) The **west**ern **w**a*v*e w*a*s *a*ll a-fl*a*me.
> The **d**ay w*a*s **w**ell nigh **d**one!
> A*l*most upon the **west**ern **w**a*v*e
> **R**est*e*d the *b*road *b*right *S*un;
> When that *s*trange *s*hape drove *s*uddenly
> Betwixt *u*s and the *S*un.

"Day" comes from II (8), "bright" I (7), "Sun" II (7), "drove" I (12), "shape" III (2).

(8) And *s*tra**i**ght the *S*un was flecked with bars,
> (Heaven's Mother send us gr**a**ce!)

> As if through a dungeon-grate he peered
> With *broad* and *burning* face.

Here is the "Sun" again with "broad and burning face", and the vowel of "wave". In (7) he was "broad" and "bright".

(9) echoes the 3rd and 7th stanzas of this part.

> Alas! (thought I, and my heart beat loud)
> How fast she nears and nears!
> Are those *her** sails that glance in the *S*un,
> Like restless gossam*e*res?

(10) Reflects (8) and (9).

> Are those *her** ribs through which the Sun
> Did peer, as through a grate?
> And is that *Woman* all her crew?
> Is that a *Death*? and are there two?
> Is *Death* that *woman*'s mate?

The last line collects sounds from the other lines, "mate", echoing from the 2nd line, "woman" from the third, and "Death" from the fourth. This gives quite a different effect from repeating words together, which have already been joined. All these sounds are recompounded in the next stanza.

(11) emphasises the sounds of (10), with "white" and "blood" and "cold" for old sounds.

> *Her** lips *were* r*ed*, *her** *looks were* free,
> Her *locks were* yellow as gold:
> Her skin was *a*s white as *l*eprosy,
> The Night-mare L*i*fe-in-*D*eath was she,
> Who thicks m*a*n's *blood* with c*old*.

There are several graded echoes here.

* Coleridge's *italics*.

Most of (12) is new, although we may remember that
the Albatross "came" through the fog in I (16), and the
sun "came" out of the sea in I (25) and II (1).

> The naked hulk alongside came,
> And the twain were casting dice;
> "The game is done! I've won! I've won!"
> Quoth she, and whistles thrice.

(13) has "Sun", "sea", "shot" I (20) and a whispering s.

> The Sun's rim dips; the stars rush out:
> At one stride comes the dark;
> With far-heard whisper, o'er the sea,
> Off shot the spectre-bark.

(14) concentrates the vowel of "ribs" (10), "lips",
"skin" (11), "rim", "dips", "whisper" (13), and rhymes
it in "sip", "drip", "tip".

> We listened and looked sideways up!
> Fear at my heart, as at a cup,
> My life-blood seemed to sip!
> The stars were dim, and thick the night,
> The steersman's face by his lamp gleamed white:
> From the sails the dew did drip—
> Till clomb above the eastern bar
> The hornéd Moon, with one bright star
> Within the nether tip.

"Night", "white" and "blood" come from (11), "stars"
from (13), "sails" from (9), "face" from (8), "Moon"
from II (7), "bright" (7). Coleridge's first draft began

> And we look'd round, and we look'd up.

"Listened" is preferred to "look'd", from having the vowel
of "whisper", "rim", etc., "sideways" that of "night",
"white", "bright". We can hear the dropping of the "dew
did drip".

(15) One after one, by the star-dogged Moon,
    Too quick for groan or sigh,
    Each turned his face with a ghastly pang,
    And cursed me with his eye.

Here are "Moon", "face", "star" and "eye". "One after one" reminds us of "Day after day", II (8).

(16) echoes (15) and (14); "drop" comes from II (9) and (6).

    Four times *fi*fty living men,
    (And I heard nor sigh nor groan)
    With heavy th*ump*, a lifeless l*ump*,
    They *d*ropped *d*own one by one.

The second last line is most gruesomely onomatopoeic; we almost feel the deck vibrate with the leaden collapse of "thump" and "lump". Part III ends with the whizz of "cross" bow, the moaning rhyme of "woe" and the rustle of spirits in flight.

    The souls did from their bodies fly—
    They fled to bliss or woe!
    And every soul, it passed me **by**,
    Like the whizz of my cross-**bow**!

Part IV—The music of Part III has drifted away a little from the colour of the opening music; it makes a gentle contrast, with sufficient of the old words to keep the pattern continuous. Now, in Part IV we go back to the opening music—"the ancient Mariner" and his "skinny hand", though "fear" has come from Part III (14).

(1) "*I fear the*e, ancient Mariner!
    *I fear th*y skinny h*and*!
    *And th*ou art *l*ong, and *l*ank, and brown,
    As *is* the r*i*bbed *s*ea-sand.

(2) reflects (1) and has "dropt" from III (16); it casts back to the beginning in "thy glittering eye", and "Wedding-Guest".

> *I fear thee* and *th*y glittering *ey*e,
> *And th*y *s*kinny hand, *s*o brown.—
> *Fear* not, *fear* not, *th*ou Wedding-Guest!
> *Th*is bo*d*y *d*ropt *n*ot *d*own.

(3) is modelled on II (9), with "soul" from III (17), and "sea" from IV (1).

> Alone, alone, all, all alone,
> Alone on a wide wide sea!
> And never a saint took pity on
> My soul in agony.

The liquidy *l*s and *w*s, the continuing sound of the *n*s, and the "o" and "y" ("wide", "My") vowels give us a feeling of the wide expanse of waters.

> (4) The *m*any *m*en, so beautiful!
> And they all *dead did* lie:
> A*nd* a thousa*nd* thousa*nd s*limy things
> Live*d* on; a*nd* so *did* I.

"Slimy" comes from II (10). "All dead did lie" imitates the meaning, stiff in "dead did", and stretched out in "lie".

> (5) I loo*k*ed upon the rotting sea,
> And *drew* my eyes a*w*ay;
> I loo*k*ed upon the rotting *deck*,
> And there the *d*ead men la*y*.

Here are "eyes" and "sea"; "dead" sounds again with *d*s and *t*s and *k*s; "rotting" comes from II (10).

(6) carries on the sounds of (5), "heart" from III (14), "whisper" from III (13), "came" from III (12).

> I look*t* to heaven, and tried to pr*ay*;
> But or ever a prayer had gush*t*,
> A *w*icked *w*hisper c*a*me, and m*a*de
> My heart as *d*ry as *d*ust.

(7) Has a near echo in "dead" (5), and a far away one in "weary" III (11), and "sea" and "sky" and "eye".

> I *c*losed my *l*ids, and **k**ept them **c***lose*,
> And the *balls* *l*ike *pu*lses *b*eat;
> For the *s*ky and the *s*ea, and the *s*ea and the *s*ky
> Lay *l*ike a *load* on my weary eye,
> And the *dead* were at my feet.

"And the balls like pulses beat"! The line beats like a fevered pulse too. "Lay like a load" drags like its meaning.

(8) echoes "rot" from (5), "passed" from III (17), "cold" from III (11).

> The **c**o**ld** sweat *m*e**l**ted from their li*m*bs,
> No*r* *r*ot no*r* *r*eek did they:
> The *look* with which they *look*ed on me
> Had never passed away.

"Nor rot nor reek did they" concentrates the *d*, *t*, *k* colouring we have had for some time, making it sound all the more for the *r*s; "reek" is a graded echo of "rot". "Look" and "looked" give us another gradation, *r* becoming *l*, already a familiar sound in this context.

> (9) An orphan's curse would drag to hell
> A spirit from on high;
> But oh! more horrible than that
> Is the curse in a dead man's eye!
> Seven days, seven nights, I saw that curse,
> And yet *I* could not *d*ie.

"Eye", "curse", "day", "night", "spirit" and "dead" are

old sounds. We do not hear many *h*s in the poem, but here are three—"hell", "high", "horrible".

(10) has "the moving Moon", and "sky" and "star", with *s* sounding very beautifully.

> The *moving Moo*n went up the sky,
> And no where did a*b*ide:
> *S*oftly *s*he was going up,
> And a *s*tar or two *b*eside—

"Moving Moon" sounds very lovely, although "mutely mused" does not. This is partly because *t* and *s* are nearly related, and *v* and *n* far enough from each other to make the contrast worth while. Two words with hardly any difference in sound do not usually please us in juxtaposition.

(11) reflects II (11).

> Her *beam*s *bem*ocked the sultry *m*ain,
> Like April h*oa*r-fr*o*st spread;
> But where the *sh*ip's huge *sh*adow lay,
> The charmèd w*a*ter burnt *a*lway
> A still and awful rèd.

(12) repeats "hoar"-y, "sh*ip*", "shadows", and "watched" and "water" echo \ "water"; "shadow", "watched" and "track" are in (13) also; "moved" comes from (10), "shining" and "wh*i*te" from III (14).

> (12) Beyond the *sha*dow of the *sh*ip,
> I *wa*tched the *wa*ter-snakes;
> They mov*ed* in tr*a*cks of *sh*ining *wh*ite,
> And *wh*en they rear*ed*, the *e*lfish light
> F*e*ll *off* in h*oa*ry *f*lakes.

> (13) *W*ithin the sh*a*dow of the sh*i*p
> I *wa*tched their r*i*ch att*i*re;
> Blue, gl*o*ssy green, and velvet bl*a*ck,

> They coiled and swam; and every track
> Was a flash of golden fire.

This reflects II (11) with a difference. There we had:

> About, about, in reel and rout
> The death-fires danced at night;
> The water, like a witch's oils,
> Burnt green, and blue and white.

"Oil" ("coil") sounds in both, not a common sound in this poem.

(14) has "tongue" II (13), "gush'd" IV (6), "heart" III (14); "saint took pity on" comes from IV (3).

> O happy living thing! no tongue
> Their beauty might declare:
> A spring of love gushed from my heart,
> And I blessed them unaware:
> Sure my kind saint took pity on me,
> And I blessed them unaware.

This Part ends on "Albatross", but the "cross" has gone.

(15) reminds us of (5); we have not forgotten "deck" and "dead", and here is "neck" and "lead"; the reminiscence is subtle but clear.

> The self-same moment I could pray;
> And from my neck so free
> The Albatross fell off, and sank
> Like lead into the sea.

Part V—(1) echoes within itself.

> Oh sleep! it is a gentle thing,
> Beloved from pole to pole!
> To Mary Queen the praise be given!
> She sent the gentle sleep from Heaven,
> That slid into my soul.

"Soul" comes from III (17).

(2) has "deck", and "dew" from III (14), but these stanzas rather introduce fresh sounds than repeat old.

> The silly bu*ck*ets on the d*e*ck,
> That had so long *r*emained,
> I *dr*eamt that they *w*ere filled wi*th d*ew;
> And *w*hen I a*w*oke, i*t r*ained.

(3) takes up old sounds.

> My lips *w*ere *w*et, my throat was cold
> My garments all were *dank*;
> Sure I had *dr*un*k*en in my *dr*eams,
> And still my body *dr*an*k*.

"Lips" comes from III (11), "throat" III (1), (4), (5), "cold" III (11), "dreams" II (12), "body" III (15), and perhaps "drank" recalls:

> Water, water, everywhere,
> Nor any drop to drink.

(4) I move*d*, and coul*d* not fee*l* my *l*imbs:
> I was so *l*ight—a*l*most
> I thought that I had died in s*l*eep,
> And was a b*l*esséd ghost.

"Moved" comes from IV (13), "sleep" V (1), "blessed" IV (14), "light", "could" and "die" are less strongly felt repetitions.

> (5) And soon I hear*d* a roaring win*d*:
> It did not come anear;
> But with it*s* *s*ound it *s*hook the *s*ails,
> That were *s*o *th*in and *s*ere.

The "roaring wind" comes from I (15), "anear" brings recollections of III (3); "sails" was in III (14); "heard" gives us the rare *h*, which we hear twice in the next stanza.

(6) The upper air burst into life!
    And a hundred fire-flags sheen,
    To and fro they were hurried about!
    And to and fro, and in and out,
    The wan stars danced between.

The "stars", IV (10), dance a little like the dance of slimy things in II. "About, about, in reel and rout", *etc*. The "sheen" comes from I (14).

(7) And the coming wind did roar more loud,
    And the sails did sigh like sedge;
    And the rain poured down from one black cloud;
    The Moon was at its edge.

Here are "wind" and "sails'" and "roar" and an *s* alliteration from (5), "rain" from (2), "Moon" IV (10), "sigh" III (16), and "black" from IV (13). "The sails did sigh like sedge" sounds just like its meaning.

(8) continues the storm music.

        The thick black cloud was cleft, and still
        The Moon was at its side:
        Like waters shot from some high crag,
        The lightning fell with never a jag,
        A river steep and wide.

Ck, g, c make noisy sounds. "The thick black cloud was cleft" is very expressive. I think "still" stands out as an exceptional liquid, and hence we recollect it when we come to "fell"; perhaps we hear *s* as a subsidiary consonant, and remember "still" when we come to "steep". There is an *h* in this stanza.

(9) also continues the word echoes from (7) and (8), bringing "wind" and "loud" close together.

        The loud wind never reached the ship,
        Yet now the ship moved on!

> Beneath the lightning and the Moon
> The dead men gave a groan.

"Moved" comes from IV (10), "dead men" IV (5), "groan" III (15).

> (10) They groaned, they stirred, they all uprose,
> Nor spake, nor moved their eyes;
> It had been strange, even in a dream,
> To have seen those dead men rise.

"Groaned", "moved" and "dead men" come from (9); "eyes" awakens sinister recollections. "Dream" comes from IV (3), "strange" from III (7). The mariner "spoke" in I (5). I think we do keep this sound in our head.

> (11) The helmsman steered, the ship moved on;
> Yet never a breeze up-blew;
> The mariners all 'gan work the ropes,
> Where they were wont to do;
> They raised their limbs like lifeless tools—
> We were a ghastly crew.

"Helmsman" gives us an *h*, which we should not notice if we were not on the look out for *h*s; "moved" was in (10), "ship" in (9); "breeze" comes from III (6); "ghastly" renews an old shudder, III (15); "up-blew" is a recollection of "uprose" in (10); "mariner" was last heard in IV (1). The *l* alliteration in the second last line gives us a very tired, listless feeling, helped by the same vowel in "like" and "life".

(12) echoes (11) a little. "Stood" perhaps reflects "steered", and we have "rope".

> The body of my brother's son
> Stood by me, knee to knee:
> The body and I pulled at one rope,
> But he said nought to me.

"Body" comes from V (3); curiously enough we have not forgotten that the Wedding-Guest "stood" still in I (4). *The Ancient Mariner* has an almost uncanny way of printing its words indelibly. In no other poem should we remember such an unimportant sound for over 300 lines.

(13) goes back to the beginning. I wonder if the arrival of "stood" sent Coleridge's mind suddenly there.

> (13) "I fear thee, ancient Mariner!"
> Be calm, thou Wedding-Guest!
> 'Twas not those souls that fled in pain,
> Which to their corses came again,
> But a troop of spirits blest:

The return to the "ancient Mariner" and the "Wedding-Guest" brings the variation that comes in Part IV: "I fear thee". "Souls" comes from V (1), "spirits" IV 9), "blest" V (4), and "came" IV (6).

> (14) For when it *d*awne*d*—they *d*ropp*ed* their arms,
> And clu*st*ere*d* roun*d* the m*a*st;
> *S*weet *s*ound*s* ro*s*e *s*lowly through their m*o*uths,
> An*d* from their bo*d*ies pass*ed*.

Here come "drop" and "mast" and "rose" and "bodies" and "passed", all old words, with *s* to make it sound beautiful.

> (15) Ar*ound*, ar*ound* flew e*a*ch *s*we*e*t *sound*,
> Then darted to the Sun;
> *S*lowly the *s*ounds c*a*me back ag*ai*n,
> Now mixed, now one by one.

(15) rearranges some of the words of (14). "Sweet sound" is repeated, then "slowly" comes, and "sounds" follows; "came again" is from (13). "Around, around", as much by its rhythm as its sound, takes us back to II (11). We have not heard the "Sun" since it dipped in III (13);

from then the "Moon" has reigned. In III (16) the bodies dropped "one by one".

(16) has "dropping", "sky", "sea", and "sweet".

> *S*ometimes a-dropping from the *s*ky
> I heard the *s*ky-lark *s*ing;
> Sometimes all little birds that are,
> How they *s*eemed to fill the *sea* and ai*r*
> With their *s*wee*t* jargoning!

In this stanza of lovely sounds perhaps none is more lovely than "jargoning", yet in other contexts "jargon" may be ugly enough. It has the vowel of "lark" and rhymes with "sing", but I think some other more subtle echo gives it this beauty.

> (17) And now 'twas like all instruments,
> Now *l*ike a *l*one*l*y f*l*ute;
> And now it is an angel'*s* *s*ong,
> That *m*akes the heavens be *m*ute.

Recollection dies down here in the presence of a more ethereal music. We do not remember that "like" or "lone" were potent words in another context; "song" perhaps refers us to "sing" of the previous stanza, but I do not think we remember that "heaven" comes from V (1). Reading the poem especially on the look out for echoes, we do of course notice these, but they do not count in the musical impression.

> (18) It *c*eased; yet *s*till the sai*l*s made on
> A pleasant *n*oise till *n*oo*n*,
> A *n*oise like of a hidden brook
> In the leafy mo*n*th of Ju*n*e,
> That to the *s*leeping wood*s* all *n*ight
> *S*i*n*geth a quiet tu*n*e.

The last two lines of (15), and (16)(17) and (18) make a sort of oasis of land music in this world of sea; it is a sailor's dream. Even "sails", "noon", "night", "sing", "made", or "sleep" from "Oh sleep! it is a gentle thing", V (1), do not destroy this sense of paradise. There is an *h* in the stanza.

> (19) Till noo*n* we quietly sailed o*n*,
>   Yet never a *breeze* did *brea*the:
>   *S*lowly and *s*mooth*ly* went the *s*hip,
>   Moved onward from *b*eneath.

When Coleridge returns to the prose of sailing on till 12 A.M., he should not have profaned his more heavenly music by using "noon" and "quietly" from the garden of his paradise. They are like strings hanging down from heaven, making prose of our descent. Repeating "quiet" spoils the lonely loveliness of it. "Three hours we sailed on steadily", or "Four" or "Five hours", would have made the break more sharply and therefore more satisfactorily. The stanza does not need these repetitions to keep the sense of contiguity. The *s* alliteration maintains the same texture, and we have "sailed" and "breeze" (11), "slowly" (15), "ship" (9) and "moved" (9). Incidentally "breeze did breathe" sounds a little out of tune; it is almost as bad as "So though", and for nearly the same reason; *s* and *th* with the same vowel make dangerous neighbours.

In (20), after the descent to the level of the poem has been made, we welcome the echoes of heavenly music.

> Under the keel *n*ine fathom deep,
> From the land of mist and snow,
> *The* spirit slid: and it was he
> *Th*at made the ship to go.
> *The* sails at *n*oon left off their tu*n*e,
> And the *sh*ip *s*too*d* s*t*ill also.

The echoings of this stanza are very subtle; "*m*ade the

ship to go" reflects "*mist* and *snow*". In II (12) the "spirit" followed

> Nine fathom deep . . .
> From the land of mist and snow.

(18) has "made", "sails", "noon", "tune". "The sails at noon left off their tune" brings them closer; it is a (metaphorical) *stretto* of stanza (18). "Keel" comes from III (6), "ship" and "sail" from (19), "stood" from (12). The vocal gesture of the stopping consonants in the last line is most beautiful.

> (21) The S*u*n, righ*t u*p above the mas*t*,
> Had fixed her to the ocean:
> But in a minu*te* she 'gan s*t*ir,
> With a short uneasy motion—
> Backwards and forwards half her length
> With a short uneasy motion.

"Sun" comes from (15), "mast" (14); "ocean" and "motion" rhymed in II (8)—

> We stuck, nor breath nor motion;
> As idle as a painted ship
> Upon a painted ocean.

> (22) Then like a pawing horse let go,
> She ma*de* a s*u*d*de*n *b*oun*d*:
> It fl*u*ng the *b*loo*d* into my he*a*d,
> And I fell *d*own in a swoun*d*.

"Blood" comes from III (14); "down" is in (7), "made" (20). We have two *h*s and a land metaphor. (21) has four *h*s and (23) has three.

> (23) How *l*ong in that s*a*me fit I *l*ay,
> *I h*ave not to decl*a*re;

> But ere my *living life* returned,
> *I heard* and in my soul discerned
> Two voices in the air.

"Heard" was used in (16), "soul" in (13), "air" in (16); perhaps we hear a faint echo of "noise" (18) in "voices".

> (24) "Is it he?" quoth one, "Is this the man?
> By him who died on cross,
> With his cruel *bow* he *laid full low*
> The harmless Albatross.

H still sounds. We know the end of Part V is near by the return to "Albatross", "cross" and "bow".

(25) harps on the same theme a little differently. "Bow" is repeated, and the vowel of "woe" rhymes; *b* and *d*, and *l* and *d* resound and there are four *h*s. "Land of mist and snow" comes from (20).

> (25) The spirit who bideth by himself.
> In the *land* of mist and snow,
> He *loved* the *bird* that *loved* the man
> Who shot him with his *bow*.

The softer voice of the second spirit has softer echoes:

> (26) The other was a softer voice,
> As soft as honey-dew:
> Quoth he, "The man hath penance done,
> And penance more will do."

This stanza has sounds from previous ones, as "soft" IV (10), "voice" (23), "Quoth" (24), "man" (25). Its characteristic music, however, depends on the even lines beginning with an echo from the end of the odd lines—"softer voice, As soft", "penance done, And penance". This is really all we want of the voices. "Voices" are all right and in place in Shelley's *Prometheus*, but a little out of the picture in *The Ancient Mariner*.

Part VI begins badly.

FIRST VOICE.

(1) "But tell me, tell me, speak again,
　　　Thy soft response renewing—
　　　Wha*t* makes tha*t* ship drive on so fas*t*?
　　　What is the ocean doing?"

"Soft response renewing" surely ought never to have been in this poem. It sounds wrong; the spirit of its meaning is wrong too.

SECOND VOICE.

(2) "*Still* as a *sl*ave before his *l*ord,
　　　The ocean hath no blast;
　　　His great b*r*igh*t* *eye* most s*i*lently
　　　Up to the Moon is cast—

This is good. "Slave", a new word, fits the music, alliterating with "still" and "silently", *imitating* the meaning. "Ocean" and "silently" are old words, "blast" and "cast" typical sounds, and "bright eye" and "Moon" *key* words of the poem.

(3) If he m*ay* kn*ow* which w*ay* to *go*;
　　　For *s*he *g*uides him *s*mooth or *g*rim.
　　　See, brother, s*ee*! how graciousl*y*
　　　She looketh down on him."

There are four *h*s here, and two in the last verse. "Smooth", "sea" (see), "down" are recent sounds. "See, brother, see" is horrid.

FIRST VOICE.

(4) "But wh*y* drives on that ship so fast,
　　　*W*ithout or *w*ave or *w*ind?"

SECOND VOICE

"The air is cut away *be*fore,
And *c*loses from *be*hind.

"Ship", "fast", "wave", "wind" and "air" are old or recent sounds.

(5) Fl*y*, brother, fl*y*! more h*igh*, more h*igh*!
   Or w*e* shall *be* *be*lated:
   For *slow* and *slow* that *s*hip will g*o*,
   When the Mariner's trance is a*b*ated."

This stanza is good in so far as it gives us the sensation of a fading dream disappearing away. But "Fly, brother, fly", like "See, brother, see", is vile. Make it feminine and it would do for a stage-witch's chant; the supernatural of *The Ancient Mariner* is of a different stuff from the supernatural of *Macbeth*; what suits one does not suit the other. Though not impossible, "Voices" are difficult, and even dangerous, in this sort of poetry. The spectre-bark was as risky an invention, but carried through with consummate art. It is first a "*s*omething in the *s*ky": then it "*s*eemed a little *s*peck",

   And then it *s*eemed a mi*st*;
   It moved and moved, and took at last
   A *c*ertain *s*hape.

This gentle introduction uses old sounds, which are then summed up or packed together in:

   A *s*peck, a mi*st*, a *s*hape, I wi*st*!

making the progress quicker and more exciting, till it becomes lively and uncanny in:

   As if it dodged a water-sprite,
   It plunged and tacked and veered.

Nothing unnatural or impossible is suggested. We return

to "throats unslaked, with black lips baked", and when we look back it is a sail.

> Without a breeze, without a tide,
> She steadies with upright keel!

Then the sun sinks—

> When that strange shape drove suddenly
> Betwixt us and the sun.

Our hearts thump with sudden fear—a ship sailing with no tide or breeze—a strange shape driving suddenly betwixt us and the sun! Coleridge has put the spell on us; we must accept anything he tells us now. He gets the strange ship away as skilfully, taking our attention to something else, and when we look again the spectre-bark is gone.

> The sun's rim dips; the stars rush out:
> At one stride comes the dark;
> With far-heard whisper, o'er the sea,
> Off shot the spectre-bark."

The stanza before this ended:

> "The game is done.   I've won! I've won!"
> Quoth she, and whistles thrice.

The voices never did anything so grotesque as whistling thrice, yet we do not notice the grotesqueness; perhaps "The sun's rim dips" before she has time actually to do it; it sounds well when the bark goes off echoing it in "whisper". Nothing jars; the music, though not the music alone, carries the strange ship through triumphantly. On the other hand, the "soft response renewing" makes the voices vulgar at once. Their first impetus is too weak to carry us over eight stanzas. No panic or apprehension covers their grotesqueness; we listen without particular emotion, and the phantasy and absurdities have not even the truth of nightmare, appearing merely out of place. We are glad to escape, which we do very easily and naturally.

(6) I *w*oke, and *we w*ere sailing on
As in a gentle *w*eather:
'Twas n*i*ght, cal*m* n*i*ght, the *m*oon was h*i*gh;
The dead men stood together.

"Sailing" comes from V (20), "gentle" V (1), "night" V (18), "high" (5) in the dream; "moon" is in (2). "The dead men stood together" is a sinister reflection of V (10) and (11).

(7) takes us further into the dread atmosphere.

All stoo*d* togeth*er* on the *d*eck,
*F*or a charnel-dungeon *f*itt*er*:
All *f*ixed on me their stony eyes,
That in the moon did glitt*er*.

"Stood together" is repeated from the previous stanza. "All" was a powerfully painful sound in, "Alone, alone, all, all alone". "Deck" has appeared in sinister contexts already, V (2) and IV (5). "Stony eyes" were "fixed" in V (21). "Moon", "glitter" and "dungeon"—a fearsome word in itself—reflect from III (8).

The reflections in (8) are little less brutal.

The *p*ang, the curse, with which they died,
Had never *p*assed away:
I could not draw my eyes from theirs,
Nor turn them up to *p*ray.

"Curse" and "eye" occur together in IV (9); "pray" comes from IV (6) and (15); "passed" from V (14).

(9) resolves us from the spell.

And now this *s*pell was *s*napt: once more
I viewed the ocea*n* gree*n*,
And *l*ooked *f*ar *f*orth, yet *l*ittle saw
Of what had else b*een seen*—

"Snapt" and "spell" are vocal gestures; "ocean" and "green" echo; "looked far forth" is a good vocal gesture also.

(10) puts the atmosphere of apprehension into a picture, derived from a land experience, with five *h*s.

> Like one that on a *l*onesome **r**o*a*d
> Doth *walk in* fear and d**r**ead,
> And having once tu**r**ned **r**ound *walks on*,
> And tu**r**ns n*o* m*o*re his hea**d**;
> Because he kn*o*ws a *f*rightful *f*iend
> **D**oth cl*o*se behind him t**r**ead.

"Fear" was last heard in V (13); "turned" in (8). We notice the variety that can be made out of echoing common *r*s, *d*s, *t*s and *n*s.

(11) But soo*n* the*r*e b**r**eathe*d* a win*d* on me,
> Nor soun*d* nor *m*otion *m*a*d*e:
> Its *p*a*t*h was not u*p*on the sea,
> In *r*i*pp*le or in sha*d*e.

This brings us back to "breathed" V (19), "wind" V (7), "sound" V (15), "motion" V (21), "made" V (18), "sea" V (16). "Soon" makes me think of V (15-18), but there is no "soon" in that passage, only *s* and "noon".

(12) *I*t ra*i*se*d* **my** ha*i*r, *i*t fanne*d* **my** cheek
> Like a meadow-ga*l*e of spri*ng*—
> It mi*ng*le*d* stra*ng*e*l*y w*i*th my *f*ears,
> Yet *i*t *f*elt like a welcomi*ng*.

"Raised" comes from V (11), "fear" VI (10), "strange" V (10).

(13) *S*wi*f*tly, *s*wi*f*tly *f*le*w* the *s*hip,
> Yet *s*he *s*ailed *s*oftly t*o*o:

*Sweetly, sweetly blew the breeze—
On me alone it blew.

S for sweetness and speed! "Breeze", "blew" and "flew" are in II (5); "ship" and "sailed" occurred together in V (20); "softly" and "sweetly", which echo "Swiftly", are in V (14), (15) and (16). "Alone" recalls "Alone, alone, all, all alone"

> (14) Oh! dream of joy! is this indeed
> The lighthouse top I see?
> Is this the hill? is this the kirk?
> Is this mine own countree?

"Joy" strikes a new note. "Dream" is in V (10). Then we jump to the opening stanzas, only "kirk", "hill", "light-house" are repeated backwards, not a purely musical in-version of course. We have two hs.

In (15) we drift over the "harbour bar" I (6), with "pray" (7) and "sleep" V (18) for recent sounds.

> We drifted o'er the harbour-bar,
> And I with sobs did pray—
> O let me be awake, my God!
> Or let me sleep alway.

(16) repeats "harbour-bar" with "smoothly" VI (3), "moon" (7), "shadow" IV (13) and "ships" (5).

> The harbour-bay was clear as glass,
> So smoothly it was strewn!
> And on the bay the moonlight lay,
> And the shadow of the Moon.

---

* I need not repeat that I neglect finicking differences in these sounds. The s of "sweetly" differs from that of "sailed", both being different from the z of "breeze". In marking the vowels, I take my own pronunciation, which is probably as near Coleridge's as the Southern English pronunciation of to-day.

332 SOUND AND MEANING IN ENGLISH POETRY

We do see the "shadow" or reflection of the moon in a pool, but, not as far as I can recollect, when the moonlight lies on it. Perhaps the "shadow" of the moon was on the dark side of the ship, while the moonlight lay on the other, though I think it more likely that the music of, "And on the bay the moonlight lay" suggested the music of, "And the shadow of the moon". "Shadow" echoes from IV (13).

In (17) we see the same sort of thing. Possibly the "rock shone bright" here, because the "Sun shone bright" in I (7).

> The roc*k* *s*hone bright, the kir*k* no le*ss*
> That *s*tands above the rock;
> The moonl*i*ght *s*teeped in *s*ilentness
> The *s*teady weathercock.

"Rock", "kirk", "cock", "steep" and "steady", "bright" and "light" are close echoes.

> (18) And the bay was wh*ite* with *s*ilent l*i*g*ht*,
> Ti*ll* r*i*sing from the s*a*me,
> Fu*ll* many sh*a*pes, that *s*hadows were,
> In *c*rimson *c*olours c*a*me.

"White" and "light" carry on the echo of "bright" and "light", with "shadows" and "bay" from (16). "Rise" was in V (10), "came" in V (13), "white" and "light" in IV (12), "shapes" in III (7).

> (19) continues these.

> A little distance from the prow
> Those crimson shadows were:
> I turned my eyes upon the deck—
> Oh, Christ! what saw I there!

"Crimson" and "shadows" are in (18); "were" is taken from (18) and rhymed to the eye, though if we pronounce "were" a Cockney *weah*, this would make the sound rhyme to "there" (*theah*); "turned" is in (10), "eyes" in (8) and "deck" in (7).

> (20) Each corse *lay flat*, *lifeless* and *flat*,
>   And, by the ho*l*y rood!
>   A man a*ll l*ight, a seraph-man,
>   On every corse there stood.

"Corse" is in V (13), "stood" V (12), "light" (18), "lay" (16).

> (21) This *s*eraph-b*and*, each waved his h*and*:
>   It was a heaven*l*y *s*ight!
>   They *s*too*d* a*s* signa*ls* to the *land*,
>   Each one a *l*ove*l*y *l*ight.

"Seraph", "stood", "light" and "each" are repeated; the *l* sound continues, with *s*; "hand" comes from I (3), alliterating with "his" and "heavenly".

> (22) This *s*eraph-b*and*, each waved *h*is *h*and,
>   *No voice* did they impart—
>   *No voice;* but *oh*! the *s*ile*n*ce *san*k
>   Like music on my *h*eart.

The first line of (21) is repeated. "Voice" echoes from V (26), "oh" from (19), "silence" from (17), "heart" from IV (14)—three *h*s again!

> (23) But soon *I h*eard the dash of oars,
>   *I h*eard the *P*ilot's cheer;
>   M*y h*ead was turned *p*erforce away
>   And I saw a boat a*pp*ear.

"Soon" echoes from (11), "turned" (8), "heard" V (23); "cheer" takes us back to I (6). We notice three *h*s. I do not think "head was turned" reminds me of "turns no more his head" of (10), though possibly it ought.

(24) The Pilot and the Pilot's boy,
I heard them coming fast:
Dear Lord in Heaven! it was a joy
The dead men could not blast.

"Pilot" of (23) is echoed twice, and "heard" repeated with "Heaven" (21) for an alliteration; "joy" comes from (14), "dead men" from (6).

(25), to close Part VI, returns to the "Albatross".

I saw a third—I heard his voice:
It is the Hermit good!
He singeth loud his godly hymns
That he makes in the wood.
He'll shrieve my soul, he'll wash away
The Albatross's blood.

"Blood" V (22), "voice" (22), "loud" V (7), "makes" V (17), "soul" V (23), "singeth" V (18) recall old sounds; the h alliteration focusses here — eight of them. They come on us like a land breeze; we have not noticed them (or at least, we should not, if we had not been looking for them) since we dropped below the horizon, and now they come with every mention of "Hermit" or "Heaven".

Part VII—(1) echoes the last stanza of VI in "Hermit", " good" and "loudly", and has older sounds, as "down", "sea", "sweet", "voice", "mariner", "countree".

This Hermit good lives in that wood
Which slopes down to the sea.
How loudly his sweet voice he rears!
He loves to talk with marineres
That come from a far countree.

(2) has "noon", *etc.*, but its sounds are rather new than old.

He kneels at morn, and noon, and eve—
He hath a cushion plump:

It is the moss that wholly hides
The rotted old oak-stump.

(3) The skiff-boat neared: I heard them talk,
"Why this is strange, I trow!
Where are those lights so many and fair,
That signal made but now?"

"Skiff-boat" is in VI (23), "neared" V (5), "heard" VI (24), "signal" VI (21), "lights" (18), "made" VI (11), "strange" VI (13).

(4) "Strange, by my faith!" the Hermit said—
"And they answered not our cheer!
The planks looked warped! and see those sails,
How thin they are and sere!
I never saw aught like to them,
Unless perchance it were

"Strange" is in (3), "Hermit" in (1), "cheer" in VI (23), and "sails" in VI (6).

(5) Brown skeletons of leaves that lag
My forest-brook along;
When the ivy-tod is heavy with snow,
And the owlet whoops to the wolf below,
That eats the she-wolf's young."

This is a new music, though "snow", "young", and "brook", etc., are old sounds, very beautifully introduced by the "interrupted" cadence of stanza (4).

(6) "Dear Lord! it hath a fiendish look—"
(The Pilot made reply)
"I am afeared"—"Push on, push on!"
Said the Hermit cheerily.

"Pilot" is in V (24), "Hermit" (4), "cheerily" (4), "made" (3), "afeared" VI (10).

(7) The boat came closer to the ship,
    But I nor spake nor stirred;
    The boat came close beneath the ship,
    And straight a sound was heard.

Almost every word of this has already been used—"boat",
"came", "ship", "spake", "stirred", "straight", "sound",
"heard".

(8) Under the water it rumbled on,
    Still louder and more dread:
    It reached the ship, it split the bay;
    The ship went down like lead.

"Water", "still", "louder", "dread", "ship", "split",
"bay", "lead" are all old sounds.

(9) Stunned by that loud and dreadful sound,
    Which sky and ocean smote,
    Like one that hath been seven days drowned
    My body lay afloat;
    But swift as dreams, myself I found
    Within the Pilot's boat.

"Loud", "dreadful", "sound", "sky", "ocean", "body",
"dreams", "Pilot's boat", and "like" are well-worn sounds
here.

(10) Upon the whirl, where sank the ship,
     The boat spun round and round;
     And all was still, save that the hill
     Was telling of the sound.

"Sank", "ship", "boat", "round and round", "all",
"still", "hill" and "sound" are prominent words in the
poem. The echoes reverberate on the trilling ls.

(11) I moved my lips—the Pilot shrieked
     And fell down in a fit;
     The holy Hermit raised his eyes,
     And prayed where he did sit.

"Moved", "lips", "Pilot", "down", "holy", "Hermit",
"raised", "eyes" and "prayed" have occurred often.

> (12) I took the o͟ars: the Pilot's boy,
> Who now doth crazy g͟o,
> Laughed *l*oud and *l*ong, and a*ll* the whi*l*e
> His eyes went to and fr͟o.
> "*H*a! *h*a!" quoth *h*e, "full plain I see,
> The Devil kn͟o͟ws how to r͟o͟w."

"Oars", "Pilot", "boy", "loud", "all" and "eyes" are old
words. *L* is expressive for laughter.

> (13) And now, all in my own countree,
> I *stood* on the *firm* lan*d*!
> The Hermit *stepped forth from* the boat,
> And *s*carcely he *c*ould *stand*.

"Countree", "stood", "land", "Hermit" and "boat" have
occurred prominently already. "Stood on the firm land"
and "stepped forth from" are imitative vocal gestures.

> (14) "O shrieve *m*e, shrieve *m*e, holy *m*an!"
> The Her*m*it crossed his brow.
> "Say quick," quoth he, "I bid thee say—
> What *m*anner of *m*an art thou?"

The repetitions here are interesting: "O shrieve me,
shrieve me", and "quick", "quoth", and "say" at the beginning and the end of the line, and in the last line "manner"
and "man". "Quoth", "holy", "Hermit", "crossed" have
occurred recently.

> (15) Forthwith this *f*rame of *m*ine *w*as *w*renched
> *W*ith a *w*oeful agony,
> *W*hich *f*orced me to begin my tale;
> And then it le*f*t me *f*ree.

"Agony" comes from IV (3); "free" and "woeful" have
also come from far.

(16) Since then, at an uncertain hour,
That agony returns:
And till my ghastly tale is told,
This heart within me burns.

"Agony" and "tale" are repeated from last stanza, "ghastly" and "heart" from further off. ·

(17) I pass, like night, from land to land;
I have strange power of speech;
That moment that his face I see,
I know the man that must hear me:
To him my tale I teach.

"Pass", "night", "land", "strange", "face", "see", "know", "man", "hear", "tale" are prominent sounds in the poem.

(18) What loud uproar bursts from that door!
The wedding-guests are there:
But in the garden-bower the bride
And bride-maids singing are:
And hark the little vesper bell,
Which biddeth me to prayer!

"Loud", "uproar", "burst", "door" (I (2)), "wedding-guests", "bride", "bride-maids", "singing", "prayer" are familiar words earlier in the poem. As we approach the close the opening sounds return.

(19) O Wedding-Guest! this soul hath been
Alone on a wide wide sea:
So lonely 'twas, that God himself
Scarce seeméd there to be.

"Wedding-Guest", "soul", "lonely", "seemed", "God", "himself", *etc.*, "Alone on a wide wide sea" are recollections.

(20) O sweeter than the marriage-feast,
  'Tis sweeter far to me,
  To walk together to the kirk
  With a goodly company!—

"Sweeter", "kirk", and "feast", *etc.*, are old sounds.

(21) repeats.

  To walk together to the kirk,
  And all together pray,
  While each to his great Father bends,
  Old men, and babes, and loving friends,
  And youths and maidens gay!

(22) strikes an unfamiliar note in "Farewell", but keeps its sense of continuity by such words as "Wedding-Guest", "prayeth", "loveth", "man", "bird".

  Farewell, farewell! but this I tell
  To thee, thou Wedding-Guest!
  He prayeth well, who loveth well
  Both man and bird and beast.

"Well", "tell" rhyme strongly where we might expect weak rhymes; and the final rhyme, where we expect strength, has only alliterating consonants, "Guest" and "beast". *Th* and *b* sound prominently. In "both", "bird" and "beast" the different vowels emphasise and beautify the consonant.

(23) repeats, emphasising "loveth", recalling *b* in "best", and echoing the vowel of "prayeth" in "great" and "made", one of the most important in the poem.

  He prayeth best, who loveth best
  All things both great and small;
  For the dear God who loveth us,
  He made and loveth all.

This stanza and the last reflect V (25).

(24) The Mariner, whose eye *is* *b*right,
Whose *b*eard with age *is* hoar,
Is gone: and now the Wedding-Guest
Turned from the *b*ridegroom's door.

This is really the ending. The sounds of the beginning are repeated to bring us round with a sense of finish; here are the Mariner, with his bright eye and his hoary beard, the Wedding-Guest and the bridegroom.

In (25) the curtain comes down and we hear the epilogue, though even it has echoes.

He went like *one* that hath been *stunn*ed,
And is of *s*ense forlorn:
A *s*add*er* and a wi*ser* man,
He *r*ose the *morr*ow *mor*n.

I have compiled this list not by mechanically picking out the repeated sounds, but have trusted my ear and memory absolutely. This probably means that I have missed many echoes—and indeed, from later readings I know I have—but it makes the array all the more significant, showing that we hear them all, that they make their effect, colouring the atmosphere of the poem. I have marked some of the more striking echoes within the stanzas; and though it would take too long to analyse every little effect, it may be worth while to note some of the more obvious stanza designs. The music is wonderful for the way Coleridge forms an exquisite vowel and consonant progress out of echoes. He combines the characteristic Spenserian way of making music by a chain of sounds lovely in sequence, and the echoing way, often echoing the sequence. In sequence his vowels sound beautiful, but the alliterating consonants and vowel assonances and rhymes make this stream of music sound more lovely. He echoes as much as possible and with the greatest variety, having sometimes a double internal rhyme:

> And he sh*one* br*ight*, and *on* the *right*.
> If he m*ay* kn*ow* which w*ay* to go.

—and still the vowels are lovely for the easy sequence they make. At other times he has assonance and rhyme, or a double assonance:

> The ship dr*o*ve f*a*st, loud r*oa*red the bl*a*st.
> We w*e*re the f*i*rst that *e*ver bu*r*st.
> The gue*s*ts are m*et*, the fea*s*t is s*et*.
> Ah wretch! sai*d* th*ey*, the bir*d* to sl*ay*.

—or alliteration and rhyme:

> The *fair* breeze *blew*, the white *foam flew*.

—and even:

> I*n* m*i*st *or* cl*o*ud, o*n* m*a*st *or* shr*o*ud.

—or alliteration and assonance:

> The *d*eath *f*ires *d*anced at n*i*ght.
> And *l*istens *l*ike a thr*ee* y*ea*rs' ch*i*ld.

—or cross alliteration:

> The *s*un now *r*ose upon the *r*ight.
> For *s*he *g*uides him *s*mooth or *g*rim.

—or single alliteration or assonance:

> The furrow followed free.
> The Wedding-Guest *s*at on a *s*tone.
> Nor *d*im nor r*e*d, like God's own h*ea*d.

—or he may have a third vowel assonating with his rhymes:

> And *i*ce, mast-h*i*gh, came floating b*y*.

Instead of rhyme or assonance, we find closely related vowels or consonants with a more subtle effect:

> We could not sp*ea*k, no more than *i*f
> We had been *cho*ked with *soo*t.

He compounds all these effects in any number of ways.

Coleridge probably thought of his longer lines in two halves, his phrasing being often in this form:

accent	accent	accent	accent
| or foot |	| or foot | |	| | or foot |	| or foot | |

accent	accent	accent
| | or foot |	| or foot |	| or foot | |

accent	accent	accent	accent
| | or foot |	| or foot | |	| | or foot |	| or foot | |

accent	accent	accent
| | or foot |	| or foot |	| or foot | |

Many of his longer lines are written in parallels, as:

> The guests are met, the feast is set,

—one echoing the other closely. These may be exactly alike:

> Day after day, day after day.

—and the third line may be built on the same plan too:

> Below the kirk, below the hill,
> Below the lighthouse top.

—or:

> The ice was here, the ice was there,
> The ice was all around.

The ends of the phrase are usually rhymed, but he sometimes alters his practice and has the beginning the same and the ends different:

> Without a breeze, without a tide.

—or he may invert his second phrase:

> For the sky and the sea, and the sea and the sky.
> Down dropt the breeze, the sails dropt down.
> I closed my lids, and kept them close.

The feet of the one phrase may echo each other, while the other phrase forms a contrast:

> It moved and moved, and took at last.

—or in a three-feet phrase:

> And still it neared and neared.

—or the feet of both phrases may reflect each other, the phrases contrasting:

> | |About,| |about,| | |in reel| |and rout.| |

—or all the feet save one may be the same:

> | |Alone,| |alone,| | |all,| |all| |alone.| |

The sounds of one line may be repeated in the next:

> O let me be awake, my God,
> Or let me sleep alway.

—though the parallelism is not often between consecutive lines, the more usual line-imitation being:

> I looked upon the rotting sea,
> And drew my eyes away;
> I looked upon the rotting deck,
> And there the dead men lay.

He prolongs his stanza by various devices, adding lines in the middle, or disarranging the rhythm of his fourth line to make a five-lined stanza, as in III (4). Sometimes he repeats two lines at the end:

> Nor dim nor red, like God's own head,
> The glorious Sun uprist:
> Then all averred, I had killed the bird
> That brought the fog and mist.
> 'Twas right, said they, such birds to slay,
> That bring the fog and mist.

This stanza makes a parallel to the one preceding.* Very often a line is taken out from one stanza and repeated in another, either exactly as it stood or slightly varied, or the

* p. 306.

first line of a stanza may echo the salient words of the last in a sort of *stretto*. We have already pointed these out. For other stanza-imitations, IV (1) and (2), and III (15), which begins with "One after one", and (16), which ends with "one by one", are worth looking at. Coleridge also varies his music by small differences in the rhythm and by altering the emphasis. He sometimes uses alliteration to help to shift the emphasis from the end of the line:

> Nine *fa*thom deep he had *f*ollowed us.
> He s*t*ruck with his o'er*t*aking wings.

Although the even lines usually have a stronger cadence than the odd and rhyme, the even line-endings occasionally only assonate and every line may rhyme, as in VI (22) and (23).

Coleridge varies his designs in many ways, yet they usually remain simple, and most of them can be paralleled from music, although he presumably did not know enough about the technique of music to realise this, and may have done most of it undesignedly. In our typical musical sentence—

```
  ⎧ foot     foot        foot     foot  = first line of stanza.
  ⎪ | a |   | b ||      | a |   | b ||
  ⎪      A                   B
  ⎨ foot   foot          foot     foot  = second line of stanza.
  ⎪ | a |   | b ||      | a |   | b ||
  ⎩      C                   D

  ⎧ foot    foot         foot     foot  = third line of stanza.
  ⎪ | a |   | b ||      | a |   | b ||
  ⎪      A                   B
  ⎨ foot   foot          foot     foot  = last line of stanza.
  ⎪ | a |   | b ||      | a |   | b ||
  ⎩      C                   D
```

—"a" and "b" in any section may be the same or different. "A" may resemble any other "A", "B", "C", or "D"; the "a" of "A" may resemble the "a" or "b" of any foot, and so on. (A + B) in the third line may repeat (A + B) of the first, or (C + D) of the second, or the second line may repeat the first, and so on exactly as in the *Ancient Mariner*, if we imagine every syllable a note. Coleridge seems to be thinking in some such divisions. He can write like this because most of his words are monosyllabic. He makes a monotony which is a subdued variety—a mosaic of few colours in myriad designs. (Stanzas III (1) and (7) are worth studying for this.) The general effect is characteristically English, and possible only to a tongue with many monosyllables. But if the choice of words is English, the designing is like music. The far-heard repetitions as well as the details of stanza-structure are like music. His ending each Part with the sound of "Albatross" or "cross" appeals to us as a musical way of keeping the unity of impression. In Part III, where there is no excuse for the "Albatross", the souls of the mariners pass by like the "whizz of my cross-bow". In Part V the "Albatross" and "cross" repetition comes in the third last stanza, not the last. The last Part ends recapitulating not the tragedy—"Albatross", "cross"—which, to take a musical *metaphor*, we might call the second theme, but the first peaceful atmosphere we started from; instead of "cross" we have "rose", though this may be an accident rather than part of the designing.

FINIS

APPENDIX

(To Page 78)

QUOTATIONS FROM SWEET'S GRAMMAR, pages 39-40

WHEN a negative interrogative sentence is used rhetoric-
ally to express affirmation, it necessarily takes the falling
tone. "Isn't it wonderful!\ " "He is very egoistical—Yes,
isn't he? \". If a complete sentence has a full-stressed tag
added, the tag is uttered in a separate fall of its own, instead of merely continuing the preceding one: "He is
stupid \ very stupid." Here the voice, after reading a low
pitch at the end of the first fall, leaps up and begins a
fresh fall.

In sequences—where there is no formal connexion—
each sentence keeps its own independent tone—whether
rising or falling—unless a rising tone is required to show
the connexion more clearly, as in "I am sorry I could not
come before / ; I had to finish writing a letter \".

When the first clause introduces a statement, *etc.*, it
takes a rising tone if it is grammatically unfinished.
"He said / he did not care \."
"The difficulty is / how are we to get back \?"
Otherwise it takes the falling. "What he said was
this \" . . .
"He speaks somewhat in this way \" . . .
Inserted or parenthetic groups or clauses naturally have
rising tones. "He is a man who / , if he chose / , might
do great things \."

This is not a real parenthesis; the real parenthesis is
usually, or at least very often, in lower tones—in a different

346

key, with a feeling of a different centre of gravity, *e.g.* "What I say is (but first let me warn you that I do not pretend to be disinterested) that, *etc.*". To return to Sweet:

If the appended or inserted words have a marked meaning of their own dependent on their intonation, that intonation is kept, which often results in broken intonation: "Which will you have\, tea / or coffee \?"

When a tag keeps its independent intonation (together with its full stress) it is either emphatic or else it is felt as detached—as if it were added with hesitation—"There is the bell again \; it is Frederick \ of course, isn't it / ?" "I will call to-morrow\, if I can / ."

Broken intonation is, of course, less frequent in the case of insertions, as insertions are generally not emphatic: "But thou / if thou shouldest never see my face again \, pray for my soul \!"

In the compound tones the second element determines the general meaning of the whole tone, and the first element only modifies this general meaning. These tones are always accompanied by extra stress, because of their emphatic meaning.

The *compound rise* expresses doubt of some implied statement, so that it expresses distrust, caution: " ∨ I will not try it." " ∨ You may take ∨ care." "If you ∨ do it, it will be at your own ∨ risk."

Hence it is used in cautious contradiction or modification of the speaker's own statements: "I am sure he will come again \; at least I ∨ think he will / ."

In its more logical uses it expresses contrast or exception: "I am what the world calls a woman-hater\; what ∨ I call a philosopher \."

It has sometimes an intensive meaning. It sometimes contradicts the meaning of the word it falls on: "Was it raining when you came in / ?" ∨ "Rather!" Rather/ would imply "only a little".

In the *compound fall* the relations between the two elements are reversed. This tone hints at a doubt, and disposes of it by a dogmatic assertion. Hence it expresses contempt or sarcasm: " ∨ *I can do it.*" " ∧ You!"

It also expresses remonstrance, contradiction, contrast, not cautiously as the compound rise does, but confidently and dogmatically. "Sunday isn't the day ╱ ; it is ∧ Monday."

"You say you are sure of finishing it ╱ , but ∧ when will you finish it?"

Sometimes the dogmatic element disappears and the intonation is simply an emphatic effect, with perhaps a trace of impatience and contempt. "You ought to have done something to prevent it." "What could I ∧ do?" "Shall we have time?" " ∧ Yes."

APPENDIX

(To Page 193)

SHOWING BY QUOTATIONS FROM WRITERS ON MUSIC AND ON POETRY HOW THE GRAMMAR AND PSYCHOLOGY OF THESE ARTS RESEMBLE EACH OTHER.

Dr. Reimann writes:

Hardly the whole of a polyphonic movement can be subjectivated; as in listening to a drama, we identify our-selves with one or a few persons who touch us sym-pathetically, and conceive the others objectively in their relation to us or to those with whom we identify ourselves —so also in instrumental work only a few prominent parts moving us sympathetically are the real representatives of the subject-matter with which we identify ourselves. . . . Naturally, as a rule, the melody proper . . . will be the part that enlists our sympathy.*

Of music, Dr. Abdy Williams says:

In many cases the first bar, or the first two bars, or even the accent only of the first bar, are merely introductory, to call attention, as it were, to the Rhythms that are about to

* *Catechism of Musical Æsthetics*, pp. 35-6.

follow. They are outside the Rhythm proper, and are equivalent to the few words that precede a speech, such as "Ladies and Gentlemen".*

Or Mr. McEwen says:

Just as words will form sense only when they express and are grouped under the relationship of a logical process of thought, any successions of combinations of sounds will form musical sense only when they are arranged subordinate to and logically expressive of musical thought.†

Yet another musical philosopher writes:

Melody comes the nearest in music to conceptual thought; musical phrases and periods are related to one another, and illustrate and explain one another, just as do sentences in discursive speech or writing.‡

Their grammars are parallel also:

In the science of grammar, from which these terms are borrowed, the intransitive statement is a movement of thought between two related ideas, and is limited to these; the transitive, on the other hand, is a movement of thought which proceeds from a first to a second idea by way of a third intermediate idea.

The same fundamental principles of classification are found in the expression of musical thought. In the one case only the strong beat is involved; it stands so distinguished from what follows it (though not necessarily in a state of isolation) that there is a feeling of opposition, rather than of connection, between it and the next strong beat. . . . In the other case there is a definite connection between the progress from one antecedent strong beat to a consequent strong beat.§

It may perhaps amuse the reader, and I hope puzzle him a little, to tell which of the following extracts refer to verbal

* *Rhythm of Modern Music*, p. 49.
† *The Thought in Music*, p. 167.
‡ Britan, *The Philosophy of Music*, pp. 213-14, paraphrased.
§ McEwen, *The Thought in Music*, p. 71.

sentences, which to musical. If he scribble down his answers, he can check them on the list which I add.

1. Occasionally the observer's apperceptive process anticipates the succession of [words or notes?] constituting the objective stimuli and forming the sentence. This phenomenon is probably often unnoticed because the premature apperception tallies with the complete interpretation, but sometimes this coincidence fails and the observer is conscious of a distinct "bias" for another form of completion.

2. The true business of the . . . artist is to plait or weave his meaning, involving it around itself; so that each sentence, by successive phrases, shall first come into a kind of knot, and then, after a moment of suspended meaning, solve and clear itself. In every properly constructed sentence there should be observed this knot or hitch; so that (however delicately) we are led to foresee, to expect, and then to welcome the successive phrases.

3. Not the least useful function of climax is the part it can play in securing continuity by avoiding an abrupt change from one emotional level to another. In many cases two separate divisions of a work, opposed or even contradictory in feeling, may be logically connected by means of a climax which leads from the one to the other. Such a process is to be regarded as a method of achieving transition from one emotional stratum to another, the division preceding the climax representing a higher—or lower—level than that which follows it.

4. The method by which a [poet or composer?] constructs a work, even of the simplest character, is a process of synthesis in which the various units are built up into a symmetrical and continuous structure. But, although the complete structure can be regarded as the sum of a large number of such small parts, the whole, as in the case of every vital organism, is more than the sum of these parts.

. . . Even in the . . . smallest work, . . . the expression of the thought and feeling is of a composite nature. Each is made up of parts, and the balancing and fitting together of these parts produce the whole.

The following are poets and musicians writing about themselves :

5. So far as he [the poet or musician?] is aware of a process which is commonly, and perhaps inevitably, obscure, the subject and the rhythm of the [poem or music in question?] came into consciousness together, the unsought but not unmediated rhythm being, of course, the only begetter of the form which Mr. —— has no difficulty in analysing. . . . Mr.—— says that recurrence, expectation raised and fulfilled, is certainly one of the secrets of good [verse or music?]. I answer that it is equally the secret of bad.

6. A poet or musician is quoted describing his procedure thus:

First bits and crumbs of the [poem or music?] come and gradually join together in his mind; then the soul getting warmed to the work, the thing grows more and more and, "I spread it out broader and clearer, and at last it gets almost finished in my head, even when it is a long piece, so that I can see the whole of it at a single glance in my mind, as if it were a beautiful painting or a handsome human being; in which way I do not hear it in my imagination at all as a succession—the way it must come later— but all at once as it were. It is a rare feast! All the inventing and making goes on in me as in a beautiful strong dream. But the best of all is the *hearing of it all at once*."

7. More than once he said that his [poems or music?] sprang often from a "nucleus"; some one [word or note] maybe, or brief melodious phrase which had floated through the brain, as it were, unbidden. And perhaps at once whilst walking they were presently wrought into a [poem or piece of music?]. But if he did not write it down on the spot, it fled from him irrecoverably.

1. refers to words and comes from *The American Journal of Psychology*, vol. xii, p. 116. Bagley, "The Apperception of the Spoken Sentence".

2. refers to words. R. L. Stevenson, *Some Technical Elements of Style.*

3. refers to music. McEwen, *The Thought in Music*, pp. 159-60.

4. refers to music. *Ibid.*, pp. 91-2.

5. Poet. The author of a poem on *Choosing Hymns, Times Literary Supplement*, Dec. 23, 1920.

6. Musician. Mozart, quoted by William James, *Principles of Psychology*, vol. i, p. 255.

7. Poet. *Memoir* of Hallam Tennyson, from the personal recollections of F. T. Palgrave, vol. ii, p. 496.

One would almost have said that No. 3 was a digest of De Quincey on the Porter Scene in *Macbeth*.